About the author

Samir Amin was born in Egypt in 1931 and pursued his higher education in Paris in the fields of politics, statistics and economics. He has a worldwide reputation as one of the foremost radical thinkers of our generation on issues arising out of the changing nature of capitalism, North–South relations and development theory. Among his many institutional roles, he has been Director of IDEP (the United Nations African Institute for Planning) from 1970 to 1980; the Director of the Third World Forum in Dakar, Senegal; and a co-founder of the World Forum for Alternatives.

He is the author of numerous books in French and Arabic, many of which have been translated into a large number of other languages, including a dozen or more in English. His most famous works are *Accumulation on a World Scale* and *Unequal Development*. Among his recent books in English are *Re-reading the Post-War World: An Intellectual Itinerary* (1994) and *Empire of Chaos* (1993).

His previous titles in English include: *The Arab Nation: Nationalism and Class Struggle* (1978), *The Arab Economy Today* (1982), *Eurocentrism* (1989), *Maldevelopment: Anatomy of a Global Failure* (1990), *Delinking: Towards a Polycentric World* (1990), *The Empire of Chaos* (1992), *Re-reading the Postwar Period: An Intellectual Itinerary* (1994), *Capitalism in the Age of Globalization: The Management of Contemporary Society* (1997) and *Specters of Capitalism: A Critique of Current International Fashions.*

SAMIR AMIN

Obsolescent capitalism: contemporary politics and global disorder

translated by Patrick Camiller

Zed Books

LONDON · NEW YORK

Obsolescent capitalism was first published by Zed Books Ltd,
7 Cynthia Street, London N1 9JF, UK and Room 400, 175 Fifth
Avenue, New York, NY 10010, USA in 2003.

www.zedbooks.demon.co.uk

Cover designed by Andrew Corbett
Set in Monotype Dante and Gill Sans Heavy by Ewan Smith, London
Printed and bound in Malta by Gutenberg Ltd

Distributed in the USA exclusively by Palgrave, a division of
St Martin's Press, LLC, 175 Fifth Avenue, New York, NY 10010.

A catalogue record for this book is available from the British Library
Library of Congress Cataloging-in-Publication Data is available.

ISBN 1 84277 320 8 cased
ISBN 1 84277 321 6 limp

Contents

Abbreviations

GATT	General Agreement on Tariffs and Trade
IMF	International Monetary Fund
MAI	Multilateral Agreement on Investment
NATO	North Atlantic Treaty Organization
OECD	Organisation for Economic Co-operation and Development
TNC	transnational corporation
UNCTAD	United Nations Conference on Trade and Development
WTO	World Trade Organization

Introduction

The triumphant discourse and formulas of neoliberalism, which were so widely applied in the last two decades of the twentieth century, are no longer in such good shape. Support for them among broad majorities, even on the left, was boosted by the collapse of the Soviet myth that had seemed the only credible alternative for much of the century, as well as by the final extinction of the fires of Maoism. Yet that support has been eroded in the space of just a few years.

The new-style liberalism promised prosperity for all (or nearly all), peace following the end of the Cold War, and a new era of democracy. Many believed it. But those who understood that its recipes could only deepen the crisis of accumulation, and that this would in turn worsen social conditions for the great majority of nations and working classes, now find an ever larger and more attentive audience. Militarization of the world order, which has been upon us not since 11 September 2001 but since the Gulf War of 1991, has dissipated the promises of peace. Democracy is either marking time or in retreat; it is everywhere under threat.

The theses in this book are not mainly intended to explain the features belying the empty promises of neoliberalism; they have the wider aim of opening a debate on the future of the world capitalist system. Are the present phenomena merely 'temporary', as the diehard supporters of capitalism claim? Do they point, beyond a painful transition, to a new period of expansion and prosperity? Or are they, rather, signs of the obsolescence of a system that must be overcome if human civilization is to survive?

The following analyses are based upon a theory of capitalism and its global dimension, and, more generally, of the dynamics of social transformation. The four key theses are as follows:

1. Economic alienation is a central feature of capitalism, in contrast to previous societies and what might constitute a post-capitalist society. It refers to the fact that a means (economics in general, capitalist accumulation in particular) has become an end in itself, dominating the whole process of social life as an objective force external to it.

2. The polarization produced by the globalization of capitalism constantly widens the gap (in terms of material development) between the

centres and the peripheries of the world capitalist system. This too is a new phenomenon in the history of mankind, as the size of the gap has become in the last two centuries quite unlike anything seen in previous millennia. It is also a phenomenon that one can only wish to bring to an end, by gradually building a post-capitalist society that really is better for all the world's peoples.

3. Crucially, our conception of capitalism does not reduce it to a 'generalized market' but locates its very essence in powers beyond the market. Instead of analysing capitalism in terms of social relations and a politics in which these powers beyond the market find expression, the dominant reductionism in economics theorizes an imaginary system based upon 'market laws' that, if left to themselves, supposedly generate 'optimal equilibrium'. In actually existing capitalism, class struggle, politics, the state and the logic of capital accumulation are inseparable from one another. Capitalism, then, is by its very nature a regime whose successive states of disequilibrium are produced by social and political conflicts beyond the market. The concepts put forward in vulgar liberal theory – 'market deregulation', for example – have no reality. So-called 'deregulated' markets are, in fact, markets regulated by the powers of monopolies situated beyond the market.

4. What I call 'underdetermination' plays a central role in history. Every social system (including capitalism) is historical, in the sense that it has a beginning and an end, but the nature of the system that overcomes the contradictions of the system preceding it is not imposed by objective laws external to the choices of society. The contradictions peculiar to the system in decline (today, those of globalized capitalism and especially those associated with its characteristic form of polarization) can be overcome in different ways, since autonomous logics govern the different levels of social life (politics and power, cultural life, ideology, the system of social values in which legitimacy and the economic dimension are expressed). These autonomous logics may adapt to one another and thus in different ways give a certain cohesion to the system as a whole, so that the best and the worst are always possible. Humanity still has responsibility for its own future.

Readers who know my previous writings will probably find these basic theses familiar. Nevertheless, as they are presented here in a highly condensed form, I should say a word about recent work that develops them at greater length.

Capitalism has developed the productive forces at a pace and scale unparalleled in human history. At the same time, it has made much wider than ever before the gap between the potential of development and the actuality of its use. The present level of scientific and technological knowledge could offer a solution to all the material problems of the whole of humanity. But the logic that transforms the means (law of profit, accumulation) into an end-in-itself has led to huge squandering of this potential and unequal access to its unprecedented benefits. Until the nineteenth century the gap between the development potential of existing knowledge and the development level actually achieved was not so great. This should not encourage us to feel nostalgic about the past, since capitalism was a necessary condition for today's level of development to be achieved. But now capitalism has had its day: the pursuit of its logic no longer produces anything but waste and inequality. In this sense, Marx's 'law of pauperization' resulting from capitalist accumulation has been ever more strikingly confirmed on a world scale over the past two centuries. We should not be surprised that, at the very moment when capitalism appears victorious on every front, the 'war on poverty' has become an inescapable obligation in the rhetoric of the dominant apparatuses.

This waste and this inequality are the other side of the coin: they make up the 'black book of capitalism', reminding us that it is only a parenthesis and not the end of history. Unless capitalism is overcome through a system that ends global polarization and economic alienation, it will surely lead humanity to self-destruction.

How was the goal of overcoming capitalism understood in the twentieth century? What lessons can we draw for the challenge now taking shape in the twenty-first century, the challenge that is the focus of this book?

The dominant view today is that, after 1917 in the USSR and after 1945 in much of the Third World and to some extent even in the developed heartlands, the twentieth century was a catastrophic period: systematic intervention by ruling political powers prevented capitalism from revealing its full benefits as a transhistorical expression of the requirements of human nature; history eventually ended such illusions and restored that complete submission to 'market laws' (a vulgar and inexact term for capitalism) that is thought, wrongly in part, to have been the norm in the nineteenth century; and this return marked a historical step forward. Chapter 1 will begin by identifying this fashionable view of history as the 'return of the *belle époque*'.

My argument is the exact opposite of what has been 'in the air' over the past period. My reading of the twentieth century is thus a first attempt to meet the challenge of development (or, to be more precise, underdevelopment), which is the term usually employed to denote the growing contrast between centres and peripheries intrinsic to the global expansion of capitalism. The existing answers to this challenge range widely from the timid to the radical, and I would not wish to minimize their diversity. But I would venture to say that they all fit into a 'catching-up' perspective in which achievements at the centre are reproduced in the periphery. In this schema, the goals and strategies pursued in the twentieth century do involve a questioning of capitalism as essentially a system of economistic alienation.

We cannot, of course, ignore the fact that the radical experiments issuing from socialist revolutions in Russia and China sought to challenge capitalist social relations. Yet that aim was gradually diluted by the prior necessity of catching up that remained as the legacy of peripheral capitalism.

The page has turned on those more or less radical attempts to solve the problem of development. Once the historical limits of what they could achieve had been reached, they were unable to rise above themselves and move on further; their collapse thus permitted a temporary but devastating restoration of capitalist illusions. In reality, humanity today faces still greater problems than those that confronted it fifty or a hundred years ago. Its answers to the challenge will therefore have to be more radical in the twenty-first century than they were in the twentieth: that is, it will have to aim for a certain kind of development of the productive forces in the peripheries of the system, but combine this with ever greater energy and rigour in overcoming the general logic of capitalist management of society. What is more, this must be done in a world that has a number of novel aspects, whose nature and scale we shall try to clarify below. The twenty-first century cannot be a restored nineteenth and must advance beyond the twentieth. The question of development will occupy in the twenty-first century an even more central position than it did in the twentieth century.

The reader will certainly have realized that my own concept of development is not synonymous with 'catching up' but is intrinsically critical of capitalism. It involves the project of a very different society, whose twofold aim would be to free humanity from economistic alienation and to end the legacy of polarization on a world scale. The project can only be universal: it must become (gradually, of course) the project of the whole of humanity, of the nations at the centre as well as the periphery of the system under attack. Whereas 'catching up' could at a pinch be conceived as a strategy that peripheral nations might implement by relying only upon their own will and resources, the twofold objective of development as it has been defined here requires the active and combined participation of peoples in every part of the world, especially as many, if not all, the problems facing humanity have an ever deeper global dimension.

One final point should be made in these preliminary remarks. Having devoted most of my efforts in recent years to certain of these problems, I shall avoid repeating myself here except when this is necessary to the coherence of the text. The reader is referred to five of my recent works in French: *L'ethnie à l'assaut des nations* (1994), *La gestion capitaliste de la crise* (1995), *Les défis de la mondialisation* (1996), *Critique de l'air du temps* (1997), *L'hégémonisme des Etats-Unis et l'effacement du projet européen* (2000), and to a previous Zed title in English: *Capitalism in the Age of Globalization* (1997), as well as *Spectres of Capitalism, A Critique of Current Intellectual Fashions*, published by Monthly Review Press, New York, 1998.

ONE
The political economy of the twentieth century

Return of the *belle époque*

The twentieth century ended in an atmosphere astonishingly reminiscent of the *belle époque* (truly *belle* for capital) that marked its beginning. The bourgeoisies of the Triad – that is, the European powers, the United States and Japan – sang a hymn glorifying their definitive victory. The working classes of the central countries no longer appeared to be the 'dangerous classes' they had been in the nineteenth century, and the peoples of the rest of the world were called upon to accept the civilizing mission of the West.

The original *belle époque* crowned a century of radical changes in the world, a century in which the first Industrial Revolution and the accompanying constitution of modern bourgeois nation-states had fanned out from the north-western quarter of Europe to conquer the rest of the continent, as well as the United States and Japan. The old peripheries of the mercantilist epoch – Latin America, the British and Dutch Indies – were excluded from this dual revolution, while the old states of Asia (China, Ottoman Empire, Persia) were integrated as peripheries into the new globalization, and the rest of the world was integrated through colonial conquest. The triumph of the centres of global capitalism was apparent in a demographic boom that raised the population of European origin from 23 per cent of the world's total in 1800 to 36 per cent in 1900. At the same time, the concentration of the Industrial Revolution within the Triad had brought a polarization of wealth on a scale never before seen in the long history of humanity. On the eve of the Industrial Revolution, the differential in the social productivity of labour for 80 per cent of the world's population had never been greater than 2 to 1. Around the year 1900 it was 20 to 1.

The globalization that was already being celebrated in 1900 as the 'end of history' was nevertheless a recent phenomenon, achieved only gradually in the second half of the nineteenth century after the opening of China and the Ottoman Empire (1840), the repression of the Sepoy Mutiny in India (1857) and the carve-up of Africa (1885 and later).

Far from accelerating the accumulation of capital, this first globalization opened with a structural crisis from 1873 to 1896 that makes us think of the one almost exactly a century later. But the crisis went together with a new industrial revolution (applications of electricity and oil, the motor car and the aeroplane), which was expected to transform human existence much as electronics is supposed to be doing today. A parallel process also saw the emergence of the first industrial and financial oligopolies – the transnational corporations of the time. Financial globalization seemed to be here to stay, in the shape of the gold standard, and the internationalization of transactions made possible by new stock markets was discussed with as much excitement as financial globalization arouses today. Jules Verne had his hero (an Englishman, of course) travel the world in eighty days; the 'global village' was in his view already a reality.

Nineteenth-century political economy had been dominated by the great classics, Adam Smith and David Ricardo, and then by the blasts of Marx's critique. The *fin de siècle* triumph of liberal globalization brought to the fore a new generation whose main concern was to demonstrate that capitalism was insurmountable, on the grounds that it expressed the requirements of an eternal, transhistorical rationality. Léon Walras – the central figure in this generation, who not by chance has been rediscovered by present-day economists – made persistent attempts to prove that markets were self-regulating. He never succeeded in doing this, any more than the neoclassical economists of our own time have done.

In reducing society to a collection of individuals, the triumphant liberal ideology asserted that market-generated equilibrium was also the social optimum and therefore a guarantee of stability and democracy. Everything was in place to substitute a theory of imaginary capitalism for analysis of the contradictions of actually existing capitalism. This economistic conception of society found its vulgar expression in the textbooks of Alfred Marshall, which served as a bible for economic studies at that time.

The much-hailed promises of global liberalism seemed for a while to be fulfilled in the *belle époque*. From 1896 growth picked up again, on the new foundations of the second industrial revolution, the formation of oligopolies, and financial globalization. This 'way out of the crisis' not only swept off their feet the ideologues of capitalism – the new economists – but also left the workers' movement at a loss to make sense of what was happening. The socialist parties slid over from reformist positions to the more modest aim of associating themselves with management of the system, in much the same way as the discourse of

Tony Blair or Gerhard Schröder a century later. Modernizing elites in the periphery, again like their present-day counterparts, accepted that nothing was conceivable outside this dominant logic of capitalism.

The triumph of the *belle époque* lasted barely two decades. A few dinosaurs such as the then-youthful Lenin foresaw that it would all end in collapse, but their voices were not heard. They showed that liberalism – that is, the one-sided domination of capital – would not reduce the intensity of the manifold contradictions inherent in the system, but on the contrary would make them more acute. While the workers' parties remained silent and the labour unions rallied to the nonsense of a capitalist Utopia, the rumblings of a divided, disoriented social movement constantly threatened to burst forth and coalesce around new alternatives. A few talented Bolshevik intellectuals wrote ironically about the anodyne political economy of a leisure class that was amazed to see its money 'making little ones'; Bukharin called it the 'economic theory of the leisure class'.[1] Liberal globalization could only lead to militarization of the system and, in relations among the imperialist powers of the time, to a war that waxed hot and cold for 30 years between 1914 and 1945. Moreover, social struggles and violent internal and international conflicts were taking shape beneath the surface calm of the *belle époque*. In China the first-wave critics of bourgeois modernization projects were clearing a path for themselves; similar critiques were still in their infancy in India, Latin America and the Ottoman and Arab worlds, but they would eventually conquer the three continents and dominate three-quarters of the twentieth century.

Three-quarters of the twentieth century was thus marked by more or less radical projects for transforming the peripheries and 'catching up' with the capitalist heartlands – a possibility that had opened up when the global liberal Utopia of the *belle époque* fell apart. It was to be a century in which the dominant capitalism of global oligopolies and their backer states would be locked in gigantic conflicts with dominated nations and classes that refused to accept their dictatorship.

The thirty years war: 1914–45

The international arena between 1914 and 1945 witnessed both a thirty-year war between the United States and Germany to inherit Britain's defunct hegemony, and a simultaneous attempt to 'catch up' through the method of building socialism in the USSR.

In the capitalist heartlands, both the victors and the vanquished of the 1914–18 war persisted against all the odds in trying to restore the Utopia of global liberalism: they reintroduced the gold standard, maintained the colonial order through violence, and restored old liberal ways of running the economy. The results seemed positive for a brief period: growth picked up in the 1920s, due both to the dynamism of the USA and to the new forms of assembly-line labour (satirized by Charlie Chaplin in *Modern Times*), which only really came into their own after the Second World War. But it was a shaky restoration, and in 1929 the financial side of things, the most globalized part of the system, came crashing down. The next ten years, up to the outbreak of war, were a terrible period. In the face of recession, the various governments responded as they would in the 1980s, through systematic deflationary policies that merely worsened the crisis and perpetuated a spiral of descent; the mass unemployment was all the more tragic for its victims as the safety-nets of the welfare state did not yet exist. Liberal globalization did not withstand the crisis. The gold-based monetary system was given up, and the imperialist powers reorganized within the framework of their colonial empires and protected zones of influence. This was the source of the conflicts that eventually issued in the Second World War.

The various Western societies reacted to the catastrophe in their own ways. Some (Germany, Japan, Italy) sank into fascism and chose war as a means of redistributing the world pack of cards. The United States, France and Sweden – that is, the New Deal, Popular Front and Social Democratic governments respectively – took the different course of market regulation, through active state intervention supported by the working classes. This involved quite timid steps, and found its full expression only after 1945.

In the peripheries, the collapse of the *belle époque* myths ushered in a period of anti-imperialist radicalization. Certain countries in Latin America that had the benefit of political independence invented forms of populist nationalism that ranged from Mexico's new course, resting upon the peasant revolution of 1910–20, to Argentina's Peronism of the 1940s. Turkish Kemalism formed a counterpart to this in the East, while China became locked into a civil war between bourgeois modernizers with roots in the 1911 Revolution (the Kuomintang) and the communists. Elsewhere the colonial yoke delayed by several decades the crystallization of similar national-popular projects; there the issue was not development but the simple pursuit of colonial exploitation.

The isolated USSR, having vainly hoped in the 1920s for the spread of world revolution, tried to develop a new self-sufficient trajectory; a series of five-year plans, under Stalin's leadership, were supposed to enable it to catch up with the West. Lenin had already defined this path as 'Soviet power plus electrification' – which, we should note, alluded to the new industrial revolution, since it rested upon electricity rather than coal or steel. But electricity (or, in reality, largely coal and steel) gained the upper hand over Soviet power, which was emptied of meaning. In spite of the social populism that characterized official policies, centrally planned accumulation was here clearly managed by a despotic state. (It should be remembered, of course, that German unity and Japanese modernization had not been the work of democrats either.) The Soviet system proved effective as long as its goals remained simple: to speed up extensive accumulation (industrialization of the country), and to build a military force capable of facing the challenge of the capitalist adversary (first by beating Nazi Germany, then by ending America's monopoly of atomic weapons and ballistic missiles in the 1960s and 1970s).

The post-war age: from boom (1945–70) to crisis (1970–)

The Second World War inaugurated a new phase of the global system. The post-war boom (roughly from 1945 to 1975) was based on the complementarity of the three social projects of the age: (1) the national social-democratic project of building welfare states in the West, based upon the efficiency of interdependent national systems of production; (2) the 'Bandung project' of bourgeois nation-building in the periphery of the system (with its ideology of development); and (3) the Soviet project of 'capitalism without capitalists', relatively autonomous from the dominant world system. For each in its way, it was a question of a project for the development of society. The dual defeat of fascism and old-style colonialism had created a conjuncture in which it was possible for popular classes and nations subject to capitalist expansion to impose ways of regulating the accumulation of capital. These regulatory forms (to which capital itself was forced to adjust) lay at the very heart of the post-war boom.

The crisis that followed (beginning in 1968–75) saw the erosion and then collapse of the systems upon which the boom had rested. This period involved not the establishment of a 'new world order', but a chaos that is still far from overcome. The policies implemented under these conditions did not correspond to a positive strategy of capital expansion, but were designed only to manage the crisis affecting such expansion. They could not achieve this, however, since the 'spontaneous' project generated by the direct rule of capital (in the absence of cohesive and effective frameworks created by social forces) remains the Utopian one of running the world through 'the market' – that is, through the unmediated short-term interests of the dominant forces of capital. Meanwhile, the concern with development has itself vanished through the trapdoor.

Modern history is such that phases of reproduction resting upon stable systems of accumulation are succeeded by periods of chaos. In the first of these phases, the post-war boom, the unfolding of events gave the impression of a certain monotony, since dynamics within the system itself reproduced a stable architecture of social and international relations. Such phases give shape to clearly defined active subjects (social classes, states, political parties, powerful social organizations) whose practices appear solid and whose reactions are predictable in nearly every circumstance, just as the ideologies driving them enjoy seemingly uncontested legitimacy. Although the conjuncture may change, the structures remain stable – and so it is possible, even easy, to make predictions. Danger appears when those predictions are continued for too long, as if the structures in question were eternal or marked the 'end of history'. Instead of analysis of the contradictions undermining those structures, one then finds what the postmodernists have rightly called 'grand narratives', which offer a linear view of movement driven by 'force of circumstance' or 'the laws of history'. Historical subjects disappear and make way for supposedly objective structural logics.

Yet the contradictions in question continue their mole-like burrowing, and sooner or later the solid-looking structures collapse. History then enters a phase that may later be described as transitional, although those living at the time experience it as a transition to the unknown. For, during that phase, new historical subjects gradually crystallize out and grope their way to new practices, legitimizing them through new ideological discourses that are initially often confused. Only when these processes of qualitative change are sufficiently mature do new social relations emerge to define the 'post-transitional' systems. I have used the word 'chaos' very early on to describe such situations, although I have thought it important not to merge this distinctive type into mathematical theories of non-linearity and chaos which, though doubtless valid in other fields such as meteorology, should not be extrapolated to the life of society, where the intervention of historical subjects is decisive. There is no history without subjects, and history is not the product of meta-historical forces prior to itself.

The post-war boom and its visions of social development enabled huge economic, political and social transformations to occur in every part of the world. These transformations were the result of social regulation imposed upon capital by the working classes and independent nations, not (as liberal ideology claims) the result of the logic of market expansion. But they were on such a scale that they defined a new framework for the challenges that peoples around the world have to face at the beginning of the twenty-first century.

For a long time – from the Industrial Revolution in the early nineteenth century through to the 1930s (in the case of the Soviet Union) or the 1950s (in the Third World) – the contrast between centres and peripheries in the modern global system was practically synonymous with the opposition between industrial and non-industrial countries. Revolts in the periphery, whether in the form of socialist revolution (Russia and China) or of national liberation, called into question that old form of polarization by involving the respective societies in a process of modernization and industrialization. Gradually the new axis of the world capitalist system, which would define the future forms of polarization, took shape around what I call the 'five new monopolies' enjoyed by countries in the dominant Triad. These concern: the sphere of technology; worldwide financial flows (controlled by the big banks, insurance companies and pension funds in the central countries); access to the earth's natural resources; the whole area of media and communications; and weapons of mass destruction. We shall return at greater length to this fundamental question defining the new development constraints.

During the 'Bandung period' (1955–75), Third World countries practised self-reliant development policies with the aim of reducing global polarization ('catching up'). This entailed both systems of national regulation and constant negotiation, including collective bargaining between North and South, over international regulatory systems. (UNCTAD, among others, played an important role in this respect.) Another aim was to reduce the 'reserves of low-productivity labour', by transferring them to modern high-productivity sectors, even if these were 'uncompetitive' on open world markets. The uneven success of these policies (not their failure, as some like to argue) resulted in a Third World that is now itself engaged in the process of industrial revolution.

The uneven results of this industrialization, imposed upon dominant capital by social forces issuing from national liberation victories, allow us to distinguish today between first-rank peripheries, which have managed to build national productive systems capable of competing in the framework of global capitalism, and marginal peripheries, which have not been able to achieve this. We shall also return to the nature and scale of this legacy from twentieth-century experiences of development, and to the implications they bear for the twenty-first century.

To complete this rapid sketch of the political economy of transformations in twentieth-century global capitalism, I should also mention the awesome demographic revolution in the peripheries of the system, which has raised the percentage of the world's population living in Asia (minus Japan and the ex-USSR), Africa, Latin America and the Caribbean from 68 per cent in 1900 to 81 per cent today.

The third partner in the post-war global system, the countries of so-called actually existing socialism, has departed from the stage of history. The very existence of the Soviet system, with its successes in extensive industrialization as well as the military field, was a major factor impelling all the great transformations of the twentieth century. Without the danger constituted by the communist counter-model, Western social democracy would never have been able to force the establishment of the welfare state; while the existence of the Soviet system and the compulsion on the United States to coexist with it greatly expanded the room for manoeuvre of the bourgeoisies of the South. Nevertheless, the Soviet system did not succeed in progressing to a new stage of intensive accumulation, and as the end of the century approached it became clear that it was missing out on the new computer-driven industrial revolution. The reasons for its failure are complex. But central among them was the anti-democratic involution of the Soviet regime itself, which never managed to internalize the fundamental progressive requirement of deeper democratization in the direction of socialism, to achieve a form higher than the limited democracy present in the framework of historical capitalism. Socialism will either be democratic or will not exist at all – such is the lesson of the first historical break with capitalism.

Marx and Keynes were the two major inspirations for the social thought and the dominant economic, sociological and political theories that legitimated post-war practices of self-reliant national development: the welfare state in the West, Sovietism in the East and populism in the South, as well as the negotiated and regulated globalization that accompanied them. Keynes's critique of market liberalism had not been read in the 1930s, when the social relationship of forces in favour of capital had, as today, inevitably fuelled the prejudices of liberal Utopianism. But the new post-war relationship of forces, which was more favourable to labour, sidelined the liberals and meant that Keynes's work became the inspiration for the practices of the welfare state. It need hardly be said, of course, that at the same time Marx towered over the discourse of actually existing socialism. But these two dominant figures of the twentieth century gradually lost their original quality of fundamental critics, becoming instead legitimizing mentors for the practices of state power. In each case, there was a slide into dogmatism and oversimplification.

From this broad outline of twentieth-century history, a few basic lessons emerge that are indispensable for any reflection about the challenges facing the peoples of the world in the new century. The first is that the development concept is inherently critical of capitalism and can never be reduced to economic growth within capitalism: the content of development therefore depends primarily upon the social forces that put it into practice and their project for society. The second is that, if the social relationship of forces is unfavourable for development – or, in other words, if capital is in a position to impose unilaterally its own project of total subordination to profit maximization – then the ending of that dictatorial power will involve truly gigantic struggles. The three terrible decades from 1914 to 1945, filled with two world wars, two great revolutions, the great crisis of the 1930s, the rise and fall of fascism, and a long list of colonial massacres and liberation wars, were necessary for a relationship less unfavourable to the dominated classes and peoples to be established. Will there be a tragedy on a similar scale in the early decades of the twenty-first century, as a challenge to the restoration of the dictatorship of capital accompanies the forceful return of liberal illusions?

The *fin de siècle* crisis

The boom in development projects did not last until the end of the century. As early as 1968–71, the collapse of the three post-war models of regulated accumulation inaugurated a structural crisis of the system strongly reminiscent of the crisis at the end of the nineteenth century. Investment and growth rates were suddenly cut in half, unemployment began to soar and poverty to spread. The ratio measuring inequalities in the capitalist world rose from 20:1 around the year 1900 through 30:1 in 1945–48 and up to 60:1 at the end of the period of post-war growth; the richest 20 per cent of individuals on earth increased their share of the global product from 60 per cent to 80 per cent during the last two decades of the century. Globalization was fine for some. But it was a disaster for the great majority – especially peoples in the South undergoing one-sided structural adjustment, or peoples in the East locked into processes of dramatic involution. Development went by the board.

As in a previous epoch, however, this period of structural crisis was also one in which a technological revolution transformed the organization of work and eroded the efficacy, even the legitimacy, of existing forms of working-class or popular struggle and organization. The fragmented social movement has not yet found formulas strong enough for it to coalesce and rise to the new challenges. But it has made a number of remarkable breakthroughs, in directions that will increase its future capabilities. Two crucial examples of this are the entrance of women into the life of society, and the new awareness of environmental destruction which, for the first time in history, threatens the whole planet.

Crisis management, based upon a sharp swing in the balance of forces towards capital, once more gave liberalism the capacity to impose its solutions. With Marx and Keynes deleted from thinking about society, the theorists of 'pure economics' replaced analysis of the real world with a theory of imaginary capitalism, critical thought with pure sorcery. But the temporary success of this ultra-reactionary Utopianism was only a symptom of decay, testifying to the fact that capitalism was objectively ripe to be overcome.

The crisis was expressed in the fact that profits derived from exploitation did not find sufficient investment outlets likely to develop productive capacity. Management of the crisis therefore consisted in finding 'other outlets' for the surplus of floating capital, so that it did not suddenly undergo a massive loss of value. An actual solution to the crisis, however, would involve a change in the social rules governing income distribution, consumption and investment decisions – in short, a coherent social project different from one based purely upon the profitability criterion.

The path of crisis management aims to impose systematic 'deregulation', to erode and, if possible, dismantle union-protected labour 'rigidities', to liberalize wages and prices, to reduce public expenditure (especially subsidies and social services), to extend privatization, to remove external trade barriers, and so on. The use of the term 'deregulation' here is deceptive. For there are no such things as deregulated markets, except in the imaginary economy of the 'pure' economists. All markets are regulated – they can function only on that condition. The only question is who regulates them and how. The term 'deregulation' thus conceals a reality that dare not speak its name: one-sided regulation of markets by capital. Of course, the fact that the liberalization in question locks the economy into a spiral of stagnation, that it is anyway unmanageable at a global level, that it increases the number of conflicts without being able to resolve them – all this is drowned out by incantations to the effect that neoliberalism is paving the way for healthy development in the future.

Capitalist globalization requires that crisis management should operate at this level, for the vast surplus of floating capital breeds submission of the economic machinery to the profit criterion alone. Liberalization of international capital transfers, floating exchange rates, high rates of interest, a large US balance of payments deficit, Third World external debt, more and more privatization: this all makes perfect sense as a policy offering footloose capital an escape into speculative financial investment and averting the danger of massive devalorization. It will give some idea of the scale of surplus capital if we consider that international transfers of floating capital average between $80,000 billion and $100,000 billion a year, some 30 times more than the annual total of world trade ($3,000 billion).

The management of the crisis has been catastrophic for the working classes and peripheral nations, but not for everyone else. Indeed, it has been quite a juicy business for dominant sections of capital. Sharply accelerating income inequality almost everywhere in the world has produced a great deal of poverty, insecurity and marginalization for some, but it has also created new billionaires who, without a hint of embarrassment, celebrate the 'joys of globalization'.

Moreover, since the crisis management does not bring a solution, the system does not tend towards a new stabilization but sinks ever deeper into chaos. This is the context in which the United States has launched a new offensive, to restore its global hegemony as the basis for organizing the economic, political and military dimensions of the global system.

The legacy of the twentieth century: the South and the new globalization

As we have seen, during the 'Bandung period' from 1955 to 1975, Third World states implemented development policies that were (actually or potentially) self-reliant, policies almost exclusively at a national level designed to reduce global polarization through a process of 'catching up'. Their uneven record of success has meant that the Third World today is highly differentiated. We need to distinguish the following three groups.

1. The capitalist countries of East Asia (South Korea, Taiwan, Hong Kong and Singapore), and behind them South-East Asian countries (principally Malaysia and Thailand), as well as China, whose growth rates accelerated just as those in the rest of the world were slackening. After the crisis that hit them in 1997, these countries are now among the active competitors on world markets for industrial goods. Their economic

dynamism has generally gone together with a less serious worsening of social imbalances (a point that would need to be discussed and carefully qualified in individual cases), a lesser degree of vulnerability (due to the intensification of regional relations in East Asia, which are as important as in the European Union), and the still decisive role of state intervention in implementing national development strategies, even where these involve an openness to the rest of the world.

2. The countries of Latin America and India have industrial capacities that are equally important. But here regional integration is less pronounced (20 per cent for Latin America), and state intervention is less consistent. The worsening of inequalities, already huge, is all the more dramatic as growth rates remain fairly modest.

3. The countries of Africa and the Arab and Islamic world are generally still locked into an outmoded international division of labour. They remain exporters of primary products, either because they have not entered the industrial age, or because their industries are weak, vulnerable and uncompetitive. Here social imbalances mainly take the form of large impoverished and excluded sections of the population. There is not the least sign of progress in regional (intra-African or intra-Arab) integration. Growth is virtually at a standstill. Although the group contains both 'rich' countries (sparsely populated oil exporters) and poor or very poor ones, none behaves as an active participant in the shaping of the global system. In this sense, they are well and truly marginalized.[2] Here the analysis might be in terms of three development models (export agriculture, mining, oil revenue), combined with different forms of social hegemony issuing from national liberation. This would show that their 'development' was no more than an attempt to hitch themselves to the global expansion of capitalism of the time, and that in their case the term is dubious, to say the least.

The factor differentiating the active from the marginal peripheries is not only the competitiveness of their industrial production; there is also a political factor. The political rulers in the active peripheries, and behind them society as a whole despite all its contradictions, have a project as well as a strategy to achieve it. This is evident in the case of China, Korea and (to a lesser extent) certain South-East Asian countries, India and a few countries in Latin America. These national projects clash with those of the globally dominant imperialism, and the outcome will decide the shape of tomorrow's world. By contrast, the marginal peripheries have neither a project nor a strategy of their own, even if a rhetoric such as that of political Islam claims the contrary. Here it is imperialist circles that 'think for them' and have the sole initiative in projects concerning the region, such as EU–ACP cooperation, the 'Middle East project' of the USA and Israel, or Europe's vague plans for the Mediterranean; they meet with no resistance from projects originating in the respective regions. The countries in question have a passive relationship with globalization.[3] Growing differentiation among all these groups of countries has thus blown apart the concept of a 'Third World' and put an end to the strategies of a common front associated with the Bandung era.

Nevertheless, there is by no means unanimity about the nature and prospects of capitalist expansion in the countries of the former Third World. Some analysts argue that the most dynamic emergent economies are 'catching up' and can no longer be considered peripheral, even if they still only occupy middle levels in the global hierarchy. Others (including myself) insist that it is these countries that form tomorrow's true periphery. The centres–peripheries contrast, which from 1800 to 1950 was synonymous with the opposition between industrial and non-industrial economies, is today based upon new and different criteria bound up with control by the US–Europe–Japan Triad of the five previously mentioned monopolies. We shall return to this point in greater detail.

What of the marginalized regions? Are they a phenomenon without precedent in history? Or do they, on the contrary, express a permanent tendency of capitalist expansion that was held in check for a while after the Second World War, when the balance of forces was less unfavourable to the peripheries as a whole? In spite of the varied nature of the countries in question, the exceptional post-war situation created a basis for Third World 'solidarity', in its anti-colonial struggles, its demands relating to primary products, and its political will to force through modernization-industrialization in the teeth of resistance from the Western powers. But it is precisely because success on these fronts was so uneven that the cohesion and solidarity of the Third World was eroded.

In any event, even where industrialization has been most marked, the peripheries still contain varying but always very large 'reserves' of labour power that are employed, if at all, in low-productivity activities. The reason for this is that modernization policies (that is, attempts to 'catch up') impose a number of modern technological choices if they are to be efficient, or even competitive, and that these choices are extremely costly in the sense of using scarce resources of capital and skilled labour. The systematic imbalance becomes even worse whenever the modernization is compounded by growing income inequality. In such conditions, there remains a sharp contrast between the centres and the peripheries: in the former, the passive labour reserve continues to exist, varying in size with the economic conjuncture, but it is nearly always below 20 per cent; in the latter, it always constitutes the majority. The only exceptions here are South Korea and Taiwan, which, for a number of reasons (including a highly favourable geostrategic position that meant they had to be helped against the danger of 'contamination' from Chinese communism), were able to notch up unparalleled levels of growth.

What are the prospects in this regard if the tendencies uppermost today remain the principal active force governing the system as a whole as well as its constituent parts? How are relations likely to develop between what I call the active army of labour (all workers employed in activities at least potentially competitive on the world market) and the passive reserve (not only marginal layers and the unemployed, but also those employed in low-productivity sectors and condemned to poverty)?

One view is that the Triad countries will maintain their neoliberal orientation, and that a strong reserve army of labour will therefore be reconstituted on their own soil.[4] I would add that the reconstituted army will be all the larger if these countries reorganize mainly around their five monopolies to maintain global dominance, abandoning whole chunks of 'traditional' industry to dynamic peripheries. In the peripheries in question, which will remain subject to the five monopolies, there will also be a dual structure involving the coexistence of an active army (here employed in 'marginalized industries') and a reserve army. In a way, then, these trends will bring the centres and the peripheries closer to each other, though within the framework of a monopoly-based hierarchy.

Much has been written on what this implies for the concept of relative homogeneity within a national productive system and even for the very contrast between centres and peripheries. We shall return to these questions, which are closely bound up with the technological revolution currently under way. Multi-speed economies and societies are everywhere establishing themselves, in both centres and peripheries. A first world of the rich, enjoying all the comforts of the new-style society, will exist alongside a second world of harshly exploited workers, and a third (or fourth) world of the marginal and excluded.

Those with the most optimistic hopes for the future will perhaps argue that the juxtaposition of an active and a reserve army in both the centres and the peripheries will create the conditions for a renewal of consistent class struggle capable of radicalization and internationalism. My own reservations on this score stem from the following two points.

1. In the centres, it will probably be impossible to reconstitute a

large reserve army on a lasting basis, and to refocus economic activity on areas linked to the five monopolies. The political system of the Triad would scarcely permit this. In one way or another, violent explosions will make the neoliberal option untenable and cause a change of tack, either leftward in the direction of new socially progressive compromises, or rightward in the direction of fascistic national populism.

2. Even in the most dynamic peripheries, for reasons given above, it will be impossible for modernized productive activities to absorb the huge reserves of labour existing within low-productivity activities. The dynamic peripheries will therefore still be peripheries: that is, they will be societies shot through with all the major contradictions resulting from the existence of modern (sometimes quite large) enclaves within an unmodernized area – contradictions that will help to maintain their subaltern position, subject to the five central monopolies. It remains true – as the Chinese revolutionaries, among others, maintained – that only socialism can answer the problems of these societies, if we understand by socialism, not a definitive ready-made formula, but a movement giving structure to the solidarity of all, through popular strategies which, by civilized means, organize the gradual transfer of the ocean of reserves to the modern enclaves. This requires delinking: that is, the subordination of external relations to the logic of a long national-popular stage of transition.

I would add, finally, that in the dominant discourse 'competitiveness' appears as a trivial micro-economic concept expressing the myopic vision of the company director, whereas in reality it is the overall efficiency of (national) productive systems that has given their constituent companies the competitive capacity in question.

Notes

1. Nikolai Bukharin, *Economic Theory of the Leisure Class*, New York: Monthly Review Press, 1972; originally published in Russian and German in 1914.

2. See Samir Amin, 'The Political Economy of Africa in the Global System', *Africa Insight* (Pretoria), vol. 31, no. 2, 2001; and M. Diouf, A. Ndiaye, B. Founou and S. Amin, *Afrique et Nord–Sud. Co-développement ou gestion du conflit?*, Paris: L'Harmattan (Forum du Tiers-Monde), forthcoming.

3. Samir Amin, *Les régionalisations, les conventions de Lomé-Cotonou et l'association UE–ACP*, Paris: L'Harmattan (Forum du Tiers-Monde), forthcoming; and S. Amin and A. El Kenz, *Le parteneriat 'euro-méditerranéen'*, Paris: L'Harmattan (Forum du Tiers-Monde), forthcoming.

5. Giovanni Arrighi, *The Long Twentieth Century*, London: Verso, 1994. See also my comments in *Les défis de la mondialisation*, Paris: L'Harmattan, 1996, pp. 127–87.

TWO
The tools of analysis and action

Historical Marxism and historical Keynesianism

It is hardly surprising that Marx and Keynes dominated thinking about society for most of the twentieth century. The formulation of social projects in the full sense of the term – projects that constitute the framework for strategies of development – was a preoccupation in the East, in the wake of the Russian Revolution; in the developed West, where the social-democratic welfare state came into being in response to the 'communist threat'; and in the South, where national liberation movements emerged victorious. Communists, social democrats and nationalist populists all needed theoretical tools to analyse the system that was the object of their social critique, as well as to generate effective development strategies consistent with the goals of their respective projects. It was Marx and Keynes who provided such tools.

1. Marx laid the foundations for a radical critique of capitalism: that is, he drew out the essential features distinguishing it from earlier social systems, as the basis for understanding its particular dynamic and its capacity to survive its defining contradictions. This is not to say, of course, that it is able to make those contradictions less and less potent – indeed, their scale and violence only increase over time. Capitalism thus appears as a stage in a history whose end cannot come before that of the human species itself. It is a stage that must be and, one way or another, will be overcome.

I shall not repeat here my reading of what Marx had to say about these fundamental questions. But let me just recall two dimensions that seem to me essential for an understanding of the challenges facing the world today. The first concerns Marx's discovery of commodity alienation as a novel and specific form governing the reproduction of society as a whole (not only the reproduction of its economic system). This unique characteristic explains in turn why, under capitalism, economics sets itself up as a 'science', whose laws of motion impose themselves 'like laws of nature' upon modern societies and the human beings who constitute them. In other words, the fact that these laws are the product not of some transhistorical nature defining 'human existence' in the face of scarcity, but of a stage in human history involving the social relations peculiar to capitalism, is erased from the consciousness of society. This, in my view, is how we should understand Marx's definition of the 'economism' characteristic of capitalism. The second dimension concerns Marx's demonstration of the instability inherent in capitalist society, such that the reproduction of its economic system never tends to bring about any kind of general equilibrium, but moves from one disequilibrium to the next in ways that can never be predicted in advance but only registered *a posteriori*. The 'competition' among capitals – whose division is a defining feature of capitalism – means that general equilibrium is an impossibility and that it would be illusory to base one's analysis on any such tendency. Capitalism is synonymous with permanent instability. The tendencies resulting from this competition of capitals, together with the evolution of the social relationship of forces (between capitalists, between capitalists and the dominated and exploited classes, and between the states comprising capitalism as a world system), can account *a posteriori* for the movement of the system from one disequilibrium to the next. In this sense, capitalism does not exist outside the class struggle, outside inter-state conflict, outside politics. The idea that one might uncover an economic logic governing the development of capitalism is an illusion. There is no theory of capitalism distinct from its history. Theory and history are inseparable, and so too are economics and politics.

I have mentioned these two dimensions of Marx's radical critique precisely because they are the dimensions of reality left out of account in bourgeois social thought, which has been economistic ever since its origins in the Enlightenment. Its conception of 'rationality' assumed that the capitalist system, in supplanting the *ancien régime*, carried a transhistorical legitimacy that made it the 'end of history'. This original economistic alienation then became more pronounced, precisely as attempts were made to find an answer to Marx. Beginning with Walras, pure economics expressed this intensification of the economism of bourgeois social thought, which replaced analysis of the real functioning of capitalism with a myth of the self-regulating market whose very logic tended towards general equilibrium. Instability was no longer seen as an intrinsic part of that logic, but attributed to the imperfection of existing markets. Economics thus became a discourse whose main concern was no longer to know reality; its only function was to legitimize capitalism by endowing it with intrinsic characteristics that it could not actually have. Pure economics became the theory of an imaginary world.

At this fundamental level, Marx's radical critique has not been surpassed; nor can it be so long as the social system remains based upon the relations defining capitalism. On the other hand, in keeping with his own methodological refusal to separate theory from history, Marx's analyses of the contradictions within the system deserve to be developed in the light of the subsequent evolution of history itself. This requires us to leave the political economy of the capitalist mode of production and to enter the broader field of historical materialism: that is, to grasp capitalism as a historical reality existing on a world scale, and not simply to see it as the capitalist mode of production extended to the level of the planet. We must break free of the Eurocentric vision of history and capitalist expansion, by analysing the ways in which the distinctive social contradictions of each sub-group of the world system (centres and peripheries) interact and combine with each other.

Marx introduced the elements of a new approach along these lines, with all the subtlety and richness of thought with which we are familiar, and they are enough to show that it would be quite wrong to accuse him of sharing the systematic Eurocentrism that characterized bourgeois thought in his time, even if its influence can be seen to persist here and there in his work. Unfortunately, Marx did not go on to develop those first hesitant steps of historical materialism. And the historical Marxism that took shape within the European workers' movement and the Second International, from the late nineteenth century to 1914, drifted instead into a crudely Eurocentric variant that equated global expansion of capitalism with universalization of the capitalist mode of production. This simplification excluded the polarization that had loomed ever larger since the beginnings of capitalist globalization: namely, the primary intrinsic contradiction between centres and peripheries. Early on, therefore, historical Marxism was transformed into a doctrine legitimizing social imperialism. The theses of Bill Warren, originally published in the *New Left Review*, belong to this tradition, which is especially powerful in Britain, and through which the ideology of imperialism has penetrated the workers' movement.[1]

From his basic discovery that capitalism was a stage in history, and not the end of history, Marx deduced the objective necessity for it to be superseded by the building of communism. Let us look at this more closely. My own standpoint does not involve any theory of historical determinism. The fact that the distinctive contradictions of a social system have to be overcome, in one of several different ways, certainly reveals the historical character of the system in question, but the characteristics of the system that succeeds it will be shaped by the particular way in which it is overcome. Communism thus appears as one possible solution to the contradictions of capitalism. This possibility, even more striking today than it was in Marx's time, arises precisely because capitalist accumulation has created the material basis for it through prodigious development of the productive forces (and the unfulfilled potential for still more prodigious development). Of course, communism should here be broadly understood as referring to a project for human equality and liberation from economistic alienation, a project negatively defined as the 'opposite' of capitalism and made possible by the development of the productive forces. To go beyond this, by trying to define its positive structures and mechanisms, would be to fall into the Utopianism that Marx so rightly criticized for failing to see that communism will have to be built through the movement of society itself. This will take place over a long period and admit of no voluntarist short-cuts, if only because it is necessary on a world scale to reverse the massive polarization of wealth created by capitalism. If development is defined as the social project annulling this capitalist polarization, who could imagine that the challenge it represents would not at best take a good part of the twenty-first century, or more?

That communism is one possibility – but not the only one. The self-destruction of human society – through the constant aggravation of commodity alienation, the decline (not the growth) of democracy, the sharpening (not the reduction) of social inequalities both local and global – is not impossible. My reading of Marx, and the thesis I derive from it concerning 'underdetermination' in history (the autonomous logics of the various levels constituting social reality), suggest that there is a wide range of possible outcomes. The desirability of one of these does not exclude but *presupposes* deliberate strategic action, to make the autonomous logics gradually converge in the construction of communism.

History, in the twentieth century, faced the challenge of incipient revolutions aiming to build world communism on the basis of peripheries of the system (Russia, then China). All of that was or should have been foreseeable; all of that confirmed what Marx had said or begun to analyse. But historical Marxism had left everyone ill prepared for it.

For the contradiction between centres and peripheries is the principal contradiction in the actually existing world capitalist system. I say 'the *principal* contradiction', as the fundamental contradiction is the one between capital and labour, whose relationship defines the capitalist mode of production dominating the system as a whole. But every fundamental contradiction manifests itself only through principal contradictions; these are the concrete forms of its manifestation. My point, then, is that polarization on a world scale is the most violent permanent manifestation of the capital–labour contradiction in the history of the expansion of capitalism; and that up to now the most radical challenges to the capitalist order have come from powerful social movements in the peripheries of the system (the Russian and Chinese revolutions). Deleted from the vision of pre-1914 historical Marxism, the problems posed by this dominant dimension of the reality of capitalism opened a new chapter in the development of historical Marxism.

The radical revolutions of the twentieth century, in the name of socialism and under the banner of Marxism (or, to be more precise, Marxism-Leninism), therefore had to face a twofold task: to 'catch up', by somehow overcoming the legacy of peripheral capitalism through rapid development of the productive forces; and to do 'something else', which was called the construction of socialism. After the Second World War, the regimes issuing from national liberation movements in the peripheries had to face similar tasks, although the nature of their dominant social blocs meant that they were much less concerned with 'doing something else'. The two tasks were anyway not so easy to marry, although that was and still is precisely what needs to be done. Little by little – and here we cannot repeat our analysis of developments – a system came into being that gave second-stage historical Marxism its content.

This system gradually narrowed its goals to the abolition of private ownership of capital and land (one of the main characteristics of capitalism) and, on that basis, the introduction of methods of rapidly developing the productive forces. Central planning, which sums up these methods, was able with some effectiveness to make a reality of general equilibrium, so that paradoxically a term that has no meaning in the analysis of capitalism now became a useful practical concept. The effectiveness of the instrument was never more than relative, however, because the actual system developed not through 'objective economic laws' (whose effect was circumscribed by public ownership of the means of production) but through the articulation of what those laws showed to be necessary with the action of social forces responding to those laws as so many challenges.

The system in question was based upon a major theoretical confusion that equated abolition of private ownership with the institution of social ownership. What this overlooked was that social ownership can only be the result of a gradual process whereby citizens emancipate themselves and become real masters of the system, establishing at every level (from the smallest locality up to the central state) capacities for management and genuinely free decision. These capacities, necessary for the construction of communism, were negated by the force of circumstance when a single party-state, invoking its vanguard origins, took sole responsibility for management of the system and drained of all real content the democracy that had been present, sometimes strongly present, in the initial revolutionary period. This ruled out any real progress in that liberation from economistic alienation that is required for significant advances in the direction of communism. I have therefore termed what was under construction as 'capitalism without capitalists'. Historical Marxism became little more than an ideology legitimizing that system and, in particular, the central planning through which it advanced.

It is not that the material achievements were insignificant during that period on which the page has now turned; they were indeed considerable, in comparison with all the peripheral societies that remained within the orbit of 'classical' capitalism. In terms of education and health, or the lessening of inequality, the comparison leaves no room for doubt: whether between China and India, Cuba and Latin America, Titoist and pre-war Yugoslavia, or the USSR and the former Russian empire. The point is further illustrated by the devastation that came with the 'restoration of capitalism' (although I would prefer to describe this as a passage from 'capitalism without capitalists' to the traditional form of 'capitalism with capitalists').

Thus, the figure of Marx – in the clothes of the historical Marxism outlined above – dominated the history of so-called socialist societies in the twentieth century and, in weaker variants, the most advanced national liberation movements of the other peripheries. As this form of historical Marxism lost impetus and legitimacy, finding it more and more difficult to make effective use of the means of development it had allowed to be mobilized, critical Marxism made headway in the 1960s and 1970s among the most radical movements of the peripheries. I have written elsewhere about the Asian and African vocation of Marxism at that time.

2. In the capitalist centres, it was Keynes rather than Marx who dominated at least part of the second half of the twentieth century. It was never Keynes's intention to put forward any critique of capitalism in general: he was not interested in whether capitalism was by nature trans-historical or historical, nor in questions such as economistic alienation or global polarization. As an archetypal British theorist, whose knowledge of philosophy was limited to strict empiricism, his only concern was to manage the system in which he lived, in what he considered to be the best possible manner. And this did lead him to offer a serious critique of the liberal apologia for capitalism.

This variant has always expressed itself in the most extreme manner. Its dogma – for that is what it is – is based upon an imaginary axiom of self-regulating markets, whose operation within a context of maximum freedom in their favour (that is, maximum deregulation) is supposed to produce that general equilibrium of which so much is heard. This is no more nor less than the core of vulgar bourgeois ideology, which, as naively expressed by company directors, scarcely goes beyond the familiar litany of calls for cost-cutting in relation to wages and social expenditure, higher productivity as the basis for greater competitiveness, a strengthening of monopoly rents through all means including open flouting of the precepts of 'fair play', and a reduction of taxes to the lowest possible level – the aim of all this being to maximize short-term profits. But it is still necessary to prove that the application of these one-sided 'rules' yields the 'social optimum'. Pure economics – that is, the theory of an imaginary world having little in common with actually existing historical capitalism – undertakes to provide such proof. That it can do this only by violating the basic norms of scientific logic is a matter of no importance whatsoever, since its legitimizing function is of a kind that it shares with religious fundamentalism.

Capitalism is always liberal when it can be – that is, when the social relationship of forces does not compel it to adapt to other requirements than the quest to maximize short-term individual profit. Such occasions do occur in history, as at the present time. But they can never last for long, because liberalism does not produce what it claims to deliver; on the contrary, it locks society into a crisis of accumulation.

Keynes saw and understood the absurdity of the dominant liberal discourse. In this respect, his demonstration that markets left to themselves are not self-regulating but explosive is both correct and central. Keynes's starting point is the common-sense observation that market operators base their decisions on what they expect their partners or competitors to do, not on any supposedly objective tendencies. Hence the market is synonymous with instability and does not tend towards equilibrium. Post-Keynesian pure economics certainly made strenuous efforts to build these inescapable anticipations into the reasoning of economic agents, but it still completely failed to demonstrate a tendency for the market to produce equilibrium. Once again, however, the scientific setback was unimportant: the ideas of pure economics, whether true or false, asserted themselves in accordance with the social interests taken into account in the real world of capitalism.

Keynes took up questions of management in a system that he recognized to be unstable by nature. His hypotheses concerning liquidity preference, as well as his attempt to relate the marginal efficiency of capital to the temperament of businessmen and the atmosphere in which they operate, gave his propositions an appearance of scientific rigour; they were an elegant if unsound way of saying why the system was unstable by nature. It cannot be denied that the recommendations deducible from them were effective in a certain set of social circumstances, but the reasons for this were not the ones given by Keynes.

It is quite revealing that Keynes's critique, which was formulated in the 1920s and 1930s in response to the deplorable consequences of the liberal management of the economy, did not have an echo at the time. But, when the social relationship of forces shifted in favour of working people – embryonically with Roosevelt's New Deal and the French Popular Front, massively with the defeat of fascism in 1945 – the conditions became more propitious for policies deriving from a certain reading of Keynes. This passage from Keynes to what we might call historical Keynesianism involved two sets of measures, each implying acceptance of the principle of market regulation and state intervention.

The first set aimed to bring the evolution of real wages (and the total wage bill) more into line with the evolution of productivity, through negotiations (where the unions were sufficiently strong and convinced of the merits), or through state intervention, or through a combination of the two. The important point is that the harmonization principle in question had nothing to do with 'market principles'; it was a socialist planning principle whose legitimization and implementation, in capitalist societies that still respected private property, had been made possible by a favourable balance of forces. Whether all the central partners of the post-war system applied this principle in a 'neutral' and identical manner between 1945 and 1980, or whether the fluctuating relationship between wage and productivity trends in accordance with local social struggles modified competitive conditions on the world market, is an interesting problem but cannot be properly considered here.

The second set of measures concerned the management of aggregate demand. A certain reading of Keynes might explain why demand was at times inadequate (leading to chronic underemployment) and at other times excessive (leading to inflation). The conclusion then easily follows that the state – by influencing the supply of credit through public expenditure, fiscal adjustments and control over the banking system – was able to regulate the appropriate volume of aggregate demand. But we do not need Keynes to show us that aggregate demand does not spontaneously settle at the level required to maximize employment and production without provoking runaway inflation. In my Sweezyan reading of Marx, the fundamental tendency resulting from a social relationship favourable to capital is expressed in aggregate demand that always tends to be inadequate, since the system does not by itself adjust the wage level to the dynamic requirements of expanded reproduction. It is therefore necessary to find other means of absorbing the surplus. These may be either socially useful in themselves (expansion of education, health care or social services) or useful in supporting the expansion of profitable markets (infrastructural development or military expenditure). Interestingly enough, although the pure economists of our time have completely turned away from Keynes, state management of aggregate demand remains at the heart of the economic policy options actually pursued by the US administration. With Reagan, social Keynesianism certainly found itself repudiated, but the beneficiary was a kind of military Keyensianism that had been a permanent feature of the landscape since 1945. After the collapse of the ostensible Soviet enemy, it then gained new legitimacy from Washington's hegemonist ambitions.

Historical Keynesianism, reduced to a simple dogma, perfectly suited the social democracy that came to the fore in the capitalist centres after the defeat of fascism. It made it possible to manage capitalism by assuring better integration of the workforce through a socially acceptable distribution of the benefits of accumulation. This system functioned well, with a remarkable effectiveness expressed in faster growth, so long as the social relationship was favourable to the workers and the threat of 'Communist contagion' could be taken seriously. But once the first of these conditions began to change and the second ceased to exist, historical Keynesianism was bound to leave the historical stage and make way for a return of the liberals. This is what happened in the course of the 1980s and 1990s.

3. It would be wrong to suggest that there was unanimous and uncritical acceptance of the theoretical instruments outlined in the preceding section. Before historical Marxism or Marxism-Leninism took the form of a vulgate, it had continually given rise to passionate debates in the communist movement – debates that, in the 1920s, were not limited to intellectual circles but involved forces active in the terrain of politics, and finally came to a head in Trotskyism. Although certainly positive in its polemics with nascent Stalinism, Trotskyism unfortunately remained incapable of going beyond repetition of the theses of Marxism-Leninism, a dead-end that left it ill suited to escape the limits of Eurocentrism

or to grasp the nature of the challenges posed by national liberation movements in the peripheries, especially in the case of China, where it overhastily wrote Maoism off as a remake of Stalinism. Nor did Trotskyism fare better in later years, when it came to an assessment of the transformations of capitalism taking place before our eyes.

Critical social thought migrated for a while, during the 1960s and 1970s, towards the peripheries of the system, where the practices of national populism (a poorer version of Sovietism) prompted a glittering explosion of critiques of actually existing capitalism. At their heart was a new awareness of the polarization produced by the global expansion of capital, which for the previous century and a half had been underestimated or even simply ignored. The critique directed its fire simultaneously at actually existing capitalism, at social theories which legitimized its expansion, and at the ways in which socialists themselves had theoretically and practically attacked it. It was a rich and variegated critique, by no means limited to so-called 'dependency theory', which marked the entrance of the peripheries into modern thought; it re-opened fundamental debates concerning socialism and the transition to socialism, as well as the necessity for Marxism and historical materialism to overcome the limits of a still dominant Eurocentrism. Inspired for a certain period by the eruption of Maoism, this new social thought also criticized Sovietism and the neoglobalism that was looming on the horizon. There was an evident conflict here between the demands of a development that would mean something to the peoples in question, and the timid proposals which the Soviet ally summarized in a curiously negative and inadequate conception of 'a non-capitalist road'.[2] Later, when the capitalist redeployment began in the context of the crisis, critical analysis originating in the peripheries of the system – whose important contribution has been neglected in most works written in the West – showed once again that a condition for fruitfully addressing the new challenges, especially the challenge of development in tomorrow's world, is that the critique should be genuinely universalist, that is, free of any West-centrism.

Perhaps all I have outlined here is what a twenty-first-century Marxism could and should be like. Enriched by a critical reading of its history (the historical Marxisms of the twentieth century), it would critically incorporate the scope and significance of the capitalist redeployment and the new elements it has introduced, as the basis for the kind of serious debate that I shall propose below. If it fails to do this, of course, it will remain stuck in nostalgia for the past and remakes of historical Leninism,

Stalinism, Maoism or Trotskyism. That will yield nothing capable of meeting the real challenges, and instead the way will be left open for reactionary liberal Utopias and various kinds of empty fixation.

Socialization through the market or through democratization?[3]

Democracy is the absolute condition for social progress, or even its very expression, yet it is only recently that this idea seems to have become generally accepted. Not so long ago the widespread dogma in both the East and the South maintained that democracy was a 'luxury' that could arrive only after 'development' had solved the material problems of society. This was the official doctrine shared by ruling circles in the capitalist world (who used it to justify supporting military dictators in Latin America or autocratic regimes in Africa), by Third World states (Latin American *desarrollismo* clearly displayed it, and the single-party idea was not the preserve of the socialist countries), and in the Soviet system.

Now the thesis has turned virtually overnight into its opposite. In every or almost every country, a concern for democracy has become the stuff of everyday official discourse, and a duly issued certificate of good democratic practice is a 'prerequisite' for the continuation of aid by the large rich democracies. The rhetoric is more than dubious, however, if one considers the extent to which the cynical use of double standards expresses the prioritization of other, hidden objectives and devices of straightforward manipulation.

Democracy is a modern concept, in the sense that modernity itself is based upon the principle that human beings individually and collectively (that is, societies) are responsible for their history. For this idea to be formulated, it was necessary to get rid of the religious and other 'traditional' (transhistorically conceived) alienations that characterized pre-capitalist forms of rule. The modernity in question was therefore born with capitalism, and the democracy it produced is, like everything else, as limited as capitalism itself. In its bourgeois historical forms, the only ones known and practised until today, it constitutes no more than one phase. Neither modernity nor democracy has reached the end of its potential development. This is why it is preferable to speak of democratization, thereby emphasizing the dynamic aspect of a still unfinished process, rather than simply of democracy (which reinforces the illusion that a finished formula can be given to it).

Bourgeois social thought has always, ever since its origins in the 'Enlightenment', been based upon the separation of different areas of social life (economic management and political management, among others), and the adoption of specific principles expressing the demands of 'Reason' in each of these areas.

In this way of looking at things, democracy is the rational principle of good political management: since men – never women in those days, and in fact only well-off educated men – are rational, they should be responsible for making the laws by which they wish to live and for selecting people to enforce them. Economic life, on the other hand, is governed by principles expressing the demands of 'Reason' (synonymous with human nature): private property, freedom of enterprise, and market competition. One recognizes here the principles of capitalism, which in themselves have nothing to do with democracy, especially if this is conceived as implying that all are equal – both men and women, of course, but also property-owners and the propertyless. (We should note that private property exists only if it is exclusive – that is, if there are also people who own none!)

The separation of the economic and the political immediately raises the question of whether their two distinct logics have convergent or divergent outcomes. Contemporary discourse assumes their convergence as a self-evident truth that stands in no need of discussion: democracy and the market beget each other; democracy requires the market, and vice versa. Nothing could be further from the truth, as the history of the real world has shown.

Enlightenment thinkers were more demanding than the vulgar minds of our own age: they asked why this convergence existed and on what conditions. Taking their concept of 'Reason' as the common denominator of both political and economic management, they argued that if men were rational their political choices could not but have the effect of strengthening the economic results produced by the market, so long as the exercise of democratic rights was withheld from women (notoriously emotional rather than rational), as well as from slaves, the poor and the destitute (proletarians), who merely obeyed their instincts. Democracy therefore had to be based on a tax qualification, so that it was reserved only for males who were at once citizens and entrepreneurs. Understandably, the way they voted in elections was probably always – or nearly always – in accordance with their interests as capitalists. But this meant that politics lost its autonomy in the convergence of the political and the economic, not to say the subordination of the former to the latter. Economistic alienation here operated to the full in masking this cancellation of the autonomy of the political.

The subsequent extension of democratic rights to other than citizen-entrepreneurs was not the spontaneous result of capitalist development, nor an expression of its requirements. On the contrary, it was the victims of the system – the working class and women – who gradually won those rights in struggle against it. There was always a danger that the system would become unstable, or even explosive, as democratic elections brought into the open the potential clash between the will of the majority (which obviously included those exploited by the system) and the fate that the market reserved for them. Or, at the very least, there was a danger that the market would have to submit to the expression of social interests that did not coincide with the economic requirement of maximum profitability for capital; that regulation of the market through means external to its own strict logic would present a threat for some (capital) and an opening for others (citizen-workers). That was a possibility, and it actually materialized in conditions such as those of the post-war welfare state.

But it is not the only way in which the divergence between democracy and the market can be rendered less threatening to the system. If a particular history has resulted in the fragmentation and impotence of critical social currents, so that there appears to be no alternative to the dominant ideology, democracy can be drained of everything that might be troublesome or dangerous to the market. It then becomes what we might call 'low-intensity democracy'. You can vote any way you like: white, blue, green, pink or red. It won't have any effect, because your fate is decided elsewhere, outside parliament, in the realm of the market. The subordination of democracy to the market (not the convergence of the two) then finds its reflection in the language of politics. Alternation (changing the faces at the top to keep doing the same thing) takes over from any presentation of alternatives (doing something different).

That is where we are at today. It is a dangerous situation, because the declining credibility and legitimacy of democratic procedures threatens to lead ever more violently to their straightforward replacement by an illusory consensus based on such forces as religion or ethnic chauvinism. In the peripheries of the system, the stark requirements of uncontrolled capitalism produce the tragic farce of a kind of impotent 'junk democracy' (Mobutu replaced by two hundred Mobutist parties!).

Democracy is a concept that does not suffer any infringement of its essential universalism. But the dominant discourse, even when articulated by forces subjectively 'on the left', trusses up democracy in a way that ultimately denies the unity of the human species, in favour of 'genders', 'communities', 'cultural groups', and so on. We shall return to the question of cultural identities in connection with the contemporary crisis of the state and democracy. We would have to descend a level to consider the curious and currently fashionable discourse of 'good governance', a mere phrase referring to a hodgepodge of administrative methods from which the real problems of political, social and economic power have, by way of precaution, been eliminated in advance. This naive jumble of pious sentiments – ranging from the ending of corruption to the improvement of various services – is expressed in the inimitable style of American 'management', with all its characteristic stupidities. Let us leave it to the learned experts at the World Bank.

If there is no convergence, then, and especially no 'natural' convergence of democracy and the market, might we conclude that development in the banal sense of rapid economic growth plus market expansion (there is virtually no experience of other kinds) is incompatible with the exercise of any moderately advanced democracy? There is certainly no shortage of facts to suggest that this is so. The 'successes' of South Korea, Taiwan, Brazil under the military dictatorship and various nationalist populisms in their period of ascent were not due to systems that held democracy in particularly high regard. Longer ago, Germany and Japan were less democratic in their 'catching-up' phase than their British and French rivals had been. And the twentieth-century socialist experiments, which notched up sometimes remarkable growth rates, were not marked by excesses of democracy. On the other hand, it might be said that post-war democratic Italy modernized with a rapidity and depth that fascism, for all its bragging, never managed to achieve; and that Western Europe, with the advanced social democracy of its post-war welfare state, experienced the most phenomenal period of development in its history. The comparison in favour of democracy might be further strengthened by pointing to the numerous dictatorships that produced nothing but stagnation or even ruinous involution.

Should we then take a more guarded attitude, rejecting any correlation of development with democracy and simply noting that whether they converge or not depends upon the particular conditions? This is an acceptable position if one is content with the banal definition of development as rapid growth within the system, but not if one sees that global capitalism polarizes by its very nature and that development is therefore a critical concept which needs to be integrated with that of an alternative, post-capitalist society. Such a society can be built only through the progressive action of peoples that have set it as their conscious goal.

Is there another definition of democracy than the one implicit in such purposive action?

Democracy really is the precondition of development. This statement, which has nothing in common with what the dominant discourse has to say on the subject, is an affirmation that without democracy there can be no socialism (no better alternative to capitalism), but also that the advance of democratization requires a commitment to the path of socialist transformation.

Commodity alienation places freedom in a privileged position among human values: individual freedom in general, of course, but also the particular freedom of the capitalist entrepreneur, whose energy is un-shackled and whose economic power is increased. There are other human values, however, such as equality. This is not directly bound up with the requirements of capitalism, except in the most immediate sense of the (partial) equality of rights which permits the blossoming of free enterprise and condemns the free worker to the status of a wage-earner selling his or her labour-power as a commodity. At a higher level, the value of 'equality' comes into conflict with the value of 'liberty' – although in the history of at least part of Europe, especially France, they are placed on an equal footing, as in the famous motto of the Republic: Liberty, Equality and Fraternity. The conflict between the two is no accident and has complicated origins. No doubt one element, most visible in the case of the French Revolution, was the intense struggles of popular classes seeking to gain autonomy from the goals of the bourgeoisie – a contradiction openly expressed when the Montagnards rightly claimed that 'economic liberalism' (freedom in the full American sense of the term) was the enemy of democracy (understood as meaning something for the popular classes).

This will help us to understand one of the differences still apparent today between the societies and cultures of Europe and America. The functioning and the interests of dominant capital on the two sides of the Atlantic are probably not as different as the well-known opposition between 'Anglo-Saxon' and 'Rhineland' capitalism sometimes suggests; the conjunction of their interests even explains the stability of the US–Europe–Japan Triad. Yet the respective judgements of society, the social projects that implicitly or explicitly haunt people's imagination, remain quite dissimilar. In the United States, the value of liberty has the whole terrain to itself without encountering any problem, whereas in Europe it constantly has to strike a balance with the value of equality.

American society treats equality with contempt: not only does it tolerate extreme inequality, it takes it as a sign of the 'success' promised by liberty. But liberty without equality is savagery. The manifold violence generated by this one-sided ideology is not due to chance and does not give rise to political radicalization – on the contrary. The dominant culture in European societies has combined the values of liberty and equality in a less unbalanced manner; this combination was indeed the basis for the historic compromise of social democracy. Unfortunately, however, the society and culture of Europe are now tending to draw closer to those of the United States, treating them as models and objects of invasive adulation.

The presidential system invented by the American Revolution serves to displace and weaken political debate, by replacing a choice of ideas and programmes with a contest between individuals (even if these are supposed to 'embody' ideas and programmes). Furthermore, the almost inevitable polarization between two individuals sharpens each one's quest for a broad consensus reaching into the wavering and least political centre ground, at the expense of radical policy options. It actively encourages conservatism.

American-style presidentialism spread without difficulty to the whole of Latin America, then to Africa and much of Asia, for similar reasons connected with the limited nature of national liberation movements in the modern age. Today it is in the process of conquering Europe, despite the fact that there it has traditionally been associated with demagogic Bonapartist populism and has left appalling memories among democrats. France, alas, began the new trend with the creation of de Gaulle's Fifth Republic, which marked not an advance of democracy but a step back, and now French society seems to have well and truly settled into the presidential system. Arguments concerning the 'instability of governments' in parliamentary regimes are here nothing but pure opportunism.

The presidential system also favours coalitions of diverse interests – ideally one coalition behind each of two candidates – to the detriment of genuine political parties, including socialist parties, which might put forward real social alternatives. Once again, the case of the United States speaks volumes in this respect. There is not really a Democratic Party and a Republican Party; Julius Nyerere said with more than a touch of humour that they were 'two single parties' – a fine definition of 'low-intensity democracy'. This is also how the popular classes perceive democracy in the United States: they do not vote, because they (rightly) think there is no point.

In my view, other contemporary trends in the institutionalization of

'Western' democracy are no less negative and are likely to give added strength to conservatism. 'Decentralization', for instance, associated with greater powers for elected local and regional authorities, serves to strengthen 'community spirit' and the power of local notables. It is well known that in France the new regional authorities have proved to be more right-wing than their equivalent at national level. Nor is this an accident. For, within the European framework, the stated aim of the decentralization principle is to 'break up nations' in favour of regions that, in varying degrees, are capable of directly inserting themselves into the EU's economic system; no attention is paid to what might happen as a result of the worsening of inequality that this strategy implies (the unity of Italy and Spain is already under threat, for example). Yugoslavia went down this road after the death of Tito, and G-7 and the World Bank welcomed it at the time. We know where that led.

The absence of permanent bureaucracies in the Anglo-American model, which Marx and Engels thought an advantage in comparison with the solidly rooted bureaucratic legacies in continental Europe, becomes a means for conservative political rulers to entrust the implementation of their programmes to *ad hoc* clientelist networks, largely stemming from business milieux, which bear no long-term responsibility and act as both judge and interested party. Is this really an advantage? Whatever else one might say of *l'Enarchie* – and there is certainly a lot of truth in criticisms of this French system of rule by graduates of the École nationale d'administration – is it not better (or less bad) to have a bureaucracy recruited in a genuinely democratic manner, until we reach the far-off day when society can do without bureaucracies altogether? Ill-considered criticism of 'bureaucracy' in general, so common a refrain nowadays, directly inspires those systematic campaigns that seek to undermine the very idea of public service and to replace it with market-based private services. Any objective glance at the real world shows that (allegedly bureaucratized) public service is not as inefficient as it is often claimed to be, as a comparison between the USA and the EU in terms of health care perfectly illustrates. Moreover, in a democracy, public service is at least potentially open to public scrutiny, whereas market-based services are protected by 'business secrecy'. To replace public service (that is, socialization through democracy) with private service (socialization through the market) is to help strengthen the dominant view of politics and economics as two rigorously separate domains, a view totally destructive of the potential for a radicalization of democracy.

An 'independent' judicial system and its extreme logical consequence, elected judges, have also shown how they can strengthen conservative or reactionary prejudices, hindering radicalization instead of promoting it. Yet the model is now being imitated elsewhere (in France, for example), with immediate results on which I shall refrain from commenting.

Right from the beginning, the basic thesis of bourgeois social thought – that democracy and the market 'naturally' converge – contained within it the danger that is now upon us. For it presupposes social reconciliation, a society without conflict, as described in various so-called postmodernist positions; convergence becomes a dogma, about which there are no more questions to be asked. We are then dealing not with an attempt to understand real-world politics as scientifically as possible, but with a theory of imaginary politics, in much the same way that 'pure economics', in its own field, is a theory not of actually existing capitalism but of an imaginary economy. Once the Enlightenment postulate of 'reason' gives way to an understanding of the historical relativity of social logics, it is no longer possible to accept the dogma of a convergence between democracy and the market.

The contradiction between the individual and the collective, which is inherent in every society at all levels of its reality, was overcome in all pre-modern social systems through negation of the first term – that is, through the taming of individuals by society, so that they could be recognized only in and through their status within the family, the clan or society. In the ideology of the modern (capitalist) world, by contrast, the terms of the negation are reversed: modernity affirms itself through the rights of the individual, even against society. This reversal is only the initial prerequisite of liberation, for it also releases a potential for permanent aggression in relations among individuals. Capitalist ideology expresses this reality in its ambivalent ethic, where the devastating effects of its glorification of competition – 'May the strongest man win!' – may sometimes be held in check by other principles originating in religion or earlier social forms. If these barriers give way, the one-sided ideology of individual rights can produce nothing but horror.

How then, beyond capitalism, will a dialectical synthesis make it possible to reconcile the rights of the individual with the rights of the collective? How will such a reconciliation make the life of individuals and society more transparent?

The reader will have noticed the analogy between the way in which Utopian liberalism related to pragmatic management in historical capitalism, and the way in which socialist ideology related to the actual management of Soviet society. The Bolshevik ideology in question, following on from pre-1914 European social democracy, involved a facile linear conception of the necessary course of history, a 'meaning of history' in which the natural convergence of different areas of social existence was never open to doubt. But this reading of historical Marxism was not the only possible reading of Marx; it is not mine, in any event. In its dogmatic conception of convergence, economic management through the Plan (rather than the market) evidently produced an adequate response to people's needs; democracy could do no more than reinforce the planning decisions, as it would be irrational to oppose them. Here too, however, imaginary socialism conflicted with what was necessary for the management of actually existing socialism, which faced real and serious problems such as that of 'catching up' through rapid development of the productive forces. The regime provided for this with cynical practices that it neither could nor did admit in public. Totalitarianism was common to the two systems and was expressed in the same way: through systematic lying. If its manifestations were more violent in the USSR, as they obviously were, this was because the development gap exerted extreme pressure, whereas the more advanced position of the West gave its societies a protective cushion (hence its totalitarianism was often 'weaker', as in the consumerism of the periods of easy growth).

To give up the thesis of convergence ('over-determination') and to accept that different realms of social existence have different, conflicting logics ('under-determination') is both analytically and practically necessary: that is, it is an essential prerequisite both for an interpretation of history that is able to reconcile theory with reality, and for the elaboration of strategies that can make action genuinely effective and permit social progress at every level.

Socialization, understood as the reconciliation of individual and society, has taken successive historical forms, each with a different logic of its own. Before capitalism, socialization was based upon consenting or forced support for common religious beliefs, as well as personal allegiance to lordly or royal dynasties. In the modern world, it is based upon the gradual expansion of capitalist market relations into all aspects of social existence, where they largely dominate if not totally suppress all other forms of solidarity (nation, family, community). Although this 'socialization through the market' permitted extraordinarily rapid development of the productive forces, it has also aggravated their destructive characteristics. It tends to reduce human beings to the status of 'people', with no identity other than that of passive consumers (*qua* economic beings) and equally passive spectators rather than citizens (*qua* political beings).

Democracy, never more than embryonic under such conditions, can and should become the basis for a quite different kind of socialization, one that is capable of restoring to integral human beings a full responsibility for the management of every aspect of social, economic and political life. If socialism (the term used to describe this perspective) cannot be conceived without democracy, the conflict between democratization and the logic of capitalism implies that the progress of democracy must be inscribed within a socialist perspective. No socialism without democracy; no democratic progress without socialism.

Notes

1. Bill Warren, 'Imperialism and Capitalist Industrialization', *New Left Review* 81, 1973; and see Perry Anderson's remarks in praise of the article in the same issue.

2. I can do no more here than refer the reader to my remarks on the subject in S. Amin, *Re-reading the Postwar Period: An Intellectual Itinerary*, New York: Monthly Review Press, 1994.

3. For a development of the points made here, see also S. Amin, 'La mondialisation économique et l'universalisme politique: une contradiction majeure de notre époque', *Alternatives Sud*, vol. 6, no. 3, 1999; and S. Amin, 'Marx et la Démocratie', *La Pensée*, December 2001.

THREE
The redeployment of capitalism

§ Even serious observation and analysis of what is new in the contemporary global economy cannot, in my view, yield a future scenario with a sufficiently high degree of probability to appear virtually certain. This is not to deny, of course, the importance of the 'new facts'. But facts never speak for themselves, and only analysis will allow us to place them in a meaningful context in which the long-term structural trends can emerge without being confused with passing conjunctural changes. The dominant discourse, in its vulgar variants, not only confuses fleeting with lasting change; it lapses into economic determinism by constantly repeating, with as much arrogance as ignorance, the Thatcherite mantra that 'there is no alternative'.

In what follows, I intend to present elements for debate that highlight what seem to me two of the major problem and questions:

1. Can we, in what is 'new', convincingly distinguish between that which will have lasting effects and that which will prove to be only a passing phenomenon, in relation to the accumulation crisis characterizing the present phase of transition?
2. How should we analyse the possible interaction between such lasting trends and the fundamental permanent logic that defines capitalism?

The unfolding of the crisis[1]

There is general agreement that the 1970s, 1980s and 1990s were marked by declining growth rates and financial hypertrophy; this is a fact that cannot be contested.

The rate of growth of global GDP, which had been above 5 per cent before 1970, fell to 4.5 per cent, then 3.4 per cent and then 2.9 per cent for the last three decades of the century. Nor is there anything to suggest that the trend will be reversed in the first two decades of the twenty-first century, even if the G-7 governments ceremonially declare each year that 'tomorrow will be fine' and pretend to forget that reality has given the lie to similar statements they made the previous year. The slackening of growth has gone hand in hand with a deepening of international competition, as the proportion of exports in GDP has risen from 9 per cent in 1960 to 22 per cent in 1996.

The slowdown has everywhere created difficulties for public finances, as tax revenue has buckled less than public expenditure under the pressure. Deficits have generally been met through an expansion of the national debt, which, in the G-7 countries, rose from 42 per cent of GDP in 1980 to 72 per cent in 1998. At the same time, governments chose to reward capital investment in the national debt, by raising interest rates from 0.8 per cent for the years 1960–69 to 6.0 per cent for 1980–89. Champions of liberalism defend this by saying that 'the market' dictated it in response to the growing demand for government borrowing.

In general, what is called financial hypertrophy involves a set of phenomena that can be easily recognized and measured: (a) a volume of capital markets (stocks and shares, government securities and private-sector loans) expanding at a rate far above that of economic growth, to reach 189 per cent of Triad GDP in 1995; (b) an extraordinary diversification of the arrangements and instruments available on these markets (through the invention of multiple 'derivatives'), together with an explosion of what can only be called speculative financial operations; (c) the growing weight of finance in corporate affairs, as financial investment outside the company takes an increasing share of resources in comparison with investment in physical assets (in the case of France, 36 per cent of company resources against 48 per cent for real investment in 1989, compared with 3 per cent and 78 per cent respectively in 1979); and (d) progressive globalization of the financial hypertrophy, expressed in stock-market capitalization in so-called 'emerging' economies (such as Hong Kong, Singapore and Malaysia), which soared from less than 70 per cent of GDP in 1983 to more than 250 per cent in 1993.

None of these trends is disputed; the disagreements appear only when we come to the underlying causes and, above all, the medium- to long-term prospects.

The pseudo-science of pure economics, inspired by liberal doctrine, can offer no more than a purely tautological explanation: the trends in question are an expression of 'market laws', as applied by liberal policy options of recent decades; they serve to correct 'distortions' created by the 'anti-liberal' interventionist policies of previous decades. This essentially circular argument is thin in the extreme. For, if earlier interventionism produced higher growth (hence less unemployment) and a more stable distribution of income (hence less growth in inequality), it is not at all clear why it was worse than the 'good principles' which produce the opposite.

Liberal doctrine sometimes falls back on an ancillary argument:

namely, that the 'difficult' current trend is due to sharper competition on world markets that are much more open than in the bad old days of 'protectionist intervention'. This opening is supposed to have happened by itself, in the wake of globalization that had the force of an objective, quasi-natural tendency independent of economic policy options. But, again, the argument lacks any substance. If sharper global competition results in slower growth for all, how is the principle of uncontrolled opening superior to the international market regulation that used to result in general growth (albeit with a smaller gap between the growth rates of GDP and world trade)? An empirical examination of the facts would logically point in the opposite direction from liberal dogma. In the past, the engine of growth was not foreign trade, and the latter grew as an accompaniment to the expansion of internal markets. Now the idea is to make exports the engine of growth, but the result is a general slowdown. So in what way is this superior?

In the end, liberal dogma can save itself only if the theories inspired by it can show that current trends are merely transitory, that the eventual new structure will ensure stronger growth for every country (whatever its level of development) that embraces liberal principles, and that the trickle-down effect will be of benefit to all layers of the population. But this has never been shown. We are simply asked to believe it, because the curative powers of the market are an article of faith.

I would like to suggest quite a different explanation for these current trends, before examining what is likely to issue from them. The core of my analysis is the relationship of social forces, which – to simplify matters – consists of two sets of relations: those through which conflicts between labour and capital are expressed in each country, and those through which conflicts between national systems participating in the global system are expressed. The evolution of these two sets of social relations governs the evolution of the structure of markets.

Now, in the period from 1945 to 1980 these relations were more favourable (less unfavourable) for labour and peripheral nations than they subsequently became. They underlay both the policy choices of the time ('market regulation', to give them a general name) and the success of those policies (high growth, less unequal distribution). The gradual exhaustion of the development potential of growth models based upon these social relations created the conditions for (as often happens in history) quite a sudden reversal in favour of capital in its relations with labour, and therefore also in favour of the 'centres' (the Triad) in their relations with the peripheries. Today, the three models of regulated accumulation – the welfare state in the capitalist heartlands, Soviet-style socialism, and the nationalist populism of the peripheries – have ceased to exist.

From the late 1960s, the fading development potential of the post-war growth models was expressed in a marked tendency for the rate of profit to decline, which prompted those in possession of capital either to delay investment decisions or, in the case of companies, to favour investment to boost their competitiveness instead of operations to expand their already under-utilized productive capacity. Those corporations (mainly transnationals) that achieved the greatest increase in competitiveness were the ones that took the lead in, and were most likely to benefit from, the 'global opening' of markets. The crisis, in this first stage, was a crisis of over-accumulation.

This crisis, which mainstream economists at the time described as 'conjunctural', was supposed to correct the 'distortions' produced at the end of the previous boom (the 'thirty glorious years') and quickly to launch a new round of growth. But that was not at all how things developed. It became a deeper long-term crisis, and from the mid-1970s mass unemployment spread throughout the OECD countries for the first time since 1945 (eventually reaching Japan in the 1990s). The crisis unfolded in a regressive spiral: constant slackening of growth, rising unemployment, greater inequality of income, 'financialization' of the economy. What were the reasons for this?

Conventional economists had no answers. They invoked either a secondary conjunctural phenomenon (the oil price adjustment of 1973)[2] or a factor such as 'technological revolution' which, in their own minds and their own theory, was 'exogenous'. I shall return to this point below. The bankruptcy of mainstream economics was caused by its fundamental prejudices, its wilful neglect of the evolution of social relations.

In reality, the long-term duration of the crisis can be explained only by reference to a shift in social relations that was increasingly unfavourable to the working classes and the peripheral nations and increasingly favourable to dominant, transnational capital. Strengthening of the power of capital, slackening of growth, sharpening of social inequalities, rising rates of profit: these interlinked trends reinforced one another in the 'deflationary' spiral. Neoliberal government policies followed the wishes of capital and produced an outcome that served its only requirement: a recovery of profit rates.

Growing social inequality – measured by the relative share of profits and earned income in value-added – upset the balance of two factors:

the structural distribution of the net product between wages and profits; and the correspondence between effective demand (determined by wages) and the investment volume required for matching levels of production. The resulting imbalance broke the engine of expanding reproduction and replaced it with the slowdown or even reversal of growth.

The nature of the crisis changed: it was no longer an over-accumulation crisis but a crisis of under-consumption or relative over-production. The only way out was therefore a set of regulatory policies that boosted demand by ensuring a distribution of income more favourable to the workers and the peripheral nations, even if this meant that the rate of profit again fell. But such a revision of the income distribution structure could come about only through a strengthening of the social power of the victims of capitalist exploitation, and in any event not through market mechanisms obeying the logic of profit maximization for capital. The 'deflationary spiral' could be broken only through a new rise of social struggles and fresh victories against capital.

Liberal discourse has no other function than to legitimize the demands of capital – first and foremost, a recovery of profit rates. The myth of a self-regulating market makes it possible to claim that such a recovery will eventually produce growth, whereas in fact it goes hand in hand with slowdown and rising inequality.

Conventional economists have never come up with anything other than rationalizations of current policies, themselves defined by the social relationship of forces characterizing successive moments in the history of actually existing capitalism. The massive rallying of these economists to liberalism is thus an expression of their wish to rationalize – and legitimize – the policies of capital at a time when there is a social imbalance in its favour. Liberalism reflects a permanent dream of capital: to gain unilateral control over society in all its dimensions and to subject it to the single logic of profit maximization. But the dream is a false Utopia, since what that single logic produces is not expansion but its opposite: the deflationary spiral. Expansion requires social relations less unfavourable to labour. The peculiarity of capitalism is that it works 'well' when its enemies are powerful and capital is forced to adapt to demands that are not part of its exclusive logic.

Liberal doctrine sets out to prove that this is not how things are, that social progress is a by-product of accumulation strong enough to subject society to the profit motive. But, in order to demonstrate this, it has to give up analysis of actually existing capitalism (which could not ignore the state of social relations) and replace it with a theory of imaginary capitalism or 'self-regulating markets' – a theory, that is, of non-reality.

The mistake, even the stupidity, of those who represented and at least partly defended the social interests of the victims of capital – I mean the social democrats – was to believe that the defeat of their rivals and adversaries (the communists of actually existing socialism and the national populists of the Third World) heralded their own triumph. For in reality it would lead to their own defeat and their rallying to liberalism, which in turn created more favourable conditions for the unilateral diktat of capital.

Financialization: a temporary phenomenon or a sign of lasting change in capitalism?

The main positions inspired by the *Zeitgeist* claim that 'financialization' will be a lasting phenomenon in the new phase of capitalism that lies ahead. The inverted commas are there to indicate that this term, like 'globalization', reflects the imprecision and incorrectness of current discourse. For the capitalist system has always been 'financialized': capitalist accumulation cannot be conceived without money and credit.

The constraint of macro-economic equilibrium is first expressed in real terms. Each constituent element of resources (gross output, imports) and expenditure (public consumption, private consumption, gross fixed capital formation, stock variations, exports) is itself the sum of real values. But capital (fixed capital and stocks) can be understood in two ways. In real terms, it is defined by the aggregate value of fixed capital and stocks of raw materials, semi-finished goods and finished goods that do not enter into final consumption. In financial terms, it is defined by the aggregate value of securities held by property-owners (shares, private bonds); public bonds give rise to another dimension of property, an entitlement to income from future production.

Based upon this dichotomy in the evaluation of capital, and the possible autonomization of the market value of securities, the term 'financialization' therefore denotes types of economic management and decision-making (and the accumulation behind them) whose aim is to maximize the growth of financial assets, as opposed to types of management whose aim is to maximize the company rate of profit. Of course the two types are not unrelated, since the appreciation of securities depends on profit, but this mediated relation does not cancel the specificity of a quite unique mode of accumulation. According to Michel Aglietta,[3] the mode of accumulation of contemporary capitalism is new in the sense that it is based upon types of management that directly aim to maximize the growth of financial assets. Hence the name 'financialization'.

In fact, the thesis of asset-centred accumulation points up the relationship between the ownership and management of capital. Harmonization of the two, though never full or trouble-free, dominated the structures of nineteenth-century industrial capitalism. Then, for a century between 1880 and 1980, they tended to go their separate ways but never fell completely out of step with each other, capitalism being based as it is on the fundamental legal principle of the sanctity of property. The relative separation, whose forms varied with the country and period, was closely linked to the formation of oligopolies and the shifting relationship between real, identifiable capital (within companies) and the financial dimension expressing forms of ownership (public limited liability companies, bank–company relationship, shareholder expansion, and so on). Within a Marxist perspective, the reasons for this separation are not difficult to grasp: it testifies to the growing contradiction between the socialization of production and private ownership of the capital that is in command of management. Others put forward different theories of this separation (Burnham, for instance, and in a 'milder' form Galbraith), and tried to show that a public and private 'technocratic class' of managers was taking over from titular owners. Keynes hailed the advantages of this trend, since it permitted the 'euthanasia of savers and *rentiers*' and thereby freed capital, for a time, from the destructive dogmas of liberalism.

The discourse currently in fashion (whose association with the liberal return in force is not accidental) argues that we are witnessing a restoration of the higher rights of property-owners, and that this category no longer consists only of a tiny bourgeois minority but includes large majorities of ordinary wage-earners, either through the institutional investments of pensions funds, unit trusts, and so on, or through direct participation in the stock market. Asset-centred accumulation is thus simply what these property-owners require for the financial profitability of their investments.

This line of argument is not very different from age-old visions of a 'people's capitalism' or 'mass share ownership', nor is it more in tune with the realities. Capital remains dominated by the oligopolies, now called transnational corporations, which are in turn dominated by a handful of out and out capitalists. The Baron de Sellières, who presides over the fortunes of the MEDEF employers' federation in France, belongs to that handful. The hundreds of thousands of Eurotunnel shareholders, duped and now regrouped into an association they themselves have decided to call *les Eurocons du tunnel*, certainly do not. Mutual funds are not 'democratically' run by their investors; those who manage them are financial technocrats who deserve to be called real partners of the dominant capital.

Reflections on the growing importance of pension funds have a natural place in the discourse of 'people's capitalism'. In emphasizing the relative ageing of the population in the Triad and the resulting demands on pension funds, such analyses present the 'creditor bloc' as if it were a fully constituted social force conscious of its distinct interests, a bloc made up of all pensioners and, behind them, stable income-earners, who benefit from financial capitalization of their funds and share the fund manager's overriding concern to eliminate the spectre of inflation. This bloc is contrasted to the 'socially excluded' bloc of the unemployed and workers without job security, so that the social divide is supposed no longer to run between capital and labour as a whole but between the 'creditor bloc' (combining capital and labour) and excluded layers of the population. The question deserves to be discussed. For the private capitalization of pension funds (the American model) is opposed to the tradition of European countries, and the left in general, which prefers the distributive system. It is true that the powers that be in Europe have now decided to replace the distributive system with the American model – a strategy for the creation of a creditor bloc which, far from being inevitable, may be precisely designed to favour the dominant forces of capital by forestalling any united front of labour.

The thesis of asset-centred accumulation seems to be little more than the ideological expression of a social democracy that has gone over to liberalism. Claiming to believe in 'people's capitalism', it actually accepts and legitimizes the strategy of capital to replace the capital/labour opposition with an effective opposition between generations (active/retired) and to deepen the divide between sections of the working class with more or less stable employment and sections with little or no job security. The aim of the thesis is to modify the fundamental relationship of forces, and to this end it calls upon people to accept the new order of things and to give up social struggles. Asset-centred accumulation is not an objective necessity imposed on society; it is a strategy of capital.

Can the appreciation of assets 'take flight' and become independent of the real economy? If the estimated value of assets is growing at a faster rate than the economy, this can only mean an increasingly unequal distribution of GDP in favour of capital. It might be said that this is possible because the 'individuals' making up the new society are both workers and property-owners, so that what they lose as the former is offset by what they gain as the latter. But this naive argument does not hold water. If the remuneration to labour is approaching zero, why should the individuals in question agree to work at all? And if they do not work, who will produce the assets on which they are supposed to live? The whole idea is just an extreme expression of the alienation peculiar to capitalism: it is no longer only real capital which is supposed to be productive in and of itself (without any consideration of its exploitation of labour); the same is supposed to be true of the abstract entitlement to the ownership of capital. This is a supreme alienation, whose workings Marx already exposed in the rentier's 'money begets money' conception of credit. The 'new capitalism' is presented as if it were a kind of cut-price socialism, acquired without struggle, in which the workers became owners of their means of production.

Over the past twenty years, the value of assets (measured by stock-exchange capitalization) has certainly increased by a degree quite out of proportion with output rises in the real economy. But what has actually been happening? The bosses have not disappeared. The objective of 15 per cent annual growth in assets – the rule of thumb for institutional investors – has enriched a tiny minority of the population and impoverished the great majority, while at the same time locking accumulation into a crisis of over-production/under-consumption.

In reality, then, this type of financialization is a purely conjunctural phenomenon. The overall imbalance between supply and demand, which defines the crisis, is expressed in the fact that a growing share of the surplus finds no profitable outlet in real investment – the investment that actually expands and deepens the productive system. The crisis-management system therefore throws up an alternative outlet in the shape of 'financial investment', so that financial hypertrophy – the growth of such investment at a rate out of proportion with investment in the real economy – comes to be the real objective. But the 'financial bubble' cannot keep swelling for ever; it has to burst sooner or later. It is worries on this score that have led certain reformists to suggest ending the incentives for short-term speculative investment. The famous 'Tobin tax' is one of the proposals they have in mind.

Could the system stabilize in the kind of 'semi-stationary' state envisaged by Mill, where low or even nil growth rates (perhaps matching population growth) applied in equal or at least comparable measure to both real production and financial assets? I personally doubt it very much.

It would mean a kind of worldwide freezing of contemporary society in all its dimensions, a stabilization of income distribution structures at the level of inequality issuing from the crisis (as if that could be the end of the story), and a stabilization of global productive structures (that is, similar growth rates in every major region of the world economy). Moreover, a stable trend of financial asset appreciation, adjusted to growth in the real economy, would mean that pensions funds would no longer be able to cover the growing proportion of retired people in the population without revising downward the level of pension payments; they would thus run up against the same difficulties that confront the distributive pension system. The principle of pension fund capitalization does not provide a miraculous answer. Yet those who defend it shrewdly try to gain time by postponing a solution and duping the public. This also allows them to shift the risks of economic decision-making on to the shoulders of 'individuals' by converting them behind their backs into unlucky speculators (the genuine capitalists, for their part, keep the profits). The stabilization scenario therefore assumes extreme passivity and acceptance of inequality on the part of popular social forces, as well as extreme passivity and abandonment of any 'development project' on the part of the peripheral nations. That strikes me as highly unlikely, I am glad to say.

If the present accumulation crisis is solved in one way or another, a renewal of vigorous growth is certainly not inconceivable. But then all possible and imaginable social forces would join the dance: the changed relationship of forces, and the rise of new struggles and conflicts, would determine the shape of any such phase of renewed expansion. Hence there are not just one but many models of expansion, depending on the evolution of the social and international relationships of forces. It is not hard to imagine on paper what they would look like, by relying on intuitions and information gleaned from here and there. The mainstream economist (not a Marxist and not a 'political economist') closes his eyes to the whole dimension of social relations, but they return to mock his attempts to leave them out of account.

At the present time, however, there is absolutely no sign that we are approaching a solution to the crisis, still less that a model of renewed expansion is taking shape. Financial hypertrophy continues on its merry way, expressed through the bifurcation of profit rates (low for real investment, high for financial investment). This simplified but correct picture becomes more complex if we build into it differentiation within the real economy, between old sectors running out of steam and new activities thrown up by the technological revolution.

In this light, the thesis of an asset-centred mode of accumulation does not seem to have much foundation. It stems from a kind of pious wish, or *a priori* belief, that capitalism as always is in the process of inventing a solution to its problems. Using dubious eclectic methods to pick out a few aspects of the new reality, it does not even raise the question of whether they are likely to last, still less what would be necessary for that to happen.

Without necessarily spelling it out, the thesis evokes the fashionable contrast between Anglo-Saxon capitalism and the capitalism of Germany, France or Japan. The tendency to financialization is, to be sure, more pronounced in the Anglo-American model and its accompanying ideology, but is it in the process of conquering Europe and Japan? That is not out of the question, but it does not suffice to define a stable new mode of accumulation.

I therefore continue to hold that, in the contemporary crisis as in others that have preceded it in history, financialization is associated with a moment of transition; it cannot be stabilized and cannot by itself (or mainly) define the phase beyond the crisis. This being said, it is possible to read in the discourse of financialization some permanent features of modern capitalism, and to pose there the question of its obsolescence. Nor is there any problem imagining 'for the future' relations between real capital and financial instruments different from those which have existed 'in the past'. But, in my view, that is a matter of quite secondary importance.

The technological revolution: myths and realities

Something new has certainly been taking shape in the current crisis – something that will leave a lasting mark on the system that ensues, whatever its precise structures may be. The novel features may be grouped under two main headings: (a) the technological revolution and its impact on productive organization and social relations (its 'civilization effects'); and (b) the redeployment of imperialism and the new terms of the 'North–South conflict' (the centre/peripheries contradiction).

The development of the productive forces – which are at the same time destructive forces – has reached a point that qualitatively changes their impact and therefore compels us to face new questions. The arsenal of nuclear weapons makes it possible to put an end to all life on earth, creating an unprecedented danger that calls for them to be dismantled and put beyond use. NATO, however, has decided the opposite and returned to the principle of solving political conflicts through war. In other areas such as biogenetics, where existing scientific knowledge would also permit untold devastation, social control is an urgent necessity, the only way of integrating into the system the ethical principles indispensable to the survival of humanity. Yet the exact opposite has been chosen by a system hell-bent on privatization. The development of the productive forces shows that the basic rules of capitalism are out of date, that they now lead not to the development of society but to its self-destruction, that they must be overcome and left behind.

The question of the environment also has a place here.[4] For the first time in human history, there is a real danger of extremely grave and irreversible damage to the framework of life on earth; one cannot imagine any viable social project that did not face this reality. But I would also make a blunt observation that capitalism, however organized, is incapable of meeting the challenge, simply because its horizon of calculation, as illustrated in its idea of 'future depreciation', extends to no more than a few years at best, whereas any serious consideration of the matter has to look to the very long term (almost to eternity). In my view, the emergence of the environmental problem is one of the proofs that capitalism as a form of civilization must be overcome. Unfortunately, that is not a view shared by many of today's Greens.

Let us focus, however, on the technological and scientific revolution currently under way, particularly on everything in it that may be connected with computers.

This contemporary revolution exerts powerful pressure for a re-structuring of productive systems, especially by scattering certain parts of it to remote locations. As a result, labour processes are being extensively shaken up, as the old assembly-line model of Taylorism is replaced by new forms that profoundly affect the structure of social classes and the way in which they perceive problems of labour market segmentation. This is a change that will have long-term effects. I have put forward a few thoughts on its implications for the scope and content of the law of value, which is (or should be) considered a fundamental element of capitalism, since capitalism cannot be conceived without it. Present trends already point to what I have suggested calling the 'withering away of the law of value' – a formulation that also implies that capitalism must be left behind. This can happen in different ways: either through socialism, the only possible humanist response to the challenge, or through a kind of general apartheid in which social distinction is based not on participation in value creation (even if this gives rise to exploitation) but on para-political or cultural criteria. I have illustrated the 'material' possibility of a system of this kind by means of a simple reproduction model of its economic base.

We cannot here review the enormous literature on changes in the organization of work related to the technological revolution. Some authors even speak of the 'end of work', or discuss the emergence of a new society where 'networking' will replace hierarchies and 'project interaction' will dissolve the old unity of the firm. This, it is suggested, will allow individuals to assert their creative autonomy and to become the only subjects of history – classes and nations now being obsolete concepts.[5]

All these projections strike me as highly naive. For the 'new society' in question is already upon us, and what are its real social consequences? The share of capital and property in national income has been increasing with extraordinary rapidity, to the detriment of labour, and caused loss of job security, impoverishment and social exclusion for a growing section of the population. The individual, far from being 'liberated' by the development of the productive forces associated with the technological revolution, remains a social being in the grip of the oppression and exploitation upon which our contemporary society is based.

Another naive claim of the anti-state discourse of our times is that the large corporation has become autonomous of the state. Of course, the giant firm is not a novelty in the history of capitalism. But even the large transnationals, whose activity goes beyond their country of origin, remain first of all national corporations (most notably in the ownership and control of capital) and continue to need the active support of their national state. At the same time, they have become sufficiently powerful to develop their own expansion strategies outside, and sometimes against, the logic of state policies – indeed, they would like to make those policies strategically subordinate to themselves. Anti-statist neoliberal discourse masks this objective, however, by legitimizing the sole pursuit of particular interests on the part of transnational corporations; what it demands is not freedom for all but only the freedom of companies to assert their own interests against those of others. In this sense, it is thoroughly ideological and misleading. For, in reality, the relationship between oligopolistic capital and the state is ambivalent, and there is nothing to say that the present situation, in which the state appears totally subordinate to private interests, will not change one day and give way to a different balance. Neoliberal discourse transforms the temporary into the lasting and irreversible.

Capitalism cannot absorb everything required by a particular trend and still remain capitalism. But it can either 'take over' some of what is required (in certain circumstances, such as those attending its present redeployment, where it is dominant and does not face any rival), or else absorb it by beginning to move towards a different system. In the second case, we are speaking of what I have called a 'long transition'. This idea of a long transition to socialism, perhaps stretching over centuries, is not for me the same as acceptance of the conventional reformist theses of the Second International; nor was it the perspective of historical Marxism in the twentieth century. But we should remember that capitalism itself, having acquired its final form with the Industrial Revolution, took two centuries to reach the stage of putrefaction that makes its transcendence objectively necessary, whereas the West European transition from feudalism to capitalism stretched over three centuries from 1500 to 1800 (the mercantilist period).

It is also true that a transition is always uncertain, and that we can answer the question 'transition to what?' only after it has been completed. By virtue of 'under-determination in history', capitalism could be overcome either through the gradual construction of socialism (the preferable alternative, which requires the development of means consistent with the end) or through a different system of oppression and exploitation. The latter would no longer be capitalism, but it would be no less appalling for that.

In any event, the technological revolution – any technological revolution – transforms the structures of the organization of work. If society remains class society, these structures are not simply abolished but undergo a change in form, to the extent that, in conditions like those of the present, the illusion may spread that they have disappeared or been diluted into different realities. Consequently, the forms of social organization and the trends expressing various projects and conflicts are in turn profoundly influenced by the technological revolution. We shall return below to the challenge that these changes pose to the society they fragment and depoliticize. A meaningful convergence of social and political action, capable of giving it cohesion, credibility and effectiveness, is at the heart of the struggle against today's unbridled capitalism – all the more since some of the crucial aspects of the technological revolution herald the obsolescence of capitalism itself.

Notes

1. The macro-economic data in this section are taken from the various sources (especially OECD publications) mentioned in Jorge Bernstein, *La larga crisis de la economía global*, Buenos Aires: Corregidor, 1999.

2. See the collective critique of such widespread explanations, S. Amin, G. Arrighi, A. G. Frank and I. Wallerstein, *Dynamics of Global Crisis*, London: Macmillan, 1982.

3. Michel Aglietta, *Le capitalisme de demain*, Notes de la Fondation Saint-Simon, No. 101, 1998.

4. Samir Amin, 'Can Environmental Problems be Subjected to Economic Calculations?', *World Development* 20/4, Washington, DC.

5. Jeremy Rifkin, *The End of Work: The Decline of the Global Labour Force and the Dawn of the Post-Market Era*, New York: Putnam's, 1995; Manuel Castells, *The Rise of the Network Society*, Oxford: Blackwell, 1996.

FOUR
The new Triad imperialism

Imperialism, the permanent stage of capitalism

Imperialism is not a stage of capitalism – not even its highest stage. It has been an intrinsic part of capitalist expansion right from the beginning. The imperialist conquest of the planet by Europeans and their North American offspring unfolded in two phases and is now perhaps entering a third.

The first phase of this devastating imperialist deployment took place around the conquest of the Americas, in the framework of the mercantilist system of the Atlantic Europe of the time. It ended in the destruction of the Indian civilizations, the Hispanicization–Christianization of the Indian peoples, or the straightforward genocide on which the United States was built. The elemental racism of the Anglo-Saxon settlers also lay behind the reproduction of the model in mainland Australia, Tasmania (history's most consummate genocide) and New Zealand. For, whereas the Catholic Spanish acted in the name of a duty to impose their religion on the conquered peoples, the Protestant British learned from their reading of the Bible that they had a right to exterminate the 'infidels'. The infamous enslavement of black Africans, made necessary by the extermination or resistance of American Indians, constituted a happy sequel for the 'valorization' of useful parts of the continent. No one today can be unaware that all the horrors were closely bound up with the expansion of mercantilist capital. At the time, however, Europeans accepted the ideological discourses that legitimized them, and the protests of Las Casas and others found little resonance.

The devastation in this opening chapter of world capitalist expansion eventually produced the liberation forces that challenged its governing logic.

The 'American Revolution', so highly thought of by many revolutionaries in 1789 and today more loudly acclaimed than ever, was only a limited political revolution with no social import. In their revolt against the British Crown, the American settlers did not seek to change any aspect of economic and social relations, but only to escape having to share the profits with the homeland ruling class. They wanted power for themselves: not to do anything differently from their colonial rulers, but to continue doing the same with greater determination and higher profits. Their main aim was to press on westward, repeating the genocide of the Indian population. Nor was it their intention to question the institution of slavery: nearly all the main leaders of the American Revolution were slaveowners, whose prejudices on this score were quite unshakable. It took almost another century for slavery to be abolished, and yet another for black Americans to gain minimum recognition of certain civil rights. Even then, the profound racism of the dominant culture was by no means broken.

The only genuine social revolution at the time in the Americas was the self-emancipation of the slaves of Santo Domingo; what later became of them is another story. The revolutions of Spanish America (nothing much was happening then in Brazil) were similar in nature to those of British America: the Creoles took power from the Castillian monarchy and went on doing the same as before. Only in the twentieth century, with the Mexican Revolution of 1910–20 and the Cuban Revolution half a century later, did Latin America begin to emerge from the system of 1492. But the process is still far from complete, as is evident from the curious public references to the rights of 'indigenous peoples', as if all peoples were not 'indigenous' to their home country.

The founding vices of 'American democracy', which is today held up as a universal model, have their origin in that first phase of the imperialist expansion of actually existing capitalism.

The second phase of imperialist devastation was built around the Industrial Revolution and manifested itself in the colonial subjugation of Asia and Africa. The opening of markets (such as the opium market imposed on the Chinese by English Puritans) and the grabbing of natural resources were, as everyone now knows, the real reasons for this. But once again European public opinion did not see these realities and (even in the case of the Second International) accepted the new legitimizing discourse of capital, with its references to a 'civilizing mission'. The lucid voices came, rather, from bourgeois cynics such as Cecil Rhodes, who advocated colonial conquest to avoid a social revolution in Britain. The voices of the real opponents – from the Paris Communards to the Bolsheviks – did not have much resonance.

This second phase of imperialist devastation was at the root of the greatest problem ever to have confronted humanity: namely, the huge polarization that has taken the inequality between nations from a range of 1:2 around the year 1800 for 80 per cent of the world's population to a range of 1:60 today (when the centres benefiting from the system comprise only 20 per cent of humanity). The remarkable achievements of capitalist civilization also set the stage for the most violent conflicts among imperialist powers. Yet imperialist aggression again produced the forces to combat it: the socialist revolutions in Russia and China (not by chance on the periphery subject to the polarizing imperialist expansion of actually existing capitalism) and the national liberation revolutions. Their victory imposed a half-century respite after the Second World War, which allowed the illusion to spread that capitalism could be forced to adapt and become civilized.

My intention here is not to reduce the whole history of modern times since 1492 to this imperialist dimension, but only to emphasize it because the dominant Eurocentrist ideology systematically downplays its importance.

Capitalism is also a culture based upon economistic alienation (this is the first main thesis I recalled in the introduction to this work), and without that alienation it would be impossible to understand its imperialist expansionism. One might then be reduced, for example, to an explanation in terms of the particular genes or culture of Europeans, similar to the theories advanced by many cultural nationalists in Asia or Africa.

Since its origins, then, capitalism has been permeated by insoluble contradictions that have led to the idea of the necessity of overcoming it. This social need was expressed very early on, and taken up at all the great moments of modern history. One finds it actively present in the three great revolutions of modern times: the French, the Russian and the Chinese. The first of these occupies a special historical place, since its Jacobin wing very soon grasped and spelled out the basic contradiction of the bourgeois project: that is, economic liberalism is the enemy of democracy. This radical current, which tried to carry a concept of popular revolution beyond the strictly bourgeois 'objective requirements' of the hour, eventually gave birth to a first generation of communist (Babouvist) critics of capitalism. Similarly, the Russian and Chinese revolutions looked towards a communist final goal that went far beyond the tasks immediately facing their societies. It is no accident, then, that each of these three great revolutions – unlike other revolutions – was followed by a restoration. Yet the advances that marked their greatest hour remained living symbols for the future, having established human equality and liberation from commodity alienation at the heart of their respective projects.

The questions of imperialism (and its antithesis: liberation and development) have continued to weigh heavily upon the history of capitalism. Thus the victory of the post-1945 national liberation movements in Asia and Africa not only put an end to the colonialist system but in a way also drew a line under the era of European expansion begun in 1492. Historical capitalism had taken the form of expansion for four and a half centuries (from 1500 to 1950), so that these two dimensions had become inseparable parts of a single reality. Independence struggles in the Americas had certainly appeared to undermine the '1492 world system' in the late eighteenth and early nineteenth century, but (with the exception of Haiti) the independence in question was won not by indigenous peoples and imported slaves but by the settlers themselves, who thus transformed the continent into a second Europe. The independence regained by the peoples of Asia and Africa had a different significance.

The ruling classes of Europe's colonial powers did not fail to see that a page of history had turned for ever: they understood that they had to give up their traditional association of domestic economic growth with successful imperial expansion. In fact, this had been the vision not only of the old colonial powers – above all, Britain, France and the Netherlands – but also of the new capitalist centres constituted in the course of the nineteenth century: Germany, the United States and Japan. Intra-European and wider international conflicts had thus mainly been conflicts for imperialist colonial redistribution within the 1492 system, it being understood that the United States reserved exclusive rights over the whole of the new continent.

The capitalist ruling classes of post-war Western Europe therefore embarked upon the new European enterprise, a project that, by its very logic, was meant to bring to an end both intra-European conflict and the 'old colonial' system of 1492. The renunciation of colonial privilege was not accepted all at once, however, but only after new colonial wars had turned to the advantage of the peoples in revolt. It is not altogether fortuitous that the Treaty of Rome setting up the six-member European Community in 1957 coincided with the law outlining the basis for the independence of France's last remaining African colonies. A few years later, de Gaulle made it quite clear that France's 'European choice' was being substituted for its traditional colonial option.

The construction of a wealthy and developed European space, with a top-rank technological and scientific potential as well as strong military traditions, seemed to hold out capitalist accumulation without colonies as the basis for a new type of globalization different from the 1492 system. It remained to be seen precisely how it would differ: whether it would still be a polarizing system, albeit on new foundations, or whether it would cease to be so.

Today, this European project is far from complete and is passing through a moment of crisis that could call into question its intended scope; it will continue to face difficulties so long as formulas have not been devised to reconcile European political unity with the weight of historical national realities. Moreover, there are still only ambivalent or hazy visions of the way in which this European economic and political space should link up with the (still to be constructed) new global system. Is the idea that the economic space should compete with the other great space created by the United States in the second Europe? And, if so, how will this competition affect the relations of Europe and the United States with the rest of the world? Will the rivals confront each other in the manner of the imperialist powers of the previous epoch? Or will they act in concert? If the latter, will Europeans choose to revive by proxy the imperialism of the 1492 system, by trailing behind the political options of Washington? Under what conditions might the European enterprise insert itself into a globalization project that puts an end to the 1492 system once and for all?

The collapse of the Soviet system and Third World national-populist regimes means that we now face the beginnings of a third wave of global devastation resulting from imperialist expansion. Although the conditions are new and in some respects very different from those that character-ized the previous phase of imperialism, the aims of the dominant capital are the same as always: to take charge of market expansion, to pillage the earth's natural resources and to over-exploit labour reserves in the periphery. The ideological discourse designed to rally public opinion in the central Triad has been revamped to focus on a 'duty to intervene' in the name of 'democracy', 'national rights' or 'humanitarian considerations'.[1] But, whereas the cynical instrumentalization and double standards involved in this discourse seem evident to people in Asia or Africa, Western public opinion has fallen in with it as enthusiastically as it did with the discourses of earlier phases of imperialism.

Redeployment of the imperialist system

While the technological revolution has given rise to a veritable logorrhoea among representatives of the dominant discourse, issues concerning the redeployment of the imperialist system and the polariza-tion through which it is expressed have been systematically ignored. Besides, the vision of the world system in this discourse is generally defined by the frontiers of the Triad, so that the only issues to arise are those concerning relations between the European project and the United

States. In this connection, we may regret that Robert Brenner's historical analysis of the evolving terms of competition among the United States, Germany and Japan (a work of considerable quality) situates itself within an excessively narrow optic, since, although it recognizes that relations among those three centres are only one dimension of post-war history, it takes them to be the main driving force behind it.[2]

To counter this silence, I would like to propose a few hypotheses concerning the likely evolution of relations between the centres and the peripheries. These will allude to what I have called the 'five new monopolies' through which the centres enjoy certain new advantages – a concept whose broad lines must first be recalled.

Polarization, like any other aspect of capitalist society, is not defined once and for all by an unchanging formula. What is certainly out of date is the formal opposition between industrial and non-industrial countries which expressed that polarization for a century and a half, before the national liberal movements compelled the centre to adapt to changes driven by the industrialization (however uneven) of the peripheries. Should we conclude, then, that East Asia is in the process of 'catching up' with the Triad centres? To say that, it would be necessary to rush the argument. My own thesis leads to a very different conclusion: namely, that through the Triad's five monopolies the global law of value produces polarization in new forms, driving the industry of the dynamic peripheries into a subaltern position. If China decides to integrate more deeply into the international division of labour, it will not escape this perspective.

For a long time – from the Industrial Revolution in the early nineteenth century right down to the 1930s (for the Soviet Union) or the 1950s (for the Third World) – the centres/peripheries contrast in the modern world system was virtually synonymous with the opposition between industrial and non-industrial countries. The revolt of the peripheries, taking the form of socialist revolution (Russia, China) or national liberation, called into question that old form of polarization by engaging the societies at issue in the process of modernization and industrialization. Gradually the axis of reorganization in the world capitalist system – the axis that will define the future forms of polarization – took shape around what I call the 'five new monopolies' of the dominant Triad.

A country's position in the global pyramid is defined by the competitiveness of its products on the world market. This truism in no way implies acceptance of the banal argument of vulgar economics that a position in the pyramid is won through 'rational' economic policies, where the yardstick of rationality is precisely subordination to supposedly objective laws of the market. Contrary to nonsense of this kind, my point is that the competitiveness in question is the complex result of a set of conditions operating in the total field of reality – economic, political and social – and that, in this uneven contest, the centres deploy their 'five monopolies', which articulate the effectiveness of their operations. These five monopolies, which engage the whole of social theory, are the following:

1. *Technological monopoly* This requires huge expenditures that only a large and wealthy state can envisage. Without the support of the state, especially through military spending – something liberal discourse does not mention – most of these monopolies would not last.

2. *Financial control of worldwide financial markets* These monopolies have an unprecedented efficacy thanks to liberalization of the rules governing their establishment. Not so long ago, the greater part of a nation's savings could circulate only within the largely national arena of its financial institutions. Today these savings are handled centrally by institutions whose operations are worldwide. We are talking of finance capital: capital's most globalized component. Despite this, the logic of this globalization of finance could be called into question by a simple political decision to delink, even if delinking were limited to the domain of financial transfers. Moreover, I think that the rules governing the free movement of finance capital have broken down. This system was based in the past on the free floating of currencies on the market (according to the theory that money is a commodity like any other), with the dollar serving *de facto* as a universal currency. A theory that regards money as a commodity, however, has no scientific foundation, and the pre-eminent position of the dollar is only *faute de mieux*. A national currency cannot fulfil the functions of an international currency unless the country in question has an export surplus that can underwrite structural adjustment in other countries. This was the case with Britain in the late nineteenth century. This is not the case of the United States today, which actually finances its deficit through borrowing that the rest of the world is forced to accept. Nor indeed is this the case with the competitors of the United States, as the surpluses of Japan and Europe are insufficient to meet the financial needs occasioned by the structural adjustment of other countries. Under these conditions financial globalization, far from being a 'natural' process, is an extremely fragile one. In the short term, it leads only to permanent instability rather than the stability necessary for efficient operation of the processes of adjustment.

3. *Monopolistic access to the earth's natural resources* The reckless exploitation of these resources now threatens the whole planet, and capitalism, with its merely short-term rationality, cannot overcome the dangers. Indeed, such behaviour reinforces the monopolies of the already developed countries, whose only concern is to prevent other countries from being equally irresponsible in their use of resources.

4. *Media and communication monopolies* These not only lead to cultural dumbing-down but also open up new means of political manipulation. Expansion of the modern media market is already one of the major elements eroding the conception and practice of democracy in the West itself.

5 *Monopolies over weapons of mass destruction* Held in check by the post-war bipolarity, this monopoly is again, as in 1945, exclusively at the service of United States foreign policy. While it may be true that nuclear proliferation risks getting out of control, the absence of democratic international control means that there is no other way of combating this unacceptable monopoly.

These five monopolies together define the framework within which the global law of value operates. Far from being the expression of a 'pure' economic rationality detached from its social and political setting, the law of value is the condensed expression of all these monopolistic determinants, which restrict industrialization in the peripheries, devalue the productive labour incorporated in their products, and overstate the value supposedly added through activities corresponding to the new central monopolies. The monopolies therefore produce a new global hierarchy of income distribution, more unequal than ever, and reduce the industries of the peripheries to the status of subcontractors. This is the new basis of polarization that is destined to shape its future forms.

The relative competitiveness of productive systems within the Triad, or within the European Union or the various peripheries, is undoubtedly a factor fraught with medium- to long-term consequences. Nearly everywhere it gives rise to economies operating at different speeds: some sectors, regions and firms (especially the transnational giants) notch up strong growth rates and high profits; others stagnate, regress or decay. Labour market segmentation corresponds to this differentiated picture.

But, once again, is this really new? Or are different speeds the norm in the history of capitalism? The post-war period (1945–80) may be seen as exceptional in this respect, since systematic intervention by the state (the welfare state, the Soviet state, the national state in the Third World of Bandung) organized large-scale regional and sectoral transfers and thereby imposed sets of social relations promoting growth and modernization of the productive forces.

In the complexity of the real world, it is not easy to disentangle major long-term trends from conjunctural phenomena. Certainly both are real enough in the present phase: the aspect of systemic change, and the aspect of 'crisis and crisis management'. But I would insist on the basic principle that systemic change within capitalism stems not from meta-social forces (to which we must bow as to laws of nature) but from social relations. Different options are therefore always available, corresponding to different social equilibria.

The current reorganization of the system of international institutions is designed to strengthen the Triad's five monopolies. We therefore face a new 'question of development', which more than ever requires us to abandon the narrow vision of 'catching up' that was paramount in the twentieth century. It is true that there is still a dimension, not of 'catching up', but of developing the productive forces, and that in this sense some lessons from the past remain valid for the future. But we must also, from the very outset, attach much more importance than in the past to what is necessary for the building of a different society on a world scale.

What about the 'Asian miracle'?

It might be asked whether the new imperialism – based on the Triad's five monopolies, and sustained by the political and military hegemonism of the United States – is not threatened in the long term by the rise of Asia. This point has often been made, but not enough attention has been paid to the reality of the Asian 'miracles' and to how they fit into the new imperialist globalization.

Let us cast our minds back to the time when many analysts of the world system claimed that Japan was the new rising power. In fact, the 'Japanese miracle' that sustained itself as the United States and Europe were entering into crisis may be put down to a combination of special factors: austere living and high levels of savings among the popular classes; state-organized authoritarian productivism, closely coordinated with the strategies of national oligopolies; and an opening of the North American market to Japanese goods in compensation for Japanese capital exports to the United States.

That 'miracle' has had its day. Suddenly, in the 1990s, the growth rates of Japanese GDP and exports collapsed: whereas, in the 1960s, they had been 10.4 per cent and 15.7 per cent respectively, they were now 0.8 per cent and 3.1 per cent. The political and even moral crisis that has since enveloped the country has, to put it mildly, put an end to dreams about some future Japanese hegemony. The foundations of the previous success are no longer there.

From the Meiji Restoration to the Second World War (1863–1945), Japanese imperialism fed on colonial expansion and militarism. In the post-war period (1945–90), with the reconstitution of the oligopolies in tandem with a seemingly democratic but still authoritarian (effectively one-party) state, the functions of the military establishment were taken over by a 'constructive' state and its projects for mass housing and infrastructural development, together with a solid educational system that encouraged the adoption of advanced technology. Nor should it be forgotten that Washington gave Tokyo decisive political support, accompanying it with economic concessions, in an international context marked by the Cold War. Today, however, the Japanese people have to face challenges for which nothing has prepared them. Will Japanese society respond in ways that take it closer to Europe and North America, not only in the organization of the economy but also in political life and culture, including class struggle and class consciousness? What can safely be said is that, here as elsewhere, trends in social relations will determine the framework in which the Japanese economy undergoes transformation.[3]

Once the Japanese illusion was over, the idea that Asia was called upon to take over the leadership of world affairs from the (Euro-American) West began to focus on China instead. I shall not repeat here my analysis of the different possible scenarios in China, nor my critique of A. G. Frank's thesis of a 'return of Asia'.[4]

In the general crisis of the past three decades, a new 'East–West' divide does indeed seem to have been taking shape. The crisis has hit hard the whole of the American continent, north and south, Western Europe, Africa and the Middle East, Eastern Europe and the countries of the former USSR. Its symptoms are: weak growth (nil or even negative for the former Eastern bloc and marginalized areas of the Third World); low investment in productive activities; rising levels of unemployment and insecure employment; a spread of 'informal' types of economic activity, and so on – all accompanied with a more unequal distribution of income. The stagnation has become entrenched, although official discourse has continued to speak of 'recessions' and 'upturns'. A few appearances to the contrary (for example, economic growth and falling unemployment in the 1990s), the supposed 'recovery' in the United States and Britain remained fragile because it was based on a process of financialization that was itself under threat. In fact, the main pillar of the American economy continued to be military expenditure. On the other hand, the countries of East Asia (China and South Korea), South-East Asia and India have for some time given the impression of lying outside the zone affected by the long crisis, and growth rates and investment in productive systems have held up over the last few decades (India) or even risen sharply (China, Korea, South-East Asia). Accelerated growth has gone hand in hand with less sharp rises in inequality than elsewhere, although there are variations that considerably qualify this general picture. Japan benefited from the climate in the 'New East', before itself later entering a crisis that, in its case, is really deep. It remains to be seen whether the financial crisis that hit Korea and South-East Asia in 1997, and threatened China in turn, will mark the end of this 'Asian exceptionalism' and the East–West division that it involves.

Much ink was spilled over the vision of Asia or the Asian Pacific, or the Chinese superpower, as the budding centre that would wrest from Europe and North America its domination over the planet. Others, in a more sober register, have drawn from trends in Asia a number of conclusions which, though still over-hasty, are deserving of serious discussion. Thus, theories have been advanced to challenge the idea that polarization (often confused with cruder conceptions of 'dependence') is intrinsic to global capitalist expansion, and to assert that the goal of 'catching up' is better served through active involvement in globalization (perhaps even, in extreme variants, 'export-oriented development') than through the kind of illusory delinking that was ultimately responsible for the Soviet catastrophe. Internal factors – cultural, among others – are thus supposed to have played an active role in shaping the world, and to lie behind the success of certain countries or the failure of others that have been marginalized and 'delinked in spite of themselves'.

To make any real progress in these complex matters, we would need to draw a clear analytic distinction between internal social structures and forces acting at the level of the world system, and to go beyond facile polemic by explaining how the two combine with each other. Active and controlled insertion into the progress of globalization is a very different option from an economic strategy that prioritizes exports; they are based upon different hegemonic social blocs. The East Asian countries have been successful precisely in so far as they have refused to adapt to dominant trends in the world economy and made their external relations subordinate to the requirements of internal development. That, in fact, is the real definition of 'delinking', which some readers have too hurriedly confused with autarky. Another reference here is the debate on 'market socialism', proposed as an alternative especially in China.

The collective imperialism of which I have been speaking is not the 'end of history', any more than were the forms prior to globalized capitalism, and the model it represents is destined to face destabilizing social struggles and international conflicts. At the forefront of the forces already challenging the status quo are the ambitions of societies and states in the active periphery (China, India, Asia in general, large Latin American countries), but we should by no means forget about social struggles both within the Triad and in the 'marginalized' peripheries. On the (doubtless optimistic) hypothesis that these anti-systemic forces combine their strategies and manage to bring their goals into line with each other, the prospect will emerge of going 'beyond capitalism'. Meanwhile, the collective neoliberal-imperialist order might either become mired in a longer or shorter period of blocked expansion, or else enter a new phase of expansion and enlarged reproduction.

The collective imperialism of the Triad

During the two previous phases of imperialist deployment (the mercantilist period from 1500 to 1800, then the 'classical' period from 1800 to the Second World War), imperialism was always a phenomenon that existed in the plural. Imperialisms had permanent relations of violent rivalry with one another, to such an extent that conflict among them occupied a central place on the historical stage.

Lenin and Bukharin, in their theory of imperialism, thought that the violence of these inevitable clashes (typified by the First World War) would lead the proletariats of the capitalist heartlands to choose the path of revolution. A general revolt of the proletarian 'cannon fodder' could – and should – put paid to the 'betrayal' by social democratic political leaderships who had gone over to their imperialist bourgeoisies. World revolution (at least in the European centres) was on the immediate agenda, beginning with the weakest chain of the system (Russia).

Lenin and Bukharin combined their critique of the imperialism of their time with an analysis that capitalism had reached its final stage of 'decay'. The domination of finance capital, which characterized the new monopoly stage, expressed the now 'parasitic' character of capital. Bukharin, with much talent and sarcastic humour, traced the process whereby the rentier (the 'leisure class') had replaced the productive entreprent as the object of admiration in capitalist ideology. He saw this as a clear sign of the senility of the system, and a further reason to think that socialist revolution was objectively necessary and possible. In this respect, history seems to be repeating itself. In the new financial-ization and the talk of a new form of asset-based accumulation, we are again witnessing an inversion that raises the new rentier mentality above that of the productive entrepreneur. But in the intervening period – from 1914 to 1980 – none of Lenin's and Bukharin's predictions came true: the world revolution did not happen; capitalism regained its expansionist thrust after the thirty-year war (1914–45); and the post-war 'golden age' saw spectacular development of the productive forces.

Today, it seems possible to identify the dual error of diagnosis com-mitted by Lenin and Bukharin. On the one hand, they underestimated the profound changes associated with the imperialist polarization between centres and peripheries – a polarization expressing the social-economic dimension of the law of capitalist impoverishment (what I call the 'modernization of poverty', with better conditions for the working classes in the capitalist centres and extreme forms of modern poverty and exploitation in the peripheries), as well as its political-ideological di-mension. On the other hand, they considered the triumph of the 'rentier mentality' to be a constant feature of late capitalism, whereas, in my view, it was only a conjunctural aspect associated with the crisis.

At another level, however, Lenin was right in his polemic against Kautsky's theory of super-imperialism, which mechanically projected into the future the tendency to centralization of capital and concluded that the age of rival imperialisms would give way to a 'single giant trust'. Lenin correctly saw that, before any such stage could be reached, capitalism was passing through an epoch of chaos and revolutions that called into question the historical viability of super-imperialism.

But then, in the aftermath of the Second World War, the conflict between imperialisms seemed to be well and truly over. To both east and west of the great divide, there was general agreement: all those who championed the so-called free world, whether victors or vanquished in 1945, could see nothing ahead but a closing of the political ranks behind their American protector; while, for his part, Zhdanov declared that there were now only two camps (capitalist and socialist) and implied that inter-imperialist conflict was a thing of the past.

There was, of course, a simple reason for this common cause among all the bourgeosies of the Triad's capitalist core: the economic might of the United States was so overwhelming in comparison with that of its wartime allies and enemies that American hegemony seemed beyond dispute. Moreover, faced with a 'communist threat' both internally and externally, the central bourgeoisies could do nothing other than take shelter beneath America's protective wing.

But this imbalance was not going to last for ever. Within a fairly short period – fifteen to twenty years – the European and Japanese partners rebuilt their productive capacity and acquired a competitive strength comparable to that of the United States. It was thought in the 1970s that history was returning to its 'normal' course, as we can recall from all that was written about 'the decline of America' and the prospects of a 'new hegemony', either European or Japanese. The partners, it seemed, were again becoming rivals, and conflict between them was inevitable. Such theses, as popular on the liberal right as among the social democrats, found a powerful echo in all currents of thinking at the time, disturbing some as much as they delighted others.

The return to global liberalism after 1980 (carrying European social democrats along with it), Washington's new push for hegemony in the wake of the Soviet collapse, and the series of wars in the Gulf, Yugoslavia and Afghanistan force us to reconsider the question of imperialism today. For, at the level both of liberal economic globalization and of political and military management of the world order, the states of the central Triad (USA, Europe, Japan) form an apparently solid bloc in which Washington's leadership is scarcely contested.

The unavoidable question, to which an answer must be given, is whether these trends express a lasting qualitative shift from plural to collective imperialism, or whether they are only conjunctural phenomena.

In favour of the latter position, it might be said that, although Europe and the United States accept the principles of global liberalism, economic conflicts persist between them (most notably on the issue of agriculture), that Europe has a potential to become autonomous both financially (as symbolized by the euro) and militarily (where the issue is whether the new European force will be fully integrated into NATO), and so on. Today's Triad 'bloc', already showing cracks, might therefore not be destined to last.

The position at the other end of the spectrum is that a genuinely transnational capital is already taking shape.[5] Until now the TNCs have been transnational only in their field of activity; the ownership and central management of these mighty oligopolies has remained strictly national – American, British, German, Japanese, French. But today, it is argued, a new round of mergers not only expresses the swallowing of the weak by the strong (still a national phenomenon) but involves real associations between equal partners, as the basis for a new and genuinely plurinational capital. The case of Chrysler-Daimler was a good example of this, and although it ended in failure it points to a trend that is destined to recur on an ever wider scale and with eventual success. Admittedly, the transnational capital in question will remain a select club excluding the countries of the East and South, whose comprador bourgeoisies will still serve as transmission belts for its domination. Admittedly, too, many companies within the Triad will continue to be strictly national. But the interests they represent will not be those of the dominant segment of capital, which will continue moving in the direction of real transnationalization.

This analysis does not seem to me very convincing. Like Kautsky's super-imperialism before it, it involves the linear extrapolation of an economic tendency and fails to take into account the political dimensions of the problem. Besides, the emergence of a collective imperialism does not imply the transnationalization of capital that the thesis supposes.

My own view, drawing on what company directors themselves write in the business school literature, is that the emergence of a new collective imperialism is the result of changes in the conditions of competition. Just a few decades ago, the large corporations waged their competitive struggle with one another mainly on national markets, whether that of the United States (the world's largest) or those of European countries (whose smaller size put them at a disadvantage); the national 'match winners' were then in a strong position to perform in the world arena. Nowadays, it is said that the market size necessary to get through the first round of matches is of the order of 500 to 600 million 'potential consumers', considerably more than either the American or the European market alone can provide. The battle therefore has to be fought out directly on the world market: those who win there carry the day, including on their respective national terrain; deep globalization sets the main framework for the activity of big corporations. In other words, the places of the national and the global have been inverted in the causal relationship: whereas national power used to determine global presence, it is now the reverse that happens. Transnational corporations, whatever their nationality, therefore have a common interest in the management of the world market. These interests are superimposed on the permanent mercantile conflicts that define all forms of competition in capitalism.

Imperialism really has become collective in its economic dimension, and in my view this is a lasting qualitative change. The option in favour of collective management of the world market – and hence of the world political system – is not merely incidental but reflects the formation of interests common to the transnational capital of all the Triad partners. The hegemonic practices of the United States, which are part of this new picture, defend the interests not only of the United States but of the whole Triad.

This qualitative transformation of imperialism is not, however, the same as 'super-imperialism', because it leaves intact and unresolved the dichotomy between the economic and political dimensions of the system. The economy is globalized, but states (in the plural) are still the main framework for political life. This is a new contradiction. In earlier periods of capitalism, the national framework constituted the main field of economic and political life, even if both these aspects of reality were inserted into a global economic and political system. The new contradiction is destined to grow sharper, not weaker.

Any scenario of a twenty-first century run according to the strict principles of collective imperialism and global economic liberalism, within a political framework of either US hegemony or shared Triad supremacy, is intolerable for the peripheral nations. Moreover, since there is no *a priori* reason why the governing political logic in European societies should not clash with the logic determining the deployment of modern capitalism, 'conflicts' between Europeans, North Americans and others are not only still possible but probable. We shall return to these questions once we have examined more closely how the hegemonic strategy of the United States operates. Only by identifying the strengths and weaknesses of that strategy will we be able to define the alternatives more precisely, and to assess the likelihood of the various scenarios.

One final point should be made here. Whereas the imperialism of all previous epochs was a conquering force – in the sense that its centres were 'exporters of capital' and thereby gave the polarized world system its shape – this is much less true (perhaps not true at all) of the new collective imperialism. We shall return to this other dimension of the obsolescence of capitalism.

Notes

1. The unilateral 'right to intervene' is humorously taken apart in Jean-Claude Guillebaud, *La trahison des Lumières*, Paris: Seuil, 1995, pp. 96–9.

2. See Robert Brenner, 'The Economics of Global Turbulence', *New Left Review*, May–June 1998.

3. See Paul Burkett and Martin Hart-Landsberg, *Development, Crisis and Class Struggle: Learning from Japan and East Asia*, New York: St. Martin's Press, 2000.

4. Samir Amin, 'Y a-t-il un projet chinois?', *Alternatives Sud*, 1996; S. Amin, 'Théorie et pratique du projet chinois de socialisme de marché' (including a bibliography of Chinese sources), in *Chine, Vietnam, Cuba* (various authors), Paris: L'Harmattan, 2001; Lin Chun, *Situating China*, Mexico City: UNAM-Mexico, 1994; Lu Aiguo, *China and the Global Economy since 1840*, New York: St. Martin's Press, 2000; S. Amin, 'History Conceived as an Eternal Cycle', *Review* (Binghamton) 22/3, 1999 (a critique of the 'return of Asia' thesis).

5. See William I. Robinson and Jerry Harris, 'Towards a Global Ruling Class? Globalization and the Transnational Capitalist Class', *Science and Society* 64/1, 2000.

FIVE

The militarization of the new collective imperialism

Two major theses

The great instability characterizing the present day contrasts with the rather remarkable stability of the post-war period. The dominant view, especially among political leaders of all persuasions, associates this change with the collapse of the Cold War bipolarity that used to 'freeze' a number of centrifugal forces within one or the other camp. I have suggested above another explanation for the half-century of stability following the Second World War: namely, the social equilibrium relatively favourable to the working classes and peripheral nations that emerged from the dual victory of democracy and national liberation (over fascism and old-style colonialism). Having exhausted their potential for development, the three models on offer – welfare statism in the West, Sovietism in the East, modernizing national construction in the South – broke down before new lines of advance had taken shape for the states, peoples and nations in question.

As far as the economy is concerned, what characterizes the present moment is the juxtaposition of the scientific and technological revolution with a deep crisis of the systems of accumulation. The social disaster produced by financialized and globalized forms of system management defines the nature of the challenge facing the working classes and the peoples of the world. As far as politics are concerned, the most salient features are: an apparent weakening of the effectiveness of state policies (and hence an erosion of their legitimacy); the retreat of Enlightenment 'grand narratives' (bourgeois democracy, socialism) before new discourses inspired by community 'identities' (especially ethnic and religious ones); the fragmentation of social movements; and the growing number of political conflicts within and between states (especially in the most vulnerable peripheral regions of the world system). The militarization of global system management forms part of this wider picture.

In what follows, I shall suggest a way of fitting together the various pieces of this jigsaw. Let me begin by drawing the reader's attention to the two (theoretical and methodological) theses that will be the guiding thread in my analysis.

The first thesis is anti-economistic in character. It is almost an article of faith in contemporary societies that economic wealth determines political strength. Empirically, we can certainly say there is a correlation between the two, but it is well known that a correlation is not an explanation. In the economistic oversimplification of reality, wealth is the outcome of wise and effective economic initiatives taken by the societies in question and implemented by their governments; the dominant neoliberal discourse adds the further point that the wisdom of these initiatives (which, at other times and places, might have been defined differently, though still within an economistic logic) nowadays depends on their fit with the requirements of liberal globalization.

My thesis is that things are not like that. The relationship between economics and politics, wealth and strength, involves a dialectical to-and-fro movement, not a one-way causal link.

Global geopolitics, then, is necessarily the framework within which the economic and political strategies of various countries are deployed. That is how it has always been, at least in the modern world – the capitalist world system – since 1492. The relationships of force that configure geopolitics in successive phases of capitalist expansion assist the development (in the banal sense) of the dominant powers and constitute a handicap for the rest.

The present moment is characterized by the deployment of a North American project for world hegemony, a project that today occupies the whole of the stage. Unlike in the age of bipolarism (1945–90), there is no longer a counter-project to limit the area subject to US control: the European project, despite its original ambiguities, has entered a period of self-effacement; the countries of the South (the Group of 77, the non-aligned nations) have given up the plan they had at the time of Bandung (1955–75) to form a common front to Western imperialism; and even China, which goes its own way, does not present itself as an active partner in shaping the world and has scarcely any ambition other than to defend its (ambivalent) national project. Everything seems in place to ensure the triumph of the strategy of US hegemony.

In conformity with this basic methodological thesis, I would say that the 'economic advantages' enjoyed by the United States are not only 'relative' but are much less the source than the product of its political hegemonism. But I shall try not to substitute a one-sided political thesis for the one-sided economism I have just criticized; I shall not take the power of one or several hegemons as a simple fact that provides the analytic starting point. The successive phases of capitalist expansion are defined not by the hegemonic power of the time (British, American), but by the nature of the permanent conflict among front-ranking states. Hegemony is always relative, vulnerable and provisional. It is therefore better to analyse problems and challenges in terms of aspirations to (rather than exercise of) hegemony, and to focus on the strategies deployed by countries aspiring to it (today the United States).

My second thesis concerns the global dimension of the contradictions of actually existing capitalism. Let me first recall my point that capitalist globalization has always been and always will be synonymous with imperialism: that is, with a deployment that, through its own inner logic, constantly produces, reproduces and accentuates the contrast between centres and peripheries. The deployment of capitalism on a world scale does not virtuously enable those who are 'lagging behind' to 'catch up' with those who are ahead. On the contrary, it blocks off paths of development that might permit the former to 'rebuild themselves' in the image of the latter. Imperialism, as I put it earlier, is the 'permanent stage of capitalism'.

On the other hand, the current neoliberal deployment of globalized capitalism is opening a new phase of imperialism. In contrast to past phases marked by permanent and violent inter-imperialist conflict, the new collective imperialism joins together the whole of the Triad (USA, Europe, Japan). American hegemony fits into this 'post-colonial' project, which, far from reducing contrasts between the dominant centres (Triad) and the dominated peripheries (the rest of the world), actually sharpens the violence of North–South contradictions. Peaceful management of the new imperialist system, simply through the economic means at the disposal of capital, becomes less and less of a possibility, as political violence, and hence military intervention, serves functions essential to a project that misleadingly describes itself as 'liberal'. This is why the new collective imperialism cannot dispense with the hegemony of the United States, the only power capable of leading the militarization of the North's intervention in the South. Of course, the United States will charge its subaltern allies in Europe and Japan for this 'service', in terms that make up a large part of its 'economic advantages'.

If this analysis is correct, it must follow that intra-Triad conflicts are not destined to occupy centre stage as long as the dominant transnational capital remains in the political driving seat. Collective imperialism implies what I have called 'obliteration of the European project', its twofold dilution within neoliberal economic globalization and Washington's political-social hegemony. Only if social struggles in Europe acquire a political dimension strong enough to impose a political and social bloc less exclusively in the service of transnational capital will a genuine 'European project' conceivably make headway both internally (through the market regulation it requires and enables) and externally (through relations of a different kind with the South). Europe will be on the left, in a serious sense of the term, or there will be no Europe.

Meanwhile, North–South contradictions are destined to grow sharper. The vulnerability and fragility of 'comprador' regimes in the South (those that consent to neoliberal globalization) make it possible, even probable, that their rule will become increasingly unstable. The peripheries will therefore remain the weak links in the chain of the world system, and the South its area of greatest turbulence. A new 'common front' of the South, imposing a more or less pronounced revision of the world system, will then become a real possibility or probability. The 'wind of Bandung' may find itself blowing again. And if the North–South divide becomes more accentuated, the conditions will be more favourable to break the united front of the North.

American hegemony: reality or aspiration?

The construction of US hegemony has roots in the distant past. In a sense it has always – since independence – been the project of its ruling class, lending an unparalleled cynicism and hypocrisy to its ideology and practice. The conquest of the West through genocide of the native Americans, together with early claims to exclusive control over the entire continent (the Monroe Doctrine, first promulgated in 1822), paved the way for Washington's wider hegemonic ambitions, which were openly proclaimed in relation to Asia when the USA intervened in the Philippines at the end of the nineteenth century. Subsequently, it derived huge economic and financial profits from late entry into the First World War, at a time when the main belligerents – Britain, France, Germany and Russia – were on the brink of exhaustion. But the ideological and political conditions did not yet exist to reap the full benefit, and the American people imposed a return to 'isolationism'. Further unilateral advantages stemming from US participation in the Second World War underpinned Washington's new doctrine of global hegemony, which it systematically pursued after 1945. Isolationism was then definitively abandoned, even if it naively lingered in the mind of many a citizen and could even be evoked at an occasional election jamboree.

The whole of the post-war period, from 1945 to the present day, has been marked by US hegemony, however much this was tempered by the military and political bipolarity of the world system until the collapse of the USSR.

The literature on US hegemony is so abundant that it is virtually impossible to present even a brief review of it here. The main emphasis has been on 'economic' aspects, perhaps at least partly because of the 'professional deformation' of conventional (and, alas, other) economists, who exclude politics from their schemas and usually restrict themselves to the competitiveness of national productive systems. Robert Brenner's analysis, to which reference has already been made, is a typical example of this.

Hegemonism is always multidimensional, relative and under threat. It is multidimensional in the sense that it involves not only economics (higher productivity in crucial sectors of production, technological inventiveness, a decisive role in world trade, the key currency in the system, etc.), but also political, ideological (even cultural) and military aspects. It is relative because the world capitalist economy is not a world empire ruled by a single power, so that the hegemonic centre has to strike compromises with other states, even dominated ones, especially if they reject its position. Consequently, hegemony is always under threat from the evolving relationship of forces among the partners in the world system.

If we take the economic dimension in the narrow sense of the term, measuring it by per capita GDP and structural trends in the trade balance, then we will conclude that the overwhelming US hegemony of 1945 began to fade in the 1960s and 1970s as a result of Europe's and Japan's brilliant successes. European leaders never cease to point out that the EU is the world's foremost economic and trading power, and so on. But this is rather a strong assertion. For, although there is a single European market, and even the makings of a single currency, there is no single European economy, no 'European productive system' as there is a single productive system in the United States. What we still largely have are the various European economies and autocentred productive systems (open, even aggressively open, though they may be) that came into being historically with the respective bourgeoisies. Here, the transnational corporations are not European, only British, German, French, and so on; the few exceptions are the result of inter-governmental cooperation in the public sector, of which Airbus is the prototype. (This is an important point, because it reminds us of the crucial role that the public sector will have to play in any structural transformation.) There is no interpenetration of capital, or, to be more precise, the interpenetration that exists is no denser in intra-European relations than in the relations that each European country has with the United States and Japan. Thus, if European productive systems are being eroded by so-called globalized interdependence, this is to the advantage of globalization and the forces dominating it, not to that of a still virtually non-existent 'European integration'.

When we take into account other aspects of economic life, such as technological innovation or the place of national currencies within the international monetary system, the asymmetry between the United States and the European Union is also striking. It may be debatable in the case of technological innovation, although the military superiority of the United States has huge research spin-offs in areas such as computers and the Internet that confer obvious advantages on the economy as a whole. As to the dollar's role as the principal means of international settlement (which allows the United States to run a permanent balance-of-payments deficit that cushions its loss of competitiveness on world markets), this does not seem to be threatened by the euro. In my view, so long as there is not one integrated European economy, the euro will remain vulnerable and have difficulties replacing the dollar at a world level. The latter's monopoly as an international currency, despite all the efforts on the euro's behalf, is due not to any superiority of the US economic system as such but to US political hegemony and the economic advantages that flow from it.

A narrowly economic analysis therefore leaves unanswered the central question I have posed. Does the political and military hegemony of the United States stem from the advantages it enjoys in finance (the dollar as the only real international currency) and in economics more generally? Or does the causal relationship operate in the other direction?

A closer look at the 1990s will enable us to find an answer. Mainstream literature claims that the 'liberal option', applied more robustly in the United States than in Europe, is at the root of the 'American miracle' that has supposedly strengthened the economic side of US hegemony; and that Europe and Japan have only to imitate the American model (as the ruling classes of the Triad partners have indeed chosen to do).[1]

It is true that, in the 1990s, the United States did record stronger growth than its partners in the triad, and that this allowed a lot of unemployment to be mopped up. The price, as we know, was an erosion of job security, cuts in real wages (from $9.59 an hour in 1968 to $8.7 in 1998), and a rise in the percentage of the population living below the poverty threshold (up from 25 per cent in 1970 to 36 per cent in 1997). Some may find it shocking (I certainly do) that this kind of tendency is being set up as a model for others to follow. But American capital does not care: if the population accepts what it takes to boost profit margins, then everything is hunky-dory (for capital).

The US growth of the 'Clinton decade' went together with a decline in the country's industrial potential. Its industrial production per capita is now only 50 per cent of Japan's, 60 per cent of Germany's, and below that of France or Italy, while its share of the total industrial production of the three major economies (USA, Japan, Germany) fell from 54.2 per cent in 1961 to 40.5 per cent in 1996. The American growth figures, then, are mainly due to an extreme shift of the economy towards the service sector.

This decline of the United States, at least industrially, has produced a huge and growing deficit in its external trade balance, which soared from $7.4 billion in 1991 to $30.5 in 1999. At the same time, the country's savings ratio neared vanishing point, falling from 8 per cent of GDP in 1990 to a mere 2 per cent in 2000. In order to sustain growth, therefore, America relied on a huge inflow of capital representing much of the surplus produced elsewhere in the world, both in the wealthy Triad and in the poorer regions of the Third and Fourth Worlds. This capital in turn fuelled a financial hypertrophy that expressed itself in public debt up from $1 trillion in 1981 to $5.5 trillion in 1999.

But we need to take the analysis further. For the neoliberal thesis that cuts in the remuneration to labour are a prerequisite of renewed growth is not confirmed by the 'American miracle', which was funded by the rest of the world to such an extent that it would be quite impossible to generalize, even within the Triad alone. Its economic growth in the 1990s was largely due to the parasitic character of the US economy and society – a parasitism that makes it highly vulnerable.

The declared aim of US strategic hegemony is not to tolerate any power capable of resisting its injunctions. This means trying to break up any country that is deemed 'too big' into a maximum number of rump states, making it easy for Washington to move in and set up 'protective' bases. Only one country has the right to remain 'big', as its last three presidents (Bush Senior, Clinton and Bush Junior) have all made clear.

It is not difficult to discover the ends and the means of Washington's project. They are displayed with the merit of candour, even if their legitimization is still shrouded in a moralistic discourse peculiar to the American tradition. The global strategy of the United States has five key objectives: (i) to neutralize and subjugate its partners in the Triad (Europe and Japan), reducing to a minimum their capacity to act outside the American fold; (ii) to establish military control over NATO and to

'Latin Americanize' the fragments of the former Soviet Union; (iii) to hold undivided sway over the Middle East and Central Asia and their oil resources; (iv) to break up China, subordinate the other large countries (India, Brazil), and prevent the formation of regional blocs capable of bargaining over the terms of globalization; and (v) to marginalize regions in the South that are of no strategic interest.

Systematic intervention to promote these objectives rests upon three principles: (i) the rapid substitution of NATO for the UN as the means of running the international order (a goal confirmed in the wake of the Kosovo war, through a redefinition of NATO's field of operations sufficiently loose to give Washington a free hand); (ii) the alignment of Europe with Washington's strategic objectives, through a return to the traditional principle prior to the creation of the UN in 1945 (that is, war as a means of solving political disputes); and (iii) a choice of military methods that strengthen American hegemony (risk-free bombing and use of European troops as possible auxiliaries on the ground).

Ultimately, then, US hegemony rests more upon military aggrandisement than upon any 'advantages' of the American economic system. Here I shall merely summarize what I have said elsewhere about current trends, placing the emphasis on America's real political advantage of being a single country, unlike the European Union. The United States can thereby project itself as the Triad's undisputed leader, making its own military strength and a US-dominated NATO the 'visible fist' for the imposition of the new imperialist order on anyone who still refuses to knuckle under.

Militarization of the US drive for hegemony

The fashionable talk in the 1970s about a challenge to American hegemony from Europe and Japan sometimes went so far as to suggest that one or another of these two Triad partners was pushing to assert a new hegemony of its own. Then, straight after the election of Reagan in 1980, the US counter-attack began. The main stages in this campaign were: America's official adoption of so-called neoliberal economic policies; the stepping up of the arms race; the collapse of the Soviet Union; George Bush's declaration on the morrow of the Gulf War that the United States, as the only remaining superpower, was able and willing to create a 'new international order'; the American armed intervention on European territory, in Yugoslavia; and finally, in response to the attacks of 11 September 2001, the opening of a new front in the heart of Central Asia. As to America's ostensible 'economic miracle' during the 1990s, I have already expressed grave doubts about its reality.

Did all this amount to a genuine revival of hegemony, or was it only a swan song? An arrogant and egoistic push by the only remaining superpower, or action for the collective benefit of the imperialist Triad?

From the Gulf War of 1991, through the wars in Bosnia, Kosovo and Macedonia, to the Afghanistan campaign, the ruling establishment in the United States has pursued an identical method of achieving its aim of political control: first, choose an 'enemy' in the coveted geo-strategic area; next, exploit the enemy's often odious behaviour (the kind happily tolerated in others), or even secretly encourage it (that is the CIA's role); then suddenly 'declare war' on that enemy through massive aerial bombardment from a safe height ('nil casualties warfare' for the United States); and finally, establish a lasting American presence in the region, on the grounds that the enemy is still there.

A cynical picture, perhaps, but no less realistic. For it must be realized that the ruling US establishment is profoundly and utterly cynical, even if it masks this with the utter hypocrisy of its moralistic discourse. American public opinion, most of it incredibly simple-minded, makes it easy for the media to manipulate it and line it up with the tactical requirements of a policy decided behind its back.

The American ideology carefully packages the goods in the ineffable language of the country's 'manifest destiny' – a tradition handed down by the Founding Fathers, who were supremely confident of their divine inspiration. American liberals in the political sense of the term, who see themselves as the left in their society, share this ideology. In their eyes, American hegemony is a benign force helping to advance democratic awareness and practice; it is of obvious benefit to those who are its beneficiaries rather than its victims. American hegemony, universal peace, democracy and material progress are presented as if they were inseparable. But the reality is quite different.

The way in which European public opinion (especially on the left) has rallied to this project beggars belief. It is a disaster that can have only tragic consequences. Media bludgeoning, in relation to Washington's chosen areas of intervention, is doubtless an important part of the story, but Westerners are generally convinced that because the USA and the EU are democratic their governments are incapable of pursuing any 'evil purpose' – that is reserved for bloody oriental dictators. So great is the blindness that people in the imperialist countries forget the decisive weight of the interests of dominant capital, and come away from it all with a good conscience.

How will nations threatened by this third wave of imperialist expansion react? It is too soon to say. But react they certainly will.

It is useful to recall here that the coveted strategic area includes the Middle East, the Balkans, the Gulf and Central Asia, and that the latter two regions contain most of the world's oil reserves. Can the close relationship between the Bush family and US oil interests simply be overlooked? Is it not strange that Bush Senior's first war was to control the Gulf (supposedly threatened by Iraq), and that Bush Junior's first war openly aimed to wrest control of Central Asia from post-Soviet Russia – and was also a war for oil? Although the opinion-forming media have never expressed more than a few suspicions on this score, the specialist literature – which the mass of the public does not know – gives abundant proof of the links between Washington's diplomatic manoeuvres to control the Central Asian pipelines, its past military support to the Taliban in exchange for approval of a trans-Afghan oil pipeline, and its support to the Chechens (who, like the Taliban, are presented as 'freedom fighters', no longer against terrible Communists but against no less appalling Russians). Pentagon strategists also viewed the Yugoslav wars as an opportunity to move into the Balkans militarily, thereby strengthening the chain that leads through Turkey and Israel to the Middle East. Washington's unconditional support for Israel cannot be explained only by natural sympathy for an expansionist country imitating its own legendary 'conquest of the West', with the Arabs playing the role of the American Indians in the dominant myth. Here, too, oil is another important consideration.

I have showed the significance that the Pentagon attaches to the region even before the Gulf War and Afghanistan made it a topical issue.[2] Like the Caribbean and Central America, it has a frontline position in US global strategy – that is, Washington reserves the right to intervene there on its own initiative, with evident disregard for international law – and it has kept this position despite the disappearance of the Soviet Union (once supposed to be the main enemy). Indeed, it is now seen as a launching pad for the conquest of ex-Soviet Central Asia. If these aims were achieved, Washington would directly control a region that, since ancient times, has both divided and linked together Asia (China, India), Europe, Russia and Africa; it would simultaneously have tightened the net around its subaltern European ally, Arab countries with a potentially 'dangerous' population (Egypt, Syria, Iraq), Russia, China and India (whose potential for autonomous development has always been regarded as a threat). The Afghan war is part of this militarization of US global hegemony.

The designated enemy must look truly hateful, and so the US establishment picks a face that fits from the many of this type who abound in these times of chaos. This choice helps to sustain a moralistic vision that portrays any conflict between the USA and its enemies as a war between Good and Evil, saying nothing about real objectives or the fact that the 'bad guy' used to belong to Washington's charmed circle of friends and protégés serving its hegemonic ambitions. Saddam Hussein and Osama bin Laden both perfectly answer to this description.

Since the real aim is to establish a permanent US military presence in the area, it is always useful if the designated enemy remains as long as needed. So it was with Saddam, justifying the US bases in Saudi Arabia, and bin Laden, who served a similar function in Central Asia. Even if he himself is eliminated, it will not be difficult to argue that other dangerous terrorists are training in the mountains of the region and that US forces must therefore stay on indefinitely.

Sparing useful enemies, American strategy hits ever harder at a population that, in reality, has few ties of complicity with its oppressors – oppressors, let us remember, who imposed their rule at least partly through the active support of the United States. Everything is now covered up with George W. Bush's stark and simple choice: you're either with us (and therefore sign up in advance to all our declared and undeclared aims), or else you're with the terrorists! In fine McCarthyite tradition, Washington thereby demonizes any opposition to its policies, including to neoliberalism and other aspects of globalization.

Of course, there is no need to imagine that the CIA concocted the whole affair from the beginning or simply manufactured the enemy in question – although, in the case of Noriega and Panama, that actually was the case. In general, all manner of horrors have appeared with the collapse of the ruling projects that gave the post-war world its stability and legitimized otherwise highly questionable regimes. This aftermath, together with the dramatic worsening of social conditions due to neoliberal globalization, is what lies behind the serious aberrations, the reactive disarray and the monstrous illusions of ethnicism or so-called religious fundamentalism. The diplomatic efforts of the G-7 powers have supported and continue to support these aberrations, because they can find no other allies among the peoples exposed to liberal globalization. The designated enemies are therefore not only yesterday's friends but threaten to rejoin the camp of the Triad's collective imperialism and US hegemonism. Washington is already desperately searching for 'moderate Talibans'; its war against them is a masquerade, however tragic it may be for the peoples who are its victims.

The Gulf War

It is no accident that the Gulf War came immediately after the collapse of the Soviet Union. Although the bloody lurch of the Ba'ath regime in Iraq did not begin in 1990, the G-7 powers had not previously seen it as a problem. Once Baghdad had played along with US strategy against the Islamic Republic of Iran (the first Gulf War, between Iran and Iraq, lasted the whole of the 1980s), it was forgiven the terror it inflicted on its whole people as well as its savage repression of the Kurds. Is it necessary to recall that Western powers had always opposed any government in Baghdad that tried to solve the Kurdish question peacefully by integrating Kurdish democrats? Certainly Iraqi and Arab opinion had not forgotten this, and it therefore gave little credence to any of the post-1990 talk of democracy or human rights.

Buoyed by the support of Western powers, Saddam Hussein made the mistake of believing that Washington would allow Iraq to become the dominant power in the Gulf and to replace Saudi Arabia as the main US ally in the region. In fact, upon learning of his intentions towards Kuwait, the US ambassador to Baghdad almost encouraged Saddam to think along these lines, but Washington continued to regard the archaic Gulf monarchies as its best clients, while the Pentagon and Israel had already decided to destroy Iraq's military strength. Saddam's aggression against a formally independent state gave the best possible pretext, ranging the UN and NATO behind George Bush and forcing Riyadh to accept a reinforcement of the US military presence in Saudi Arabia and the rest of the Gulf. It even meant that this American war could be funded by the oil-producing countries of the Gulf! The massive blind bombing of all Iraqi towns, complacently shown on CNN news broadcasts, served an important function for the 'new international order' arrogantly proclaimed by Bush Senior: that is, it terrorized people around the world. Saddam himself was left in place, so that there would be justification for a permanent economic blockade of Iraq to finish off the country's destruction, to the accompaniment of further bombing ordered by the Pentagon and its faithful British servants. It was the Iraqi people who paid the price. Meanwhile, American troops stayed on in Saudi Arabia, continually delaying their promised withdrawal after the end of the war against Iraq.

In the short term, this first American victory was total. In the longer term, however, it produced some fresh difficulties for the hegemonic project. Arab governments had been naive enough to believe American promises that, in exchange for their support against Iraq, Washington would make every effort to solve the Palestinian question once and for all. The Madrid conference held in the aftermath of the 'Desert Storm' victory, then the Oslo accords of 1993, gave the impression that the promises were going to be fulfilled, but the sequel showed that Washington was actually continuing its policy of support for the expansion of Israeli settlements. The intifada soon showed Arab public opinion that it had been cruelly deceived. Indeed, far from pacifying it and smoothing the advance of neoliberal globalization (with all the social catastrophes that would involve), the Gulf War and its aftermath up to the intifada brought 'hatred of the Americans' to a fever pitch. The consequences inevitably stretched deep into the Arab ruling elites, however aligned they were with the comprador option complementing liberal globalization. This even affected the Saudi ruling class, Washington's main ally in the region, which began to look so shaky that its collapse sooner or later would come as no surprise.

The Yugoslav wars[3]

The disintegration of Yugoslavia has its roots inside the country, in the period after Tito's death, when his successors embarked on an uncontrolled opening of the economy that soon led to stagnation and a sharpening of inequalities between the constituent republics and regions of the federation. Here as elsewhere (in the USSR, for example), the ruling communist 'nomenklatura' lost its legitimacy and began to splinter, as each of its segments scrambled to prop itself up on the basis of 'ethnic' and religious factors that Titoism had to a large extent begun to overcome. Europe, egged on by Islamic secessionists in Bosnia (and later in Kosovo and Macedonia), moved in the opposite direction and added fuel to the fire by hastily recognizing the independence of Slovenia and Croatia. Moreover, by suggesting that NATO impose a military solution, the Europeans gave that organization's real boss (the United States) an opportunity to involve itself directly in European affairs and to establish a military presence of its own in the Balkans, another priority area (after the Middle East and Central Asia) for its project of global political and military hegemony. Following the 'victory' in Kosovo, Washington had no difficulty in getting its subordinate European allies to swallow an expansion of NATO's functions, thereby ensuring in advance that they would rally behind its project.

I cannot here go into further details and must refer the reader to my *L'Hégémonisme des États-Unis et l'effacement du projet européen*.[4] A closer study of the responsibilities of individual EU countries (especially

Germany) in the Yugoslav affair, as well as the role of the papacy, would once again illustrate the fundamental shortcomings of the European project, in the absence of a political centre capable of giving even minimal cohesion to the policies of the member states of an area that does not deserve the name of a union.

Nor shall I recall the reasons given to justify the forms of NATO intervention, the light-minded and manipulative arguments, and the choice of, to say the least, dubious local allies such as former Croat fascists, Izetbegovic's islamicists, or the UCK Kosovars who would have been treated as terrorists under other circumstances. All the peoples of the region now have to cope with the deplorable outcomes: the dislocated societies and economies with no prospect of reconstruction, the 'ethnic cleansing' that has hit hardest those who were first accused of it, the failed promises of democracy, and so on. But, in compensation for all that, the United States does now have its secure military base in the area for a good while to come.

War in Central Asia[5]

Since the collapse of the Soviet Union, Washington has had its eye on the Muslim oil-producing region of Central Asia, as a natural extension of the already US-dominated Gulf. Is the Caspian Sea a second Gulf, in terms of oil and gas reserves? Many experts doubt it: those in the former USSR, for example, thought the West Siberian basin much more promising. In any event, the Caspian has become the object of conflict both among the states that border on it and among the oil corporations able to operate in the region. Other disputes concern possible pipeline routes for the region's output: north through Russia, or south through Turkey, Iran or Afghanistan. There is a wealth of documentation and analysis on all these matters.

Even if Central Asia is far from being an El Dorado, its resources certainly excite the greed of the Bush family, and the rents might provide a basis of survival for the various countries and allow their ruling classes to keep their autocratic power indefinitely. All the talk about democracy of which the West is so fond nowadays will here be put on ice, as it has been in the Gulf. Political Islam and ethnicity, backed up by the oil rent, might then provide the legitimacy for the local post-Soviet regimes.

If the whole operation also established the United States politically and militarily in the region, Washington would be able to wrap it up and eliminate any danger of a Russian comeback. To tighten the military net around Russia, Iran, China and India is anyway one of the main priorities of its hegemonic strategy – an objective first outlined during the first Afghan War, against the Soviet Union and local national-populist modernizers who improperly called themselves communists, much to the glee of Western propaganda. At the time, Washington supported Islamicists of various ethnic stripes and even described them as freedom-fighters, despite their ultra-reactionary anti-democractic and anti-female programme. In fact, the main thing they held against the communists was that they had opened the schools to girls. The hanging of Najibullah in 1996 by the Taliban – after they had cut off his genitals and stuffed them in his mouth – did not give rise to any protest in the West, just as their closing of girls' schools did not really shake the major feminist movements. Everyone was supposed to 'respect traditions'.

During the first Afghan War, as well as during the second war – following the Soviet withdrawal – which pitted the Taliban against what would later become the 'Northern Alliance', the United States entered into an agreement with the Taliban and their mentor, Osama bin Laden. Had it not been for the direct military intervention of Pakistan, a loyal ally of Washington, the Taliban would probably have been incapable of taking Kabul and imposing their odious dictatorship on the Afghan people. At the time, bin Laden played the role of an efficient middleman for the funding and supply of heavy weapons; his training camps for 'fanatics' were never condemned. In fact, the Arab 'terrorists', having been trained under the supervision of the CIA and Pakistani intelligence, were supposed to act only where it fitted in with US foreign policy: in Algeria and Egypt to keep up pressure on the local regimes and show them that the USA had another possible team in reserve; in Yugoslavia and Russia (via the Chechens); and perhaps even in France (neither the USA, nor Britain, nor Germany, nor Sweden refused to house the operational centres of 'terrorist' Islam). Relations between the Bush family and bin Laden went as far as exchanges of compliments. And did bin Laden not help finance Republican election campaigns?

Things later started to go wrong, of course. Washington is supposed to have promised bin Laden, in return for his invaluable services, nothing less than the government of Saudi Arabia – which would mean that the USA was then remarkably sure of him, more than it was of the Saudi royal family itself. The extreme form of Wahhabism embraced by bin Laden also gave him the legitimacy, in both his eyes and the Americans', to aim at substituting a rejuvenated dictatorship for the corrupt monarchy that had betrayed 'Wahhabi purity'.

The United States achieved victories beyond its expectations: not only did the Soviets pull out of Afghanistan, but the USSR itself collapsed soon after. Washington then began to set its sights higher, with Central Asia as the new prize. As bin Laden lost his usefulness, the Americans decided to drop him and to go on backing the Gulf monarchies. It was probably this terrible disappointment that led him to send his regards by striking on America's home ground. The attacks of 11 September again posed the so-called question of terrorism, which had ceased to be an object of easy manipulation by the American state. We shall return to this point below.

The US strategic objectives in Afghanistan were clear, but the success of the operation was quite a different matter. New and huge difficulties appeared, first of all at a strictly military level, where the United States – for all the official bluster – will increasingly need allies willing to act on the ground. Will the French with their Foreign Legion, the British with their Gurkhas or other European governments be prepared to supply cannon fodder, after the lesson the Soviets received in the mountains of Afghanistan? Now that the Northern Alliance has recaptured the country, or at least Kabul and the main cities, does it not threaten to display a new autonomy *vis-à-vis* the Western powers that long preferred the Taliban? Does it not threaten a new 'neutralism' in the good old Afghan tradition, equidistant from Russia and the United States? Is there not a danger that Putin will join the game and strengthen his alliance with the republics of Central Asia? Interestingly enough, the main media have hastened to point out that the Northern Alliance is ethnically skewed towards the Tadzhiks and Uzbeks and is therefore incapable of running the country – as if good government has ever been a concern of Western diplomacy in Afghanistan! In this curious talk, the Taliban are supposed to be the genuine representatives of the Pathans – but that is false: they exercised their odious dictatorship as much over the Pathans as everyone else. The truth is that, for the United States (and therefore, alas, for its European camp followers), an indulgent attitude to the Taliban is the best way of avoiding trouble for its allies in Pakistan. Washington is therefore desperately seeking a 'moderate Taliban': that is, a Taliban which agrees to exercise its terrorist expertise, if at all, only under the control of the CIA.

It is unlikely that the operation could ever be completed without sacrificing Pakistan. Some time ago, after New Delhi had lost the Soviet support traditional since the time of Nehru, the US establishment decided to modify its alliance strategy to favour India rather than Pakistan, and, in a further move, to strengthen India against its Chinese 'adversary'.

Part of the Indian establishment was certainly attracted by this new perspective, but another part – not only the communist left – remained on its guard. Aware of Washington's record of cynical duplicity, it feared that the United States would support India as the rope supports a hanging man, and would at the same time continue to bank on an 'ethnic' fragmentation of India by backing the demands of the southern states. This fraction of the Indian political class prefers the alternative of a Russia–India–China rapprochement: the wind of Bandung blowing anew.

It is also unlikely that the United States will be able to prevent huge shocks to its allies in the Gulf, especially if the Afghan operation gets bogged down. The Saudi regime is already seriously threatened, and it would be no surprise if it went the way of the Shah of Iran. Of course, society in the Arabian Peninsula is not the same as in Iran, and the ways and means of change, as well as the nature of any ensuing regime, are still open to doubt. Nevertheless, a regime that wishes to distance itself from Washington, perhaps even to end its embarrassing military presence, no longer belongs to the realm of the unthinkable.

Another new headache for Washington is the question of who will foot the bill for the war in Afghanistan. In addition to the direct costs, there are the financial concessions that the USA has already made to Pakistan, and will probably extend to India, Russia and the Central Asian countries, to keep them within the grand 'alliance against terrorism'. Previously, Washington had no trouble getting the oil-producing monarchies to pay for the Gulf War, or European governments to fund the wars in Yugoslavia. But who will cough up for Afghanistan? One idea, no doubt, is that the money could be extracted from the Gulf states, whose massive investments in the world financial system are always open to seizure. Bush's declaration of 'financial war' against the terrorist sources of supply has come just in time for a possible grab at Arab investments in the USA and elsewhere. But this is a double-edged weapon. It could indeed frighten the Gulf monarchies, and their billionaire clienteles, into putting a brave face on things and paying their 'share' for the war on terrorism. But it could also make them realize that the vulnerability of the investments in question requires other long-term economic and financial options to be considered.

Last but not least, there is the Palestinian question.[6] Up to this day, the United States has never treated Israel other than as a privileged ally whose aims, whatever they may be, must be unconditionally supported. The promises made by George Bush Senior during the Gulf War therefore came to nothing. But it seems that, this second time round, it will be more difficult for Washington to delude not only Arab opinion in general (which now has a real and deserved hatred of America) but even the ruling political classes in the region, which are prepared to serve as loyal allies and to accept the injunctions of liberal economic globalization. Will the United States in the end recognize the right of the Palestinians to a state? If so, within which frontiers: those of 1967, as UN Resolution 242 demands, or those that began to be negotiated in Oslo and were later brutally rejected by Sharon, the same man whom Washington continues to support against allcomers? What is clear is that in future the United States will be judged not by its promises (which it is in the habit of shamelessly breaking) but by the positions it takes in practice.

Notes

1. The macro-economic data are again taken from Jorge Bernstein, *La larga crisis de la economía global*.

2. See Samir Amin, 'La géopolitique de la région Méditerranée Golfe', in S. Amin et al., eds, *Les enjeux stratégiques en Méditerranée*, Paris: L'Harmattan, 1992, pp. 11–112.

3. See Samir Amin, *L'ethnie à l'assaut des nations*, Paris: L'Harmattan, 1993; Ivan Ivekovic, *Ethnic and Regional Conflicts in Yugoslavia and Transcaucasia*, Ravenna: Longo Ed., 2000; Catherine Samary, *La déchirure yougoslave*, Paris: L'Harmattan, 1994; and F. Chesnais, T. Noctiummes and J. P. Page, *Réflexions sur la guerre en Yugoslavie*, Paris: L'Esprit frappeur, 1999.

4. Samir Amin, *L'Hégémonisme des États-Unis et l'effacement du projet européen: face à l'OTAN, le combat pour un monde multipolaire et démocratique*, Paris: L'Harmattan, 2000.

5. See Robert Ebel and Rajan Menion (eds), *Energy and Conflict in Central Asia and the Caucasus*, New York: Rowan and Littlefield, 2000; Raja Anwar, *The Tragedy of Afghanistan*, London: Verso, 1988; and Gilles Dorronsoro, *La tragédie afghane*, Paris: Karthalla, 2000.

6. Samir Amin, *Le monde arabe, État des lieux, État des luttes*, forthcoming; especially the section on the Palestinian intifadas.

SIX
Obsolescent capitalism and the new world disorder

§ Can the historical phase through which we are passing be analysed as phase B of a Kondratiev long cycle, to be inexorably followed by a new phase A of expansion? The previous phase A, based on the social equilibria of the three post-war modes of accumulation and their accompanying international equilibria, eventually exhausted itself, so that now the system has all the aspects of structural crisis associated with phase B. By no means, however, does this allow us to conclude that it will *necessarily* be followed by a new phase of expansion. Such a conclusion would require us to accept that capitalism is eternal, to ignore its grave and visible signs of ageing.

This ageing means that the system has entered a state of permanent disorder, which will lead either, in the best case, to a long transition to socialism or, in the worst case, to catastrophe and the suicide of humanity. Moreover, my thesis concerning 'under-determination' in history – which emphasizes the autonomous logics governing the various dimensions of social existence – prevents us from concluding that political societies in both the centres and the peripheries will be happy simply to adapt to the laws of capital accumulation defined by the new conditions of the system today (especially those governing accumulation on a world scale in our era of collective imperialism).

The chaos, then, will express itself in a proliferation of conflicts, with a variable geometry allowing any number of imaginable scenarios. All the various 'projects', whether just begun or already far advanced, find their place in this general framework. The 'European project' might either gradually fade away if current trends continue, or else find a new lease of life and even acquire new political and social dimensions (whose conditions would need to be identified). Similarly, the Chinese kind of 'market socialism' project might either assert itself in a more rigorous form and become part of a long transition to socialism, or else crumble into nothingness (and again the conditions for each scenario would have to be specified). The hegemony of the United States might maintain itself in an 'American twenty-first century' (as some imagine and even hope), or it might collapse.

In its social dimension, the chaos necessarily expresses itself in the decline of democracy, which can take a number of forms according to the precise time and place: for example, contempt for the law, or the rise of culturalist replacement ideologies that betray impotence in the face of the real challenges. The peoples of the world may also, of course, react against these forms of social, political and cultural regression, enabling elements of alternatives to crystallize within a long transition beyond capitalism.

Obsolescent capitalism

The structural crisis of contemporary capitalism probably does not involve the kind of transition that will be overcome through a new phase of globalized capitalist expansion. What we see, rather, are signs of the obsolescence of capitalism, and therefore of the objective need for humanity as a whole to set out on the road to socialism. I say 'set out on the road', the road of a long transition, and not 'build socialism' in one place or another.

The first element of obsolescence lies in the long-term significance of the scientific and technological revolution. If this revolution – and, in particular, the computer technology and automation that it promotes – is expressed in the fact that greater material output can be achieved with less labour and simultaneously less capital, then we must conclude that the capitalist mode of production has exhausted its historical role. For capitalism is based on the domination of labour by capital, and there is less and less basis in reality for that domination. In other words, capitalist social relations no longer allow pursuit of the continual accumulation that used to be their historical function; they have become an obstacle to the enrichment of human societies. Different relations, based on abolition of the private ownership of capital, are now an objective necessity: not to 'correct' (in favour of labour) a pattern of income distribution that capitalism tends to make ever less equal, but, more fundamentally, to enable the renewed growth of material wealth, which has become impossible on the basis of capitalist social relations. In other words, socialism has never before been such an objective necessity for the progress of civilization as it is today.

The second element of obsolescence lies in the fact that the collective Triad imperialism operating on the whole world system no longer allows the pursuit of 'dependent' capitalist development in the peripheries.

In previous historical phases of global capitalist expansion, the centres played an active role by exporting capital to the peripheries and shaping an asymmetrical development that may correctly be described as dependent or uneven. In turn, of course, these 'exports' made it possible to extract a surplus from the exploited surplus labour of the peripheries, so that the 'return of profits' could be greater than the outflow of capital.

The collective Triad imperialism, especially in its American 'centre of centres', no longer functions in this manner. The United States absorbs a considerable part of the surplus generated throughout the world, and the Triad is no longer a significant exporter of capital to the peripheries. The surplus that it pumps out in various forms (including debt repayments from developing countries and the former Eastern bloc) is no longer offset by new productive investment. The parasitic character of this imperialist system is itself a sign of obsolescence that brings to the fore the 'North–South' contradiction between centres and peripheries.

Ideologists and manufacturers of media discourse herald this withdrawal of the centres from the peripheries as proof that there is no longer such a thing as imperialism, since the North can perfectly well do without the South. But the facts refute this daily (why do we have the WTO, the IMF and NATO interventions?) and they also give the lie to the 'universal vocation' that was originally an important part of bourgeois ideology. If that vocation has been abandoned for the sake of a new, 'postmodernist' discourse of culturalism, does this not symbolize the obsolescence of a system that has nothing to offer 80 per cent of the world's population?

These two elements of obsolescence together express themselves in the replacement of 'creative destruction' (to use Schumpeter's term) with a type of 'uncreative destruction'. Borrowing from Beinstein's analysis,[1] I would argue that the destruction produced by any technological innovation is creative when it begins with the acceleration of demand, but that it is no longer creative when it begins with the slackening of demand. Another way of analysing this might be in terms of a passage from 'expanding capitalism' to 'shrinking capitalism', as proposed by Ankie Hoogvelt.[2]

The world system has not entered a new 'non-imperialist' or 'postimperialist' phase; on the contrary, it has the nature of an imperialist system carried to the extreme (pumping out of surplus with nothing in return). Unfortunately, Toni Negri's analysis of an 'empire' without imperialism – in fact, an empire limited to the Triad in which the rest of the world is ignored – falls within a certain 'occidentalist' tradition as well as sharing elements of today's Zeitgeist.[3] I very much hope that Negri will correct this false move on his part. The real difference between the new and the older imperialism is that the latter was a plural phenomenon ('imperialisms' in conflict with each other), whereas today we are talking a collective Triad imperialism, albeit in the shadow of US hegemony. Hence, conflicts among the Triad partners unfold in a minor tone; it is conflicts between the Triad and the rest of the world which set the major tone. The obliteration of the European project in the face of American hegemony finds its place here.

The most serious political conclusion from the above analysis is that the strategies of Triad transnational capital will require stepped-up military intervention by the United States and NATO, and that this will reproduce Washington's hegemony and push Europe and Japan to fall more closely into line. A new phase of capitalist expansion within this collective imperialist framework remains unlikely, even if one can always construct such a phase in theory and construct a scenario in conformity with it. The geometry of what I have suggested as possible conflicts will have to take this conclusion into account.

The obsolescence of capitalism is expressed not only in its spheres of economic and social reproduction, but also in political practice and ideological discourse. The decline of democracy, the replacement of (even bourgeois) civic culture with a 'culture of spectacle',[4] are also signs and effects of this obsolescence.

Apartheid on a world scale

The Triad's new collective imperialism, and the hegemony of the United States with which it is inseparably bound up, have generated a distinctive conception of world government both economic and geopolitical.

The idea that the world's affairs cannot be left to depend only on the relationship of forces between countries, and that the gradual construction of elements of a supranational order is the only alternative to the law of the jungle, is in itself certainly attractive and deserving of support. The UN was created in this spirit, with the institutions of the General Assembly and Security Council and a charter that prohibited recourse to war as a means of solving political disputes. Immediately after the Second World War, in the field of the regulation of international economic life, the United States used the advantages of its position to impose organizations directly under its control (the Bretton Woods organizations) and to take action outside the framework of the UN (the Marshall Plan for Europe, the famous Point Four Programme offering US aid to Third World countries that joined the anti-Soviet camp). Subsequently, the growing weight of Third World countries led to the creation of special institutions, UNCTAD among others, which applied themselves to correcting the fundamental imbalances generated by the history of capitalism. That whole page of history has been turned.

As early as 1975, in response to the rise of the Non-Aligned Movement, President Giscard d'Estaing of France took the initiative of setting up the G-7, with a composition perfectly expressing the idea of collective imperialism. The transformation of the GATT into the World Trade Organization at the end of the Uruguay Round lies at the heart of the new conception of global economic 'governance' by this collective imperialism.

The precise idea behind the WTO was to strengthen the 'comparative advantages' of transnational capital and to give them a degree of legitimacy: industrial and intellectual property rights would perpetuate the monopolies of the TNCs, guarantee their super-profits and erect almost insuperable barriers to any attempt at autonomous industrialization in the peripheries. The task of the WTO is not, as its name might suggest, simply to regulate world trade (that is, trade across frontiers). Its functions go much further than that. It seeks to create uniform rules for the management of both internal markets and the world market, to eliminate any distinction between them, in the name of an extreme vision of free trade that has no precedent in history. The result can only be a reorganization of productive systems to the advantage of the strongest – that is, of transnational capital. The WTO, then, seeks to organize not only world trade but production on a world scale, gearing it not to development requirements (at least partial 'catching up' by the poorer countries) but to the maximization of TNC profits through more asymmetrical and unequal productive systems. The WTO's plan for world economic government is an ultra-reactionary project in the full sense of the word: it means returning to earlier forms of the international division of labour. For this reason, I think of the WTO as the G-7's new colonial ministry, whose role *vis-à-vis* the peripheries is everywhere the same: to prevent the colonies from becoming competitors, by denying them the right to legislate and regulate in connection with the activities of metropolitan capital in their own countries.

The guiding principle of actually existing capitalism is systematically to protect the most powerful monopolies. The fantasy discourse of vulgar economics, which trumpets the supposed virtues of free trade, is just propaganda in the most ordinary sense of the term: it is a lie. I, with Braudel, am among the few who define capitalism not by 'the market' but by the powers beyond the market.

The methods used by these powers beyond the market are as diverse as the circumstances in which force can be employed. Intellectual property, for example, as interpreted by the *ad hoc* judges dreamed up by the WTO, can allow a (transnational) corporation to get its hands on traditional but 'unprotected' peasant know-how (the virtues of a strain of rice, for instance) and to impose its own monopoly on the marketing of the seeds in question – even in relation to farmers who have been growing that particular strain for centuries. Indians will thus have to buy the seeds for their basmati rice from a US corporation. This and other cases analysed by Vandana Shiva show that the major economic decision-makers of the contemporary world have a side to them very similar to that of Mafia racketeers: they impose an obligation to trade.[5] For this analogy, I refer the reader to the work of Carlo Vercellone.[6]

The scandal of the drugs companies that claim free and exclusive access to the world market, denying anyone else the right to produce cheap medicine in the countries of the South, is a particularly good example of this apartheid on a world scale. It means that only people in the rich countries will have the right to effective treatment, while people in the South will be refused the right to life itself. Similarly, the WTO plan to 'liberalize' agriculture completely negates the food security policies of countries in the South and condemns hundreds of millions of peasants to extreme poverty and forced migration to urban shanty towns, with no hope of any kind of activity in the formal economy.[7]

We find the same logic in the WTO's plan to develop 'international business law', with precedence over all other elements of national and international law, as well as in the OECD's secretly hatched project for a Multilateral Agreement on Investment (MAI).

The function of the other international institutions is simply to consolidate the strategies handed down by the WTO's political bosses. The World Bank, for instance, pompously described as a 'think-tank' for development strategies, is in reality little more than a kind of G-7 propaganda ministry responsible for speech-writing; any major economic decisions are taken within the WTO, while NATO handles the political and military side of the show. The International Monetary Fund (IMF) has greater importance, though less than often claimed. Since the adoption of the flexible exchange-rate system, which means that it no longer manages relations among the main currencies (dollar, euro, yen), this institution has been little more than a colonial monetary authority serving the Triad's collective imperialism.

The mention of NATO in the previous paragraph leads us on to the other dimension of world government. At no moment in its history has capitalism been able to dispense with state action, nor world capitalism with the political and military means at the disposal of the imperialist centres. In this respect, our epoch is no different from others before it.

Far from believing in the virtues of the market's 'invisible hand', the American establishment knows that it has to be backed up with the 'visible fist' of military might. In this connection, let me quote the magnificent insight that 'globalization will only work if the United States acts with the almighty (!) force of its position as superpower'. As an example, we are told that 'McDonald's cannot prosper without MacDonnell Douglas, which makes the F-15. The hidden fist that guarantees a safe world for Silicon Valley is called the army, air force, navy and Marine Corps of the United States.' The author was not a practical joker but Thomas Friedman, adviser to Madeleine Albright.

This is a long way from the soothing vision of fashionable economists, in which a self-regulated market guarantees universal peace. One savours in passing the use of McDonald's corporate profits as a criterion of the progress of world civilization; only a little later, Bush Junior was speaking in similar vein of the World Trade Center and the Pentagon (the targets of the 11 September attacks) as two 'symbols of civilization'. More important, the American ruling class knows that economics is politics and that the relationship of forces (including military forces) is ultimately in command of markets. There will be no 'world market' without an American military empire, they say. If such frankness, repeated in hundreds of articles, is possible in the United States, this is because the media are sufficiently well controlled for US strategic objectives never to become the object of real debate. The field of free expression, sometimes bordering on the farcical, covers only matters pertaining to individuals, behind which the conflicts within the ruling class remain perfectly opaque. No political force is capable of 'wising up' a public opinion that can be so manipulated.

More curious is the silence of European governments and certain others who pretend not to read the press on the other side of the Atlantic (I do not think they are in the dark about what is said). These people forbid anyone even to mention that Washington has a global strategy, all too readily accusing infractors of a 'conspiracy theory of history' or even of a fanatical vision that sees the 'Great Satan' lurking everywhere.

NATO's role as the main instrument serving Washington's chosen strategy explains why it has survived the collapse of the adversary against which it was originally directed. Nowadays, NATO speaks in the name of the 'international community', thereby expressing its contempt for the UN's democratic principles that are supposed to steer that community. In the American debates on global strategy, it is rarely a question of human rights or democracy; they are mentioned only when useful for the implementation of that strategy. Hence the blinding cynicism and the systematic employment of double standards.

The Kosovo war provided President Clinton with the opportunity to flesh out the principles of the new political order outlined by Bush Senior at the time of the Gulf War. In fact, there was a dual coup: NATO replaced the UN as the institution for the management of world politics; and the USA reasserted its leading role as the ultimate decision-maker. This crucial function of the Kosovo war was confirmed by the complete capitulation of European governments to Washington's 'new strategic concept', which NATO adopted on 23–25 April immediately after the 'victory' in Yugoslavia. In this new concept, NATO's missions are extended to virtually the whole of Asia and Africa (the USA retaining sole right under the Monroe Doctrine to intervene in the Americas), so that NATO ceases to be a defensive alliance and becomes an offensive tool of the United States. Moreover, its new missions are defined in the vaguest terms that include all manner of 'new threats' (international crime, terrorism, dangerous arms programmes in non-NATO countries and so on), making it possible to justify any act of aggression useful to the United States. Thus Clinton's talk of pre-emptive strikes against 'rogue states' carefully avoids spelling out what he means by 'roguery'. NATO is thereby freed of the obligation to act only with a UN mandate, the latter organization being treated with a contempt strikingly similar to that which the fascist powers reserved for the League of Nations. Now profiting from the attacks of 11 September, Washington is using the pretext of terrorism to forge ahead with its expansionist strategy for militarization of the so-called 'liberal' world order.

Alignment with this strategy of the United States and its subaltern NATO allies has a number of dramatic consequences. First of all, the United Nations is in the process of undergoing the same fate as the League of Nations. Although American society is happily not the same as Nazi Germany's, the rulers in Washington, like those in Berlin before them, have elevated force to the status of a supreme principle, scornfully replacing international law with a curious 'duty to intervene' that disturbingly recalls the 'civilizing mission' of nineteenth-century imperialism. I shall return to the issues of international law that this raises.

Globalization, so often presented as an imperative of 'economic progress' and positive social change, is actually a strategy to secure US control: (a) over 'world economic government', through institutions such as the WTO which, though nominally international, are in fact run by mainly American transnationals and the US government; and (b) over global political and military government, by means of NATO. Kissinger admitted as much when he coolly said that 'globalization is only another word for US domination'.

Europe's strategic support can only be explained by an acute sense of the common interests uniting the servants of the dominant capital, in Europe and Japan as well as the United States. This is what I mean by the collective imperialism of the Triad, the framework within which the dominant forces have developed an overall vision of 'global governance' around two basic pillars. The first of these is direct management of the world economy by the transnationals, via the WTO and other mechanisms. We should note, by the way, that Washington's idea of global economic governance has nothing to do with the speeches regularly made on the subject: the United States seems less convinced than its European allies of the virtues of competition and fair play, as it violates them with impunity whenever its own interests are on the line. Besides, Washington knows that without military hegemony it cannot artificially maintain its economic position by getting the rest of the world to make up its savings shortfall. The second pillar of global governance is quite simply the substitution of NATO (in reality the United States, with which other NATO countries have to associate themselves) for any other political or military expression of the 'international community'. The UN General Assembly, the Security Council, regional organizations such as the OAU in Africa, even the OECD rich men's club or the European Union – none of these (which Americans know is a union only in name) has any say whatsoever in implementing the political and military requirements of one-sided 'governance' by the dominant capital. NATO is being substituted for all of them. All over Asia and Africa, people think it obscene when the secretary-general of that military organization speaks in the name of the 'international community'. Europe's left-wing majorities, however, lap up all the insipid talk of democracy and national rights that accompanies each one of Washington's aggressive initiatives. A fig leaf is all they ask for.

The Triad's collective imperialist sanctioning of global governance enables Washington to affirm that only US hegemony can provide the coalition with the services it requires, and to speed up the obliteration of the European project. Nevertheless, the collective imperialist project of worldwide apartheid will not prevent a proliferation of revolts by its victims, and therefore an increasing number of wars of intervention against them.

Obliteration of the European project

The rallying of (both left and right) European governments to neoliberalism since the 1980s is naturally bound up with internal factors – essentially, the sharp shift in the social relationship of forces in favour of the dominant capital. Local political conjunctures may have varied considerably, as have electoral programmes (often either silent at the hour of key choices, or put on ice immediately after the polls), but the rallying itself is an indisputable fact. In my view, the only explanation for it is that the dominant political forces in Europe embraced the logic of collective imperialism, to which the transnational capital of the EU countries had gone over some time before.

Whether the political classes that made this choice realized it or not, the inherent logic of the system soon displayed itself in all its rigour. It is possible that, when the governments of all the Triad countries rallied round the flag in the 1980s, they did not foresee the growing difficulties they would have to face in implementing the neoliberal programme, both within their respective countries and in the management of globalization. Mainstream economists were not equipped to explain the (rather obvious) reasons why it was impossible to realize the wonderful Utopian vision of capital, to achieve its simple world in which every dimension of human reality, both social and international, complied with the exclusive demands of the maximization of transnational profits.

As the project became mired in economic stagnation – despite the apparent success of the Clinton years in the United States – the resulting social disaster could not but erode the legitimacy of the public authorities, especially in the most vulnerable peripheries. And this destabilization inevitably meant that the economic system, however liberal, ceased to function effectively. Although liberal discourse cannot understand why, no economy can be viable without a state.

The need to militarize liberal economic governance became clear long before 11 September, as the wars of the 1990s testify. The turn of European governments to global neoliberalism, reflecting the common interests of dominant capital within the new collective imperialism, therefore required them to fall into line politically and militarily with the United States. For it was US hegemony that in turn guaranteed Triad hegemony over the world system. The Europeans agreed to sail on in the American wake, without even any 'cultural' qualms on the part of Britain, Germany or Japan. But then the speeches concerning Europe's economic might – the staple fare of the continent's politicians – suddenly lost all hold on reality. By focusing its disputes purely on trade issues, Europe was always bound to lose. And Washington was well aware of this.

Thus the *ralliement* by European governments meant nothing less than obliteration of the European project, both economically (the advantages of European union dissipated in globalization) and politically (Europe's political and military autonomy lost in NATO). As things stand today, there is no European project; instead there is a North Atlantic (or perhaps a Triad) project, under American command. When first suggested by a European commissioner – Leon Brittain – it caused general uproar. But now it is the only show on the road.

The surrender of the European project to a revamped Atlanticism (with US hegemony lurking behind it) ought nevertheless to be a problem for at least some sectors of the public and some segments of the political classes in certain European countries, especially France. The European enterprise has been so much associated with wealth, power and independence that it ought to be difficult to make people swallow the pill: that is, to accept that US 'military' protection, via NATO, is today more necessary than ever.

NATO, we know, was created in 1949 with the ostensible aim of defending Western Europe from Soviet attack. I personally doubt that the threat ever existed – Moscow never dreamed of advancing beyond the frontiers outlined at Yalta – and would rather argue that it was a pretext for the United States to establish its political hegemony over the rest of the capitalist world, thereby complementing the economic supremacy it enjoyed at the end of the Second World War. But, in any event, these are historical questions that I shall not examine here, if only because the disappearance of the Soviet Union has made the alleged threat a non-issue.

I do not deny that Europeans have the right to ensure that they are defended – an imprescriptible right at the current level of human civilization, even if no one actually threatens them at present. European nations, whether individually or collectively (as the European Union), share with all other nations on earth the right to have armed forces capable of resisting or deterring any aggressor. But NATO is not the right way of addressing the problem, since it is not an alliance of equals but places the European allies in a subaltern position and forces them to line up behind the objectives of the United States. De Gaulle was the only major European post-war politician who understood this fatal defect of NATO. The history of the last decade, from the Gulf War to Afghanistan, shows that it does not and will not act in any other way than to serve Washington's interests. Whether it intervenes or takes no action, this will be decided by Washington alone. NATO can only be the instrument of the US project of global hegemony.

American military might was systematically built up after 1945 to cover the whole planet, through a chain of regional 'US military commands'. Until 1990, Soviet military power forced Washington to accept a kind of peaceful coexistence – but that is no longer the case. Here again I can only refer the reader to my previous writings on the subject, where I contrasted the global reach of US military strategy after 1945 with the Soviet Union's defensive strategy that had absolutely no ambition to 'conquer the world for communism', as Western propaganda claimed with regrettable success.[8]

Faced with these blinding realities, those who unconditionally support the European project 'as it is' adapt their arguments to the audience of the moment. Some apparently ideological considerations are put forward with candour (or false candour?): for example, that NATO is an association of democratic nations, or even the only solid democratic nations around, with the exception of semi-members such as Israel, Australia and New Zealand. But why is it actually needed? Its champions do not always dare admit that a new enemy has taken the place of communism: namely, the 'nationalism' of the countries of the 'South'. To say that would be to acknowledge that Europe conforms to the Triad's new collective imperialism. And so, no more is said is about NATO's real function of making the peoples of the South accept (through a permanent military threat) the dictatorship of transnational capital. What we hear instead is pure fantasy about NATO's noble mission to defend democracy or national and human rights – such a farcical argument that it cannot be taken seriously for a moment. Another claim that might seem plausible is that the purpose of NATO (or of the US armed forces) is to eradicate terrorism; bin Laden fits in here, just at the right time. But this whole issue of terrorism makes it possible to keep quiet about the real aims of American intervention in Central Asia.

In the present conjuncture, the 'united front against terrorism' has permitted an incredible 'Western' mobilization around such elastic (not to say dubious) themes as 'the sharing of common values'. 'We are all Americans' is one thing we hear – an affirmation that might command respect if its authors had had the courage, after the massacres at Sabra and Chatila, to say that they were 'all Palestinians' and to demand firm action against the Israeli state. As things stand, however, most people in Asia and Africa take it as one more expression of the racist solidarity among 'Caucasians' (the official term in the United States to characterize Arians *and* Jews!). Besides, whether one is 'Western' or not, one has the right to say: 'No, I don't share Mr Bush's values, I don't think of him as a democrat, he sounds more like a McCarthyite to me.' The manipulation of 'solidarity' is here perfectly consistent with the 'clash of civilizations' strategy advocated by the reactionary Washington establishment, which stresses the unity or 'democratic consensus' of Western societies as a way of getting them to accept the neoliberal diktat at home and aggression overseas against the peoples of the Third World.

Another set of arguments, intended for sections of European public opinion less susceptible to the US model, place the emphasis on Europe's supposed efforts to shake off American tutelage through the creation of the euro and the decision to set up a unified military force as part of the European enterprise.

As regards the euro, what this overlooks is that the single currency can be an effective instrument only if there is someone to make use of it. Behind the dollar stand not only the American transnationals but also the US government. Behind the euro stand, perhaps, the European transnationals, but without a European government. Moreover, under its statutes, the bankers' assembly in Frankfurt has to give an account of itself not to any public authorities, national or international, but only to 'the market' (that is, the corporations). If political Europe came to realize the absurdity of the choice it made at Maastricht, which political authority could it entrust with management of the euro?

The question of the European military force is of a similar nature. With a touch of posturing that is supposed to strike one as cynical, a few pundits have suggested without fear of ridicule that Europe could use the Americans as 'mercenaries' in its service. This may possibly satisfy European vanity, but it does not correspond to any reality. The only purpose of American military might is to underpin US hegemony; it makes no sense otherwise. Faced with this obvious fact, our European ultras go on to argue that the EU is pressing ahead with plans for an integrated rapid deployment force. Now, it is true that the European countries, with their solid military traditions, would have no problem putting together an intervention force potentially as capable as anything Washington could put into the field. I would even say that a solution could be found in a few days. But who will assume political leadership of such a force? Who will decide where it should intervene? Who will define its political objectives? Which European head of state? Unless these questions are answered, can a European summit do more than any other before it: register the disagreements among member states, or endorse a common denominator of alignment with Washington?

Without a European state, there will be no European currency or military force worthy of the name. The twofold dilution of the European project, through economic globalization and acceptance of US political and military leadership, will ensure the permanence of American hegemony.

These choices have been disastrous at every level: they have stripped all credibility from the talk of democracy and national rights, and they have ended the illusions of European autonomy by lining the EU up more heavily behind the United States than in the days when the Cold War served as a pretext.

The only option that would have made sense for Europe would have been to embrace the perspective of a multipolar world, with a margin of autonomy which, in the best European humanist tradition, made it possible to develop a viable project for society. This would have meant recognizing the same margin of autonomy for Russia, China and each of the major regions in the Third World, as well as accepting that NATO had had its day and should be replaced by a European defence force whose degree of integration kept pace with the European enterprise as a whole. Unlike the formulas lying behind Bretton Woods, the WTO or the MAI, the mode of regulation implicit in this conception would have been adapted to the level of Europe as well as the level of the world system. But, in opting for liberal globalization instead, Europe has foregone using its economic competitive potential and fallen into line with Washington's global ambitions.

All this reveals the fragility of the European project itself, which is actually not such a high priority in the dominant policy visions. Britain's basic choice since 1945 has been to console itself for the loss of empire by vicariously reviving it through the United States. Germany's, after giving up the mad Nazi dream of world conquest, has been to limit its ambitions to its traditional sphere of influence in Eastern and South-Eastern Europe, in the wake of Washington's strategy of global hegemony. And Japan, facing China and even Korea, has for somewhat similar reasons kept to strictly regional ambitions, within the same perspective of American global hegemony.

Can the European project be saved from the débâcle? My provisional response to this question is neither to endorse the simple 'Euro-optimist' belief that successive miracles will enable progress to be made, nor to embrace the 'Euro-pessimist' criticisms which, though correct in themselves, inspire little more than nostalgia for the various national pasts. My own fundamentally critical position is that European countries, like other parts of the world, need regional institutionalization to meet the challenges of the future, but that the European project as it stands today does not answer that need. For it still bears the marks of the American anti-communism which conservative forces gobbled up after the war in order to win pardon for their (at least) ambivalent attitudes to Nazi occupation and local fascist regimes. There needs to be a root-and-branch review of the whole project, focusing on the social dimensions offered to the peoples of Europe and the terms of a new historic compromise between capital and labour. A new basis must be negotiated for effective democratic ways of reconciling national realities with pan-European priorities; it is necessary to get away from formulas that say as little as possible, to stop rewarding those whose immobility vis-à-vis the United States allows it a monopoly of initiatives. I do not think that such a turn would be 'impossible' or 'too late', as Europe's faint-hearted politicians currently claim. On the contrary, I think that political forces that took strong initiatives in this direction would soon arouse a great deal of enthusiasm. But courage is required to make a start.

The main political conclusion from the analysis outlined above is that Europe cannot make any different choices so long as the political alliances which define its ruling blocs remain centred on the dominant transnational capital. Only if social and political struggles succeed in creating blocs with a new content, and in imposing new historic compromises between capital and labour will Europe be able to take some distance from Washington and renew its regional project. If that were to happen, Europe could – and should – also strike out on a new path in its relations with the East and the South (a path different from the one defined purely by the requirements of collective imperialism) and start to join the 'long march' beyond capitalism. To repeat what I said before: either Europe will be on the left in a serious sense of the term, or there will be no Europe.

The geometry of international conflicts

The structural crisis of accumulation has not been, and is not in the process of being, overcome. This provides fertile ground for a proliferation of conflicts, including violent conflicts, in the foreseeable future. It is a simple but pointless exercise to imagine a future situation in which phase B of the long cycle is followed by a new phase A of relatively stable capitalist expansion such as those we have seen in the past.

To be sure, it is not difficult to think of a globalized world consistent with the new form of the law of value and the five monopolies analysed above: the traditionally dominant centres would retain their advantage by reproducing hierarchies already visible to us today; the United States would retain its global hegemony, based on its R&D, its dollar monopoly and its military preponderance; and secondary powers would provide a flanking role in support (Japan facing China, Britain as the political and financial associate of America, Germany in control of Europe); and East Asia, Eastern Europe and Russia, India and Latin America would be active as the main peripheral zones in the system. In the centres themselves, the emphasis on activity related to the five monopolies would entail a two-speed management of society, in which large sections of the population would be marginalized through poverty and petty employment as well as straightforward unemployment.

Within this general framework, there could be a new phase of capitalist expansion involving faster growth in the active peripheries and some recovery in Western and Eastern Europe and the former USSR, while the marginalized African and Islamic world was abandoned to its convulsions. Higher volumes of trade among the dynamic regions of the world would sustain the project. In my view, however, as the world moved in this direction and trade expanded among the regions in question, the new polarization based upon the triad's five monopolies would become more and more extensive. Development gaps between regions would not narrow; the gulf between centres and peripheries would widen. The active peripheries would export on a massive scale, achieving a trade surplus that could then largely be transferred back to the wealthy countries. This would be the new form of imperialism. I have not the slightest doubt that the peoples of the active peripheries in question – even their ruling classes – will make this 'apartheid on a world scale' impossible to realize.

But what if the Triad partners in the developed centres started doing it anyway? What if they decided to go for deindustrialization and to concentrate growth on the 'new economy'? This is the scenario I envisaged in my analysis of the five monopolies: the centres would 'specialize' in activity linked to these monopolies (mainly research and the development of new technologies), while the peripheries were allocated the role of subaltern producers. In France, for example, Alcatel has gone down this road by turning itself into a 'mastermind' company that does not directly produce anything at all. None of the grave social problems that are with us today would be solved as a result.

For the moment, Europe is fully behind this strategy, in all its political, military and economic dimensions. Even with regard to Africa – long the preserve of former colonial powers, especially France and Belgium – the European Union has fallen into line with Washington through the intermediary of the World Bank, as the new Cotonou Convention signed in 2000 testifies.[9]

Doubtless this alignment does not exclude an intensification of the regular 'market conflicts' between the EU and the USA (Airbus, bananas, hormones in meat, and so on), although it may not be possible for the authorities in Washington to keep up their arrogant posture indefinitely. Such contradictions anyway strike me as secondary in comparison with those that will oppose the new peripheries (especially China, India and tomorrow perhaps Russia) to the Triad, whose cohesion is maintained through alignment with Washington.

The G-7 came into being to coordinate management of the global system by the major capitalist powers, yet it has had only very limited success in stabilizing exchange rates. As Gustave Massiah put it, the G-7 is a 'global executive without any overall project for the world'.[10] It was content in 1976 to lay down the principles of unilateral adjustment for the periphery, in 1980 to organize the recycling of petrodollars for the benefit of speculative finance and to encourage lower prices for primary products (a major reason for the Gulf War), in 1982 to organize debt rescheduling without creating the conditions for a solution to the problem, in 1992 to include Russia and other parts of the former Eastern bloc in its unilateral adjustment strategies, and most recently to engage in crisis management in relation to the former Yugoslavia and 'terrorism'.

Thus no variant of the 'great recovery' scenario offers the chance of any development worthy of the name – not even for the inhabitants of the developed centres, still less for those of the peripheries.

There will be no lack of spoilsports in each of the scenarios. A renewal of serious class struggle has already been visible in France (December 1995) and South Korea (January 1997), and if the trend continues it may pave the way for the kind of progressive alternative that we shall examine later. But in some countries the ruling classes, too, may try to widen their room for manoeuvre and to push the model in a direction more favourable to themselves. I am thinking here of China – especially if the social solidarity that gives its project a national character is strengthened by popular forces hitherto left out of the picture – but also of Korea, India, Brazil and, tomorrow, perhaps Russia.

It might be thought that, in the prevailing global disorder, the main contradiction will be between two rivals in violent competition with each other – the United States and Europe – and that the USA and Japan will strengthen their strategic alliance by pulling in the semi-peripheries of Asia (especially China) and Latin America, while Europe integrates the new Russian semi-periphery into its sphere of domination. This does not seem to me a likely scenario, mainly because it assumes that Europe exists as a unified political force (which it does not, for the foreseeable future at least). Most probably, therefore, the United States will retain its hegemony in spite of its weaknesses, and will head the Triad's collective rule over the rest of the world. Besides, it seems most doubtful that China will agree to fall in behind a US–Japanese bloc: my own guess is that it will try to go it alone by exploiting any intensification of the US–Europe conflict. The same will probably be true of India and Russia (if it manages to overcome its crisis).[11]

The 'big project' anyway includes an element of 'burden-sharing' and neo-imperialist regionalization, so that each of the Triad's constitutive powers has a geostrategic space in the South: USA/Canada/Latin America (beginning with Mexico's integration through NAFTA); EU/ North Africa/sub-Saharan Africa; EU (or Germany)/Eastern Europe, or else Germany/USA/Eastern Europe/ex-USSR; Japan/ASEAN, or Japan/USA/Asian Pacific.

This neo-imperialist project is perfectly compatible with the emergence of fifteen or so regional and sub-regional poles that, while enjoying privileges in their part of the world, remain loyal intermediaries in the process of open-ended globalization. Here one thinks immediately of Germany and Japan, which are brilliant seconds-in-command for the United States, but also of Brazil, Turkey (and/or Iran) in Western/Central Asia, or South Korea in East Asia (assisted by second-rank powers such as Egypt, Nigeria, South Africa, Pakistan and Malaysia). It is also quite possible that we shall see 'revolts' by some of these sub-regional poles, as they seek to expand their autonomy in conflict with globalization and American hegemonism. Here one thinks of Brazil and the Mercosur initiative, if this ever takes a greater distance from liberal dogmas.

The various alliance networks and clashes of interests soon become extremely complex if one thinks that the three poles of the central Triad are partly in conflict, but also associated, with the American leader, that each one's sphere of influence in the peripheries is not stable, that regional poles seek to push their own pawns, and so on. Alliances and oppositions then form and break up in a variable-geometry global system, and anything more than short-term prediction becomes impossible. There is a great temptation to rise above the difficulties by grouping conflicts of interest and the power of the protagonists into minor and major categories. But that would mean simplifying a lot of things, such as the fact that it is not only states that act within the system but also transnationals and ideological movements capable of grounding solidarity (on a common religion, for example). In so far as the centre/periphery polarization remains key, the dominant powers (the United States and/or the Triad) may be forced to 'flatter' the regional poles in charge of maintaining discipline in their spheres of influence and intervention. It has thus been tolerated when Turkey has massacred Kurds, Brazil destroyed Amazonia, Israel ethnically cleansed its conquered territories, or apartheid South Africa pursued expansionist policies ('reinforcing the mould', as Hein Marais called it).[12] Nevertheless, a certain number of countries, though peripheral within the economic system of global capitalism, have had or may have ambitions that are incompatible with respect for the core systemic hierarchies. Here one immediately thinks of China, India and Russia. This may be why the leaders of the United States or the Triad will often, if not always, treat them as potential adversaries, or even enemies.

With or without US hegemony, it seems unlikely that a new period of capitalist expansion will stabilize on the basis of the technological revolution and collective Triad imperialism, especially as the factors of capitalist obsolescence to which I have drawn attention make the development of society more fragile in the centres and, above all, the peripheries. The future will therefore depend more on factors other than those governed by the new-style logic of accumulation on a world scale. I have in mind political factors, first and foremost the choices – whether rational or not – that the peoples and even ruling classes of the peripheries (particularly China) will be able to impose, and the choices that the peoples of Europe might want to make in the projects for their own society.

The evolution of China will weigh heavily in the global balance, precisely because of the weight of that gigantic country. I have tried elsewhere to clarify the internal and external conditions for a number of equally possible scenarios.[13] These are:

1. Break-up of the country into a 'marginalized' north and west and

a comprador south integrated into the South-East Asian industrial constellation dominated by Japan and the United States (the strategic scenario that both of the latter favour).

2. Continuation of the Chinese national project, based on the success of the 'three positives': social redistribution of income to maintain national solidarity; regional redistribution to strengthen the inter-dependence of China's internal regional markets; and control over relations with the outside world in accordance with the priorities of the national project.

3. A worse variant of the last scenario, in which attempts are made to continue the national project without leaving the framework of the 'Leninist' one-party state. This 'big negative', as I have called it, could lead either to the break-up of the country (the first scenario) or to the crystallization of a more straightforward (and probably undemocratic) form of national capitalism.

4. A leftward evolution of the current project, strengthening popular social forces and moving forward in the long transition to socialism.

These different scenarios will in turn vary according to what happens in India, the other great Asian partner in the world system. Once again, almost anything is possible: break-up of the country (favoured by the USA in a not too distant past), stagnation, assertions of autonomy and a new beginning. Relations between India and China (whether open hostility, tolerance or mutual support) will play a role here, as will imperialist strategies to make them as bad as possible.

As to Europe, the big corporations that have so far been dominant there gear their strategies to unbridled globalization. Hence they are not capable of actively challenging American global hegemony, or of develop-ing a different vision of North–South relations. The new relationship between Western and Eastern Europe falls naturally into a perspective of 'Latin Americanization' of the East, not one of integrating it on an equal footing. Will the components of the European left, in both the East and the West, be capable of together working out a new strategy that meets the need for a progressive pan-European social pact? The neoliberal options and the ongoing Latin Americanization of Eastern Europe, which are sharpening the imbalance within the EU in favour of Germany, perpetuates American global hegemony, since Germany is playing the card of a regional power aligned with the United States on issues of global import. Alternatively a rapprochement between Germany, France and Russia enhances an independent European project.

For reasons connected with history and Europe's legacy of human-ist and socialist traditions (which I mentioned earlier in comparing the French and American revolutions), it is not out of the question that a project for a different, 'social' Europe will take shape and eventually impose itself. But we need to think what this would mean. Beyond magical formulations such as 'neo-Keynesianism', whose content remains vague, is the social vision one of a fortress, or of an open Europe? And how would it handle its relations with the United States, Japan and the peripheries?

The law under contempt, democracy under threat

The period through which we are living today, marked by a structural crisis of capitalist accumulation, a major technological revolution and a redeployment of imperialism, is naturally one of great confusion for the oppressed peoples of the world and the exploited working classes. For the dominant capital is able to impose its interests and them alone, without having to strike a compromise with their victims.

Because of the deconstruction of the old ways of organizing produc-tion and work, the old, inherited ways of organizing social and political struggles are also losing their effectiveness and hence their legitimacy. New forms of the organization of work can take decades to stabilize at a point of relative equilibrium, and in the meantime disarray and fragmentation hold centre stage among the victims of the system.

It is also, therefore, a period of intensified violence – first of all, the violence of the dominant forces of capital, which seek to impose their own solutions both nationally and internationally. Hence the 'militar-ization' of globalization. Against this, the counter-violence can take the most diverse forms: some may be described as positive, when they are part of front-building among popular forces and herald a political awareness capable of rising to the new challenges; others may not be so described, when they confine the victims of the system to dead-ends where there is no possibility of correctly identifying the nature of the challenges. Of course, the ruling powers make every effort to muddy the waters and to stave off their worst nightmare: a positive politicization of popular social movements.

What is considered a likely scenario for the future largely depends on one's view of the major objective trends and how popular social forces should meet the challenge they represent. Hence there is inevitably an element of subjectivity and intuition – which is just as well, because it means that the future is not pre-programmed and that the inventive imagination – to use Castoriadis's strong term[14] – has its place in real history.

'Foresight' is more difficult in a period when all the ideological and political mechanisms and reflexes that used to govern people's behaviour are no longer present. The structure of political life was turned upside down when history turned the page on the post-war world. Political life and struggles used to be part of the framework of states whose legitimacy was not in question (governments perhaps, but not states); and, behind and within the state, the political parties, trade unions, a few other major associations such as the employers' federations, and what the media call the 'political class' constituted the backbone of the system in which political movements, social struggles and ideological currents were expressed. Today, nearly everywhere in the world, all these institutions have lost much if not all their legitimacy; the people no longer 'believe' in them. Instead, a variety of 'movements' have come to the fore around the demands of the Greens and women, campaigning for democracy and social justice and often basing themselves on ethnic or religious identities. The articulation of these demands and movements with a radical critique of actually existing capitalist society, and of neoliberal 'global governance', has to be the object of detailed discussion. Some of the movements in question are, or may become, part of a conscious rejection of the dominant social projects, whereas others are not interested in fighting against them. The ruling powers certainly know how to make this distinction: relentless hostility in the one case, manipulation and open support in the other, are the rule amid the chaos and turbulence of political life as it exists today.

The political strategy for 'global governance' seeks to fragment any forces that might present a challenge to the system, and therefore to break up the forms of the organization of society within individual states. As many Slovenias, Chechenias, Kosovos and Kuwaits as possible! The use, or manipulation, of identity claims is here most welcome.

The question of identities based on community, ethnicity, religion or the like is one of the key issues of our times.[15] The basic democratic principle of respect for national, ethnic, religious, cultural and ideological diversity must not be violated, and in fact that diversity cannot be handled except through the sincere practice of democracy. Otherwise, it inevitably becomes a tool that the adversary can use for his own ends. The historical left has often fallen down in this respect – though not always, and much less than many have claimed. To take but one of many examples, Tito's Yugoslavia was almost a model of coexistence among different nationalities on a basis of equality; but that was certainly not true of Romania. In the Third World in the Bandung era, national liberation movements often succeeded in uniting different ethnic groups and religious communities against the imperialist enemy, and the first generation of rulers in African states were often genuinely trans-ethnic. On the other hand, few regimes were able to handle this diversity democratically, or to preserve whatever gains had already been made. Their weak democratic propensities had consequences as deplorable here as in other problem areas for their society. When the crisis hit, the ruling classes found themselves powerless to do anything about it – indeed, they often fanned the flames by using communalist identity to prolong their control over the masses. It is also true, however, that the whole issue has by no means been handled correctly in a number of genuine bourgeois democracies: Northern Ireland provides the most glaring example.

The successes of culturalism have been commensurate with the shortcomings in the democratic management of diversity. By culturalism, I mean the position that such differences are 'primal' and should be treated as more important than class differences, for example; sometimes, even that they are 'transhistorical' – based on unvarying historical factors – so that, as in the case of religious culturalism, it easily slides into obscurantism and fanaticism.

Anglo-American communitarianism is a perfect example of a false (reactionary) response to a real problem (inequality). In naively, and perhaps with the best intentions, celebrating forms of 'community development' as an expression of the democratic will of the community in question (for example, West Indians in London, second-generation North Africans in France, or blacks in the United States), this ideology confines individuals to those communities and locks the communities themselves into the hierarchical straitjacket imposed by the system. The result is nothing less than a kind of apartheid that does not speak its name.

Those who support this model of 'community development' put forward both pragmatic arguments ('something needs to be done for the deprived victims who make up these communities') and a democratic case ('communities should assert themselves as such'). It may be true that much universalist discourse has been purely rhetorical, involving no real strategy to change the world and therefore no attention to real struggles against the oppression suffered by particular groups. But that oppression cannot be eradicated if it is made part of a framework that permits its indefinite reproduction, albeit in a milder form.

Culturalist attachment to a community, however worthy of respect in the abstract, is still the product of the crisis of democracy. It is because the efficacy, credibility and legitimacy of democracy are being eroded that people seek the illusory protection of particular religious, ethnic, sexual or other identities, each with its own irreducible values. Culturalism is not a complement of democracy that allows it to be applied in practice; it is the antithesis of democracy.

In order to see more clearly in the thicket of identity claims, I shall propose what seems to me an essential criterion: those demands which link up with the fight against social exploitation and for greater democracy in every dimension are progressive; those demands which are not part of any social programme and are not hostile to globalization (on the grounds that both are 'unimportant'), and *a fortiori* those that regard democracy as an alien 'Western' concept, are frankly reactionary tools serving the aims of the dominant capital. In any event, capital knows what it is doing when it supports the latter claims, even if the media exploit their content to denounce those who are its victims. The movements are there to be used and manipulated.

The facts show that, in these conditions, the granting of so-called ethnic demands does not advance the cause of democracy and social progress. On the contrary, in the former Yugoslavia and USSR it helps create the base for a new ruling class, which assumes all political and economic power for itself in the name of defending 'ethnicity'. Political Islam serves similar reactionary functions useful to the domination of transnational capital.

The offensive of the dominant collective imperialism has called into question the principle of national sovereignty, using NATO as its military instrument in place of the UN, the only institution representing the nations of the world.

The democracy and people's rights that the G-7 powers invoke to justify their interventions are only political means for them to manage the crisis of the contemporary world, complementing in this respect the economic means of neoliberal management. The democracy of which they speak is only incidental, their cynical talk of 'good governance' wholly subject to the strategic priorities of the USA/Triad.

Nor is it only a question of brow-beating and media manipulation. The aim is to force people to choose between unacceptable alternatives: accept oppression, disappear, or place yourselves under a protectorate of the imperialist powers. For this purpose, not a word must be said about the policies that led to the drama in the first place.

The principle of respect for the sovereignty of nations must remain the cornerstone of international law. Originally, the decision to proclaim it in the United Nations Charter was precisely a response to its denial by the fascist regimes. In a poignant speech to the League of Nations in 1935, Emperor Haile Selassie lucidly explained that violation of the principle – which the democracies of the time accepted in a cowardly way – sounded the death knell for that organization. The fact that today the democracies themselves are violating it with the same brutality is not an extenuating but an aggravating circumstance. It has already signalled the beginning of an equally inglorious end for the United Nations, which is now treated as a body to rubber-stamp decisions taken and implemented elsewhere. The solemn adoption of the principle of national sovereignty in 1945 logically went together with a ban on recourse to war: states were permitted to defend themselves against anyone violating their sovereignty through an act of aggression, but they were condemned in advance if they were the aggressors.

No doubt the UN Charter gave an absolute interpretation of the sovereignty principle. On the other hand, the potentially conflicting principle now upheld by democratic opinion – that governments do not have the right to do anything they please with human beings under their jurisdiction – marks a certain advance of universal consciousness. So, how should these two positions be reconciled with each other? Certainly not by suppressing one of the terms: national sovereignty or human rights. For, not only is the path chosen by the United States and its subaltern European allies not the right path; it also masks the real purposes of the operation, which, for all the media hype, have nothing to do with respect for human rights.

The UN should be the locus for the elaboration of international law; no other can possibly command the same kind of respect. This certainly requires that organizational reforms are undertaken, that some consideration is given to ways and means of enabling real social forces to be represented alongside governments (which at best are only imperfectly representative), and that efforts are made to weave into a coherent whole the rules of international law concerning individual and people's rights as well as the economic and social rights overlooked in neoliberal dogma that necessarily imply some degree of market regulation. It is an agenda filled with questions, and any answers I might give here would inevitably be too truncated. We are speaking of a long process, then, but there are no short-cuts. Human history has not yet reached its end: it cannot advance faster than the possibilities allow.

The project that the collective Triad imperialism and US hegemony seek to impose on the whole world conflicts with the principle of people's sovereignty and ignores the need for it to exist alongside democratic, political and social rights in a harmonious and institutionalized relationship. The project in question also makes the elaboration of 'international business law' a top priority, to which all national rights in every sphere are supposed to subordinate themselves. The plans concocted by shadowy 'study groups' within the WTO and the OECD (such as the Multilateral Agreement on Investment, or MAI) are part of this general drive to foist the rules of economic 'liberalism' on all the peoples of the world, challenging their right to organize their social existence in any other way. As I said above, the WTO is in this sense an organization whose main aim is to reorganize every aspect of production within individual countries, and to subject every aspect of their social and political life to what is needed for the penetration of the dominant transnational capital. In thus attempting to deny every government the right to regulate its own activities, the WTO deserves to be called the 'colonial ministry' of the collective imperialist.

The US/Triad project is the opposite of what the peoples of the modern world actually need: that is, a higher law that ensures that everyone on the planet is treated in a dignified manner, so that they can participate actively and creatively in the building of the future. This means a full set of laws covering every dimension: the rights of the human person (men and women equally, of course), political rights, social rights (employment and security), rights of communities and nations, and rights governing relations among states. An agenda for decades of reflection, debate, action and decision.

Finally, with regard to issues of security and disarmament, the dominant discourse trotted out in the media highlights the dangers of the proliferation of nuclear and other weapons – not the right focus, we have to say, since Washington uses its military might to engage in terror bombing and would not hesitate to use nuclear weapons if it thought them necessary. Faced with this major threat, other countries in the world can react only by choosing to build up a military capability of their own to deter imperialist aggression. That is the price of peace.

For all the above reasons, the present is a time not of democratic advance but of threatened decline. The substitution of cultural (ethnic or religious) 'collective identities' for a recognized plurality of interests and ways of expressing them, the denial of national sovereignty, nor the attempt to subordinate all aspects of economic and social life everywhere in the world to some kind of neoliberal business law: none of these is creating favourable ground for the progress of democracy.

Returning to the conflictual rather than complementary nature of the relationship between market and democracy, I would say that at the present time it is manifesting its full destructive potential as the dominant capital asserts its dictatorial powers. In the developed capitalist countries, the model of what I have called 'low-intensity democracy' – in which submission to 'the laws of the market' drains away all potential for the democratic invention of citizenship – has made disturbing advances in the past two decades. Europe now finds itself facing the threat of alignment with the wretched model of the United States.

In the countries of Asia and Africa, any talk of democracy, national rights, and so on loses all credibility once people realize that it is coming from 'the West'. Unfortunately, the democrats of Europe do not wish to see this. No one in Asia or Africa – I exaggerate not – thinks that what Western governments and media say about such matters is anything but a web of duplicity to conceal their real imperialist objectives. It changes little that a few timorous diplomats plus NGOs whose survival depends on Western funding refrain from spelling things out. It can also happen that a particular community finds itself in a situation where Western intervention, regardless of its motives, is seen as the only lifeline. But then we are talking of small groups which, despite themselves or perhaps without realizing, have been instrumentalized by the dominant powers within the world system.

That is certainly no cause for rejoicing, as it is a serious obstacle to the development of an international front in the struggle for democracy. Yet the peoples of Asia and Africa do hope to achieve not only material well-being but also (in varying degrees) the democratization of their societies. The hypocrisy and deception practised by NATO countries are most effective allies of those opposed to the cause of progress and democracy. The fact that most of the European left has now fallen into line with Washington's interventionist strategy and methods of terror adds a further obstacle to any universalist cause. Today Blair and Schröder appear not only as the most dangerous gravediggers of traditions that have been the honour of the European left, but as servile agents of the American project for the world. Their 'third way' association with Clinton should not create any illusions on this score.

The issue of so-called 'terrorism' fits into the crisis of democracy. The term itself is so awkward to define that anyone can engage in whichever interpretations or manipulations they currently wish to promote: for example, it can be used to describe legitimate struggles such as that of the Palestinian people, which is engaged, with very unequal forces, in a fight to achieve liberation from the Israeli occupiers; or it can be used to pass in silence over acts of violence committed by the imperialist states (above all, the United States), which authorize themselves or others to kill political figures who are not to their liking (Salvador Allende among so many others), or to bomb and terrorize civilian populations while claiming to come to their rescue from the very regimes that the same imperialists imposed (as was the case with the Taliban). 'State terrorism' is a perfectly appropriate term to describe such operations.

As we know, the attacks of 11 September 2001 made it possible to take an extra step in manipulating people's fears and getting them to accept grave breaches of democracy. A new version of McCarthyism in the United States is not impossible, given the need the country apparently feels every half-century to wallow in a fundamentalist affirmation of what pass as 'American values'. G. W. Bush is not, alas, the only one to make an amalgam between 'terrorists' and all those opposed to any part of the neoliberal project. Has not the Italian prime minister, the far from brilliant Berlusconi, echoed this idea of 'tightening the vice' on all European protest movements?

What has to be said on the question of terrorism may be summed up in one sentence: we do not need a 'global front against terrorism'. What the peoples of the world need is a global front for social and international democracy. If they get it, terrorism will disappear by itself.

Notes

1. See Jorge Beinstein, *La larga crisis de la economía global*.

2. Ankie Hoogvelt, *Globalization and the Postcolonial World: The New Political Economy of Development*, Baltimore, MD: Johns Hopkins University Press, 2001.

3. Antonio Negri and Michael Hardt, *Empire*, Cambridge, MA: Harvard University Press, 2000.

4. See Guy Debord, *La société du spectacle*, Paris: Champ Libre, 1971; *The Society of the Spectacle*, New York: Zone Books, 1994.

5. See Vandana Shiva, *Stolen Harvest: The Hijacking of the Global Food Supply*, Cambridge, MA: South End Press, 2000.

6. Carlo Vercellone, *La Mafia comme expression endogène de l'accumulation du capital*, Matisse University of Paris 1, 2001.

7. Marcel Mazoyer and Laurence Rondart, *Histoire des agricultures du monde*, Paris: Éditions du Seuil, 1997.

8. See Samir Amin, 'La géopolitique de la région Méditerranée Golfe'.

9. See Samir Amin, *Les régionalisations, les conventions de Lomé-Cotonou et l'association UE-ACP*.

10. Gustave Massiah, *Le G7 en 1993, le crépuscule d'un mythe?*, Paris: Centre d'études et d'initiatives de solidarité internationale, 1993.

11. See the collective work *The World We are Entering, 2000–2050*, Luxembourg: Institute for International and European Studies (IEEI), forthcoming.

12. Hein Marais, *Southern African Cooperation: Breaking the Mould*, forthcoming (FTM).

13. See Samir Amin, *Les défis de la mondialisation*, pp. 225–36.

14. Cornelius Castoriadis, *The Imaginary Institution of Society*, Cambridge: Polity, 1987; and *La montée de l'insignifiance*, Paris: Seuil, 1994.

15. See Samir Amin, *L'ethnie à l'assaut des nations*; *Capitalism in the Age of Globalization*, London: Zed Books, 1997, ch. 4; and 'Political Islam', Appendix six, below.

SEVEN
Basic requirements for a non-American twenty-first century

Strengths and weaknesses of the liberal project of obsolescent capitalism

The post-war period (1945–80) was marked by a hegemony of the left bearing models of socially regulated accumulation to which the right had to adapt. The erosion and then collapse of the social relations governing those models allowed a new right to ram home its hegemony, bearing with it the project of the dominant transnational capital in the countries of the Triad.

This hegemony involved a widespread idea that it was necessary to overcome the present phase of structural crisis, with its characteristic imbalances and resulting disorder, but without abandoning the basic rules governing the capitalist organization of economic and social life. In other words, a new phase of global expansion would polarize as previous such phases had done, but would be 'acceptable' and 'accepted' because it ended in widely, if unevenly, shared advances.

Although such an issue might be conceivable on paper – and in earlier chapters I tried to identify its prerequisites and the kind of future to which it might give rise – the reader will be aware that I have major doubts about its feasibility. The elements of obsolescence that are part of this system make unlikely any 'rejuvenation' of capitalism through the technological revolution and its accompanying mode of 'asset-based accumulation' and globalization.

The fact is that the strategies of the new right, shaped exclusively by the interests of dominant capital, have nothing to offer the working classes and the peoples of the world and do not even recognize the legitimacy of their interests and views.

Susan George has expertly uncovered the 'rationale' behind the project of the new right. The 'Lugano Report'[1] shows that all the policies of the G-7, and the tools it uses to implement them, hold out the prospect of poverty and death for billions of human beings around the world. The ruling classes of collective imperialism know this; any notion that they are so stupid as not to realize it is quite unacceptable. The strategy taking shape behind the so-called clash of civilizations is a strategy to solve problems by exterminating whole swathes of its victims.

No doubt the victims are not to be found only among the peoples of the periphery: the subjection of all societies on earth to the maximization of profit for the dominant capital produces a declassed, unemployed, insecure, impoverished and excluded section of the population in the centres themselves. For some time, the ruling classes there have thought it possible to ignore the potential for revolt among the direct victims of their policies, as well as the danger that all the popular classes and even a significant part of the middle classes will eventually take up criticism of the system. In actions stretching from Seattle to Genoa, the wrongly named 'anti-globalization movements' have forced the powers that be to take stock of this potentially anti-systemic rising bloc.

Nevertheless, the victims of the project of the new right exist in incomparably greater number in the peripheries. There, hundreds of millions already live in poverty in shantyized urban areas, and hundreds of millions of peasants will soon join them as a result of the liberalization of agriculture. Capitalism today is no longer capable of developing programmes to feed the world's rising population; it has to devote all its forces to maintaining the artificial consumption of the well-to-do. With nothing to offer the vast majority of people in the three continents, who in turn form the great majority of humanity, capitalism tells billions of human beings that they *are* nothing. This adds up to a huge potential for revolt.

Here too, of course, the masters of the world have thought they could ignore the danger of a 'rejectionist front' in the South. As the old answers of national populism have crumbled, the relief has so far come at best from fragmented movements, or else from culturalist aberrations based on ethnicity or ostensibly religious expressions which represent so many dead-ends. But there are signs that solidarity among African and Asian peoples, with the aim of building an anti-imperialist common front, is again becoming a possibility. The political masters of contemporary imperialism know that a new internationalism joining together the workers of the North and the peoples of the South would be fatal to it.

But that front does not yet exist. The fragmentation of social movements and struggles, their inadequate politicization (the fact that they are not part of a coherent and effective vision of society on a level with the challenges), the ideological confusion and aberrant direction of certain responses to the attacks of capital: these are the short-term strengths of regimes serving the dominant capital.

The new right, which first announced itself in the 'conservative revolution' begun by Thatcher and Reagan in 1980, has gained considerable weight in all the societies of the Triad, constituting an 'International of Capital' spearheaded by the US establishment, especially its Republican wing. A group of ultra-reactionary associations with solid roots in the US tradition – ranging from fundamentalist defenders of 'American values' (read: racism, contempt for equality, and so on) to para-religious sects – relay the discourse of this new right into the middle and popular classes. Meanwhile, in various European countries, the right has gained a new lease of life from the same ostensibly liberal discourse and its eulogy of market deregulation and various kinds of communitarianism.

The strength of this new right should not be underestimated. It stems first of all from the (false) idea that there are no alternatives, since its project is part of the inexorable march of history and corresponds to the objective requirements of the technological revolution (computerization), its accompanying social relations (the 'network society') and its characteristic economic forms (financialization and globalization). The fact that left-majority governments have rallied to this project, and painted a rosy picture of the future to which it will lead, has evidently increased the credibility of the discourse in question – especially as the new right avoids the fascist language of yesterday for which more populist currents feel a certain nostalgia. The new right is neither Le Pen nor even Haider, Berlusconi and their Danish or other emulators. Those are, in fact, embarrassing allies. The new right proclaims itself democratic, and a huge ideological output continually strives to popularize an American-inspired concept of democracy, which is essential to the so-called liberal perspective.

In 1990, with its communist adversary seen off, the new right declared in theory and in practice (the Gulf War) that the 'civilized world' had a new enemy in the South, thereby expressing an acute awareness that its project had nothing to offer four-fifths of humanity. All the talk of a 'clash of civilizations', again at the heart of the American citadel of the new imperialist system, exactly corresponded to what the strategies of the new right needed for their deployment. In the view of Samuel Huntington, who is not an 'independent academic' but a functionary in the service of the US establishment, the future will be dominated neither by class struggle nor even by conflict among nations but quite simply by a 'clash of civilizations'. This culturalist, anti-universalist conception assumes that each of the identified civilizations forms a coherent whole different from the others, leaving out of account the changes that all societies on earth have undergone as a result of participating in capitalist globalization, as well as the contradictions and conflicts of interest within each and every component of the modern world system. The societies in question are supposed to confront each other as blocs welded together by their distinctive 'system of values'. This is not a scientific approach to reality, but an ideological tool to enclose the world's peoples in culturalist myths and to get them to behave as Washington wishes.

The advantages of this 'world view' are evident. North Americans, Europeans and others in the same category (Israelis) constitute, together with the Japanese ('honorary whites' in South Africa's former apartheid classification), a 'civilizational space' with the same shared values of 'democracy'. The Others have 'other values', which, by definition, are not and cannot be those of the West. Moreover, the Others are themselves diverse – blacks, Indians, Chinese, Muslims – and have relations of latent or overt hostility to each other which prevent the formation of a front of the underprivileged. The West can therefore be sure of emerging victorious from the 'clash of civilizations'.[2]

Every effort is made to ensure that reality conforms to the schema, by flattering the 'culturalisms' of various peoples who are victims of Pentagon or CIA strategy. The fundamental alliance between Washington's diplomacy and reactionary (or even fanatical) political Islam has its place in the plans. And if this political Islam strays from the terms of the contract, then that is all to the good – for it proves the correctness of the 'clash of civilizations' thesis and justifies collective action to defend the truly 'civilized' nations against attack from other nations supposedly responsible for the aberrations of their Taliban.

The new right project thus necessarily falls in with the hegemonic aspirations of the United States. The new right has to be – and is – 'pro-American', because an increasing number of military interventions are required to control the peripheries of the system.

The United States deliberately uses its comparative advantage – military power – both to impose the programme of the Triad's collective imperialism and to assert itself as leader of that imperialism. The main trump card of the 'new economy' and the new collective imperialism is precisely the capacity of American bombing to instil terror.

After the Gulf War and the wars in Yugoslavia and Central Asia, President Bush has already promised us more to come. Against whom? Against Arab states? Iran? Russia? China? Anything is possible in the long run. Of course, the initial effectiveness of such a programme requires that 'the West' remains fused together as a single bloc.

This is scarcely the first time in history that political and military means have been mobilized to impose a new economic and social order – a fact that 'liberal economists' seem to want to ignore as a matter of principle. Until today, however, imperialisms and hegemonic aspirations have always been plural phenomena. Hitlerite Germany and Imperial Japan were the last to have tried to impose by military force their project for a 'new order', and both clashed not only with the victims of the project but also with other imperialisms and would-be hegemons. After the Second World War, the very existence of the USSR compelled the United States to exercise restraint. But today, when acting on its own account as well as that of collective Triad imperialism, Washington thinks that it no longer has to answer to anyone.

Clinton's talk of 'rogue states' was intended to provide some *ad hoc* justification for this posture. No doubt some governments thoroughly deserve to be called by this name, but it has only ever been invoked as a pretext for intervention in the interests of the new global strategy. Besides, the terrorist methods and the contempt for other peoples displayed by the 'cowboy state' place it in the front rank of 'rogue states', trailed by the British and supported by every new right government in Europe. Many intellectuals, by giving it succour and attacking any condemnation of imperialist arrogance as 'outdated nationalism', rejoin the camp of the International of Capital and the new right. The appeal to racism is here the means *par excellence* of consolidating the bloc of the imperialist Triad: the civilized nations ('we') are threatened by the barbarians (potentially all the peoples of Asia and Africa, and even the Russians).

In this sense, the 'clash of civilizations' theme recalls *Mein Kampf.* The crude reasoning is exactly the same: the superior peoples (yesterday the Nazis, today the 'Caucasians' of North America and Europe) have a duty to subject the savages to their dictatorship; they can expect to continue enjoying their 'way of life' only if all others are deprived of its pleasures. This trivial racist argument is expressed with all the vulgarity of which men such as Bush or Berlusconi are capable. But *Mein Kampf* was also a crude and vulgar text; that was part of its power. In both cases, what is expressed is a criminal fantasy, but one which, unfortunately, comes true when public opinion is naive enough to believe in it.

Will a direct appeal to racism be sufficient to weld together the Western bloc? The political leaders of the system are not convinced – which is why they are also seeking to muzzle social and political movements at the very heart of the West. The pretext of the struggle against 'terrorism' is paving the way for a second McCarthyite wave in the United States, where, as one might expect, amalgams are used to present the erosion of democracy as a 'necessary evil' enjoying some semblance of legitimacy. Are not the 'anti-globalization' protesters, from Seattle to Genoa, somehow akin to Osama bin Laden's terrorist henchmen?

Since militarization is now inseparable from 'liberal' globalization, the building of an international front of the world's peoples against the criminal project of obsolescent capitalism and US hegemonism now requires systematic struggle against both economic liberalism and war. It is not possible to fight one dimension of economic liberalism here (especially in the centres of the system) while ignoring military intervention there (in the peripheries), as if the latter had a logic of its own and had nothing to do with issues raised by the deployment of liberal economics.

But the militarization of globalization does not only indicate the power of the new right; it may become the Achilles' heel of obsolescent capitalism. For, the strategy of collective imperialism and the American hegemony that provides it with direction have a chance of continuing to score points only if NATO forges ahead from one easy military victory to another, and if the US–Europe–Japan bloc not only holds but gains additional strength.

I do not think that the wars now brewing will be as straightforward as we are led to believe. Nor do I think that the American armed forces are invincible. One reason for this is that, despite the ultra-sophisticated military means at its disposal, the Pentagon is severely handicapped by the fact that the American public will only tolerate a 'risk-free war' (zero deaths on the US side, not on the other side, of course). This means that auxiliaries who accept the normal risks of warfare will have to be found among the subaltern allies. Moreover, are the much-heralded victories really military victories? Or has success in the field each time been possible because a favourable political situation in Washington allowed the enemy to be completely isolated? If diplomatic action on the part of the victims makes such configurations more difficult to achieve, the classical scenario of a colonial war that drags on and on could well come back on to the agenda.

Another problem is the funding of wars and interventions in the foreseeable future. The common view that arms manufacturers are the real forces pushing for war is a little simplistic, but it is true that a serious cut in military expenditure would plunge the US economy into a crisis at least as bad as that of the 1930s. Like Sweezy and Magdoff, I am of the view that capitalism is a form of society which generates a permanent tendency to overproduction; 'crisis' is therefore its normal state, whereas prosperity is an exception that has to be explained by special factors.

In line with this analysis, we may note that the United States emerged from the crisis of the 1930s only through the huge arms drives during and after the Second World War. Today the US economy is monstrously deformed: almost a third of economic activity there depends directly or indirectly on the military complex (a proportion that only the USSR attained before it, during the Brezhnev era). 'Military Keynesianism' is today's substitute for the social Keynesianism rejected by the dominant capital. It is also true that hegemonism is a paying proposition, precisely because of the privileges that come with the dollar's function as global currency. A scaling down of the US role on the world arena, or even a 'sharing of responsibilities' with Europe and Japan, would therefore entail a reform of the international monetary system and a loss of some of the dollar's privileges. Far from allowing 'economies' to be made, this would stem the flow of capital in its favour.

I am not suggesting that the main quarrel between Americans and Europeans will centre on how the militarization of globalization is to be funded, only that this is another element that might help to deliver a salutary jolt to the peoples of Europe. The main reason why such a jolt is both possible and desirable, however, lies in the facts that the European political tradition has not yet descended to the level of electoral farce which characterizes democracy across the Atlantic.

Finally, the attacks of 11 September 2001 revealed the vulnerability of the United States itself, by showing that its own territory was not inviolable. Will the American public, having been shaken in this way, become more vigilant and distrustful of the arrogance of its ruling classes? Or will it agree to close ranks behind them and accept the dynamic of a new McCarthyism?

The global war that US hegemonism has brought on the world is a war without end, a war without peace, because it is fought against a nameless enemy. Behind the apparent enemy (the sundry 'rogues' and 'terrorists') looms the real adversary in the shape of potentially all the peoples of the South. Will European public opinion go along with the United States in this never-ending adventure? That would require it to lose for ever any sensitivity to the imperialist nature of the project. Such may perhaps be the case today – but for ever?

What seems to me more likely in the immediate future is that the system will simply remain in its present deadlock, where more and more displays of American power are mounted to weld together the new collective imperialism and to compel Third World governments to rally behind it. The deadlock is bordering on the grotesque. American society – whose 'survival', in its existing forms, depends upon a contribution from others to fund its waste – speaks as if it were in a position to order the rest of the world about. The global economic conjuncture hangs on the continuation of American waste: a recession there would soon affect the exports of Europe and Asia, which are themselves in part a tribute to the new Rome. Having chosen to base their development on these senseless exports instead of strengthening their own systems of production and consumption, the Europeans and Asians find themselves caught in a trap. For only one country – the United States – has the right to be sovereign and to apply the principles of a self-reliant development opening out to conquer the world. Every other country is expected to remain within a model of extraverted development: that is, to become an appendage of the United States. This is the vision of the 'American twenty-first century'. I do not think that such an absurd situation can last for ever.

Meanwhile, the political strategy of the world's dominant power will not solve any problems. As it seeks to bully the Europeans into giving up their own project, to bring the whole of mankind under the rules of a systematic apartheid, and to violate on a daily basis the rights of others, democratic and social, national and international, it will generate mounting opposition to the American model – even hatred of it.

The US ruling class knows that its economy is vulnerable, that the country's total consumption far exceeds its means, and that the only way of making the rest of the world cover its deficit is to bring this about forcibly by deploying its military might. It has no other option than this headlong assertion of hegemony. To this end it mobilizes its own people – the middle classes, above all – by declaring its intention to 'defend the American way of life, whatever the cost'. The cost may involve extermination of whole swathes of humanity. That has absolutely no importance. For this ruling class believes that it can drag all its partners in Europe and Japan into its bloody adventure (by offering its services to the 'community of the overprivileged'), and that it can obtain their agreement to cover the US deficit. For how long?

The G-7 apparatuses work hard to present the 'new age of capitalism' and its global order as both inevitable and positive; any damage is merely collateral and transitory. Fortunately, however, there is no lack of lucid analyses to show that the real logic of obsolescent capitalism is towards genocide (since it treats most of humanity as a useless burden), towards the exacerbation of false 'communal' consciousness, and towards an explosion of the kind of wild individualism that is destructive of civil and social democracy. The actual economic running of this system – which is based on absolute protection of monopoly profits – bears no resemblance to what liberal economists say about the virtues of competition and the market. It is not a genuinely new phase of capitalist expansion that we are witnessing, but a barbarous attempt to solve its contradictions. Liberalism here appears for what it is: the Viagra of senile capitalism.

As a counterpoint, the optimism of reason allows us to identify the conditions in which a new left might rise to the challenge and defeat the ruling forces of the right. The building of such a left will, as I have already argued, require an international front of dominated classes and peoples in both North and South. But that front does not yet exist. The fragmentation of social struggles and movements, their lack of an adequate and coherent vision of an alternative society, and the ideological disorientation evident in certain responses to the attacks of capital, remain in the short term sources of strength for the forces serving the dominant capital.

A new left equal to the challenge would, in my view, have to aim first at the rebuilding of a multipolar world: only that can open up areas of autonomy for progressive forces to advance, at an inevitably uneven pace according to the possibilities of the country and the period. By definition, a new multipolarity of this kind assumes the dismantling of US hegemony and therefore a quest for minimal convergence of all the political and social forces opposing it.

In a longer time frame, the advances resulting from greater autonomy will make it possible to envisage a deepening of those genuine forms of civil and social democracy that go beyond the single-minded logic of capital. This, not the 'clash of civilizations', will be the real civilizational conflict of our times – a conflict between capitalism and the socialism that is more necessary than ever for the progress of humanity.

For a multipolar world

The political economy of development, as it was conceived and implemented during especially the second half of the twentieth century, was the product of powerful social movements in revolt against the logic of capitalist expansion. Its defining background was thus one of major social reforms, such as nationalizations, welfare programmes, land reforms, and so on.

Of course, the range of strategies was so wide that it would be absurd to mix them all up in a single model. The socialist experiments in systematic industrialization, which claimed to be guided by Marxism, were a long way from the efforts of neocolonial countries to use their 'comparative advantage' in primary products not as a base for diversification but only, at best, to achieve faster growth rates. Between these two extremes lay a host of national-populist experiences in the Third World.

The frontrunners did at least share the goal of building a modern, efficient and self-reliant system of national production. This brought them up against the permanent hostility of the dominant forces of world capitalism, both economically and politically. The consequences seem to me clear enough: the development concept involves a critique of actually existing capitalism; the goal of self-reliant national construction must still be addressed; and strategies towards that goal require delinking. Perhaps the latter term is not so well chosen, as it might suggest some absurd idea of autarky. But, in fact, it is meant as shorthand for a rather longer formula: namely, the subordination of relations with the outside world to the requirements of internal construction, and not, vice versa, one-sided adjustment to tendencies operating at a global level. In this sense, delinking remains as a fundamental necessity in the twenty-first century, even if the framework in which it must be implemented has undergone important changes.

The dominant ideology today, corresponding to the dictatorship of transnational capital, attacks any idea of 'self-reliance', 'delinking' or 'national construction' as a symptom of 'regressive protectionism', 'nostalgia for a bygone era', 'antiquated thinking', and so on. The strategy deployed by the Triad under the leadership of the United States has the aim of building a unipolar world on the basis of two complementary principles: dictatorship of the dominant transnational capital, and deployment of a US military empire to which all nations have to bow. No other project can be tolerated – not even the European project of the subaltern NATO allies, and certainly not a project, such as China's, to establish any degree of autonomy. That must be crushed, if necessary by force.

To this vision of a unipolar world, we must oppose multipolar globalization as the only strategy offering sufficient room for acceptable levels of social development in the various regions of the world, and therefore a democratization of societies and a reduction of the grounds for conflict between them. The hegemonist strategy of the United States and its NATO allies is today the main enemy of social progress, democracy and peace. The project of liberal-military imperialism is a reactionary Utopia which, by eliminating virtually any prospect of development for vast areas of the contemporary world, is bound to widen the gulf between centres and peripheries intrinsic to both today's and yesterday's capitalism.

A humanist response to the challenge posed by capitalist globalization is not 'Utopian'. On the contrary, it is the only realistic project, in the sense that the first steps towards it would soon rally powerful social forces in all parts of the world that could actually bring it about. If there is a Utopia, in the banal and negative sense of the term, it is the idea of running the system simply through regulation by the world market. There is no way in which a loss of national coherence will give way to global coherence.

A multipolar world is the necessary framework for alternatives that will enable that gulf to be narrowed. The creation of new conditions through development of the forces of production, in both their productive and destructive dimensions, is the only meaning we can attach to the objective side of the deepening of globalization. This being so, the building of a multipolar world will have to pass through a process of regionalization; the rise of new forces committed to 'delinking' can no longer be conceived or defined only at national levels, but will have to be completed and consolidated at regional levels.

In today's conditions, then, a multipolar world is first and foremost a regionalized world.[3] Regional interdependence, negotiated and organized in a way that permits nations and dominated classes to improve the terms of their participation in production and their access to better living conditions, constitutes the framework for this building of a polycentric world. It certainly implies action beyond the nation-state, especially small to medium-sized states, and forms of economic and political regional organization that allow for collective negotiation between regions. The challenges facing regions and countries are too different for the same formulas to be feasible for all.

The European Union might move down this road, although it got off to a bad start with its purely economistic goal of a single market, which has left it facing the problem of an inadequate political structure. As long as the social component of the project remains an empty shell, the single market will give rise to insurmountable social conflicts that will also express themselves in conflicts between member states. This is another reason why I insist that either Europe will be on the left, or there will be no Europe.

Could Eastern Europe be integrated into this system? Possibly – but only if West Europeans do not see it as their Latin America. An overcoming of the uneven development of the two Europes would therefore require subregional forms of organization in the East, linked to pan-European institutions but having their own ground rules, so that the final phase of pan-European economic and political integration would come about only after a fairly lengthy transition. Russia and the other states of the former USSR are in a similar position, even if Russia's size means that it remains potentially a great power. Cooperation and integration among the countries of the former USSR will be a necessary stage if a sharpening of their uneven development is not to result in explosive tensions.

The problems of the Third World vary from region to region. There are several reasons for this:

1. The degree to which Third World countries and regions are integrated into the globalized productive system is by no means uniform. With South Korea, Taiwan and Singapore as perhaps the only major exceptions (Hong Kong now being part of China), all other semi-industrialized parts of the Third World have only a limited segment of their productive system integrated into the new global economy.
2. The countries of the Third (and especially the 'Fourth') World are less integrated among themselves, and in some cases are not integrated at all.
3. The post-war boom made their levels of development even more uneven than before, widening the gap between the group of semi-industrialized countries and the Fourth World.
4. For all these reasons, North–South regional associations exert a considerable pull that tends to work against their collective autonomy.

The regionalization I have in mind seems to me the only rational and effective way to combat the polarizing effects of the Triad's five monopolies, each of which can help us define the main priorities that regionalization projects should serve. These, in turn, will enable us to propose the themes and objectives of the major processes of negotiation to organize controlled interdependence in the service of the peoples of the world. At least six issues need to be considered:

1. The renegotiation of 'market shares' and the rules governing their allocation. Of course, this is a challenge to WTO rules, whose talk of 'loyal competition' serves only to defend the privileges of oligopolies active on a world scale.
2. The renegotiation of capital market systems, with a view to ending the dominance of financial speculation and gearing investment to productive investment in the North and the South. This project calls

into question the functions, perhaps even the existence, of the World Bank.

3. The renegotiation of monetary systems, with a view to establishing regional arrangements and systems that provide relative exchange stability and organize their own interdependence.

4. Moves towards a global tax system, involving, for example, the taxation and international redistribution (for suitable purposes) of profits associated with the exploitation of natural resources.

5. Demilitarization of the planet, beginning with cuts in the most powerful weapons of mass destruction.

6. Democratization of the United Nations and the drafting of a body of law under UN auspices to protect the rights of the world's peoples.

The regions that one can imagine participating in such changes would not only be economic areas with preferential tariffs; they would also have to be built as political areas that helped to strengthen the collective social position of underprivileged classes and subregions. It is a question not only of the continents of the Third World (Latin America, the Arab world, sub-Saharan Africa, South-East Asia, China and India), but also of EU Europe, Eastern Europe and the former USSR.

Of course, this whole project has a chance of gradual realization only if social forces and projects first crystallize at the level of nation-states and advance the much-needed reforms that are impossible within a framework of liberalism and polarizing globalization. Whether it is a question of sectoral reforms (in such areas as government administration, the revenue system, education and support for participatory development) or wider visions of democratization and the political and economic running of society, these preliminary stages cannot be ignored. Without them, a reorganization capable of saving the planet from crisis and disorder and 'restarting development' would remain utterly Utopian.

It is therefore necessary to advance proposals for immediate action around which real political and social forces can be mobilized, primarily at local level, but with the wider aim of 'globalizing' struggles. Here I am thinking of the long list of regulatory forms that could be swiftly introduced in every domain: in the economy (taxation of financial transfers, abolition of tax havens, cancellation of debt, and so on), in the environment (protection of species, prohibition of toxic products and methods, moves towards global taxes on the consumption of certain non-renewable resources), in social matters (labour legislation, investment codes, peoples' representation on international bodies), in politics (democracy and the rights of the individual), and in culture (refusal to commodify cultural goods).

It may seem that, with the existing range of possible governments in Europe and the Third World, the prospect of building a multipolar world can be the stuff only of innocuous declarations not deserving serious consideration.

When European governments face protest movements against their alignment with globalized liberalism, they can claim some legitimacy from the fact they were elected under conditions generally held to be acceptable. The great majority of Third World governments cannot even do this, being the representatives and defenders of comprador interests and the subaltern associates of transnational capital. Some ruling classes in the peripheries – I am thinking mainly of China and India – consider that they still have sufficient bargaining power and room for manoeuvre to accept the ground rules of 'globalization' without having to bow to the diktat of those with the greatest power. For my part, I think they underestimate the consequences of their option, but anyway that is how things stand today. The public is doubtless as badly informed in the peripheral countries as it is in wealthier societies, and in addition it has to contend with powers of control that are not limited to the means of manipulation. Nevertheless, the huge social dramas caused by the alignment with global liberalism cannot fail to have a growing impact on the peoples of the peripheries, while their governments will in turn have to take them into account.

Thus, on the occasion of the WTO ministerial conference held at Doha in November 2001, the unofficial fifteen-member secretariat acting on behalf of the 'Group of 77' (the Third World) called for rejection of the Triad's proposed new round of talks to integrate agriculture into the WTO programme and to expand the field for liberalization to industrial and 'intellectual' property rights, financial and other services. The countries in question eventually backed down, thereby abandoning the firm positions of principle they had adopted at Seattle. This was undoubtedly due to blackmail on the part of Triad diplomats ('anyone who's not with the WTO is with the terrorists'), since there had been no change in G-7 strategy between Seattle and Doha. We shall see whether, in the course of the talks now under way, the Group of 77 countries plus China will be able to pull themselves together again.

Not long before, on the eve of the attacks of 11 September, hopes had been higher in Durban at the world conference against racism. Indeed, the wind had seemed to be blowing for a renewal of the solidarity of

Afro-Asian peoples, one of the main prerequisites – perhaps *the* main prerequisite – for a global system more just than the one the G-7 seeks to impose on the peoples of the world.

The Durban conference was not the anodyne demonstration 'against racism' that its organizers (the UN establishment) had hoped it would be. Africans and Asians forced discussion of two issues that Western diplomats did not want to hear.

The first concerned so-called 'reparations' for the ravages of the black slave trade. American and European diplomats, with condescension and a touch of scorn for 'professional beggars', had led a sabotage operation to focus only on the 'amount' of reparations demanded by the formerly colonized peoples. But that is not how Africans saw things. In their eyes, the issue was not money but a recognition that colonialism, imperialism and slavery were largely responsible both for the 'under-development' of their continent and for the spread of racism. Such ideas did not fail to anger representatives of the Western powers.

The second concerned the activities of the state of Israel. On this issue, Africans and Asians were clear and precise: the continuation of Israeli settlement in the occupied territories, the eviction of Palestinians (amounting to straightforward ethnic cleansing) and the planned 'Bantuization' of Palestine inspired by South Africa's apartheid past were but the latest chapter in the long history of an evidently racist imperialism.

At the same time, Asian and African governments – some of them undemocratic, complicit with neoliberal policies and prone to social or racial discrimination – could not simply turn a deaf ear to what most people thought in their own countries, and to the mounting anger at the arrogance of Western diplomats.

The new wind cast minds back to the Bandung Conference of 1955, the founding moment of Afro-Asian solidarity and the Non-Aligned Movement (now increasingly non-aligned with liberal globalization and US hegemonism), which had ushered in a first cycle of national liberation from colonialism. Whatever the limits of the post-liberation systems and the illusions they inspired, it was their exhaustion that enabled the dominant capital to mount a counter-offensive and to deploy the new imperialist globalization. The conditions for a second and more extensive wave of liberation are now ripening before our eyes. Durban was one proof of that. And it was because Durban was a peoples' victory that the G-7 made every effort to play down its importance.

Together with Seattle, Nice, Gothenburg, Genoa and Porto Alegre, the Durban conference was part of a chain of major positive events.

The time has come for all who condemn the global neoliberal strategy of the dominant capital to realize that the struggle of the peoples of the South against imperialism and US hegemonism is no less important than the struggle of victims in the developed capitalist countries against injustice. And, after the symbolic attacks on the World Trade Center and the Pentagon, it is time to realize that there cannot be a united front against terrorism without a united front against international and social injustice.

'Catching up' or building a different society?

In the twentieth-century challenge to the basic driving forces of capitalism, the two tasks – 'catching up' and 'doing something else' – were combined in ways that varied from period to period and place to place. But we can say, without forcing things too much, that the first task became so dominant that development was virtually synonymous with strategies of 'catching up' (and later overtaking, perhaps). These strategies lost impetus and began to fall apart, once conditions in the surrounding world changed and the general boom that had assisted dynamic insertion into the world economy gave way to a structural adjustment crisis. The 'failure' – if that is the right word for it – was not due to excessive radicalism of the twentieth-century experiments, but, on the contrary, to an insufficient degree of radicalism (which may be explicable in terms of objective factors). In future, then, more emphasis must be placed on 'doing something else', although this should not make us forget that some elements of 'catching up' remain a necessary part of the agenda. In other words, the twenty-first century will have to be more radical than the twentieth.

Will it be capable of this? And what are the likely stages of its progressive radicalization?

Here we need imaginative thinking, not only to accept a variety of visions and proposals, but actually to solicit them and to be glad that there are more than one. Just as, in the twentieth century, different responses to the challenge came from historical Marxism, historical Keynesianism and national populism (itself a kind of degraded form of historical Marxism), we are today witnessing criticisms of globalized liberal capitalism that may easily be grouped under the headings 'neo-Keynesianism', 'neo-Marxism' and 'post-capitalism'. The prefixes 'neo' and 'post' certainly indicate that the content of these alternative strategies has not advanced sufficiently to permit a finished theoretical formulation. But the categories also indicate that some individuals and currents of thought or action will always be more preoccupied with the immediate side of things (the short to medium term), while others concentrate more on a long-term vision of what needs to be achieved. Why not, indeed?

Even within each of the broad families, we should stress the aspect of debate and the diversity of what is proposed. As far as the short to medium term is concerned, all kinds of elements come up for consideration: the various social interests in play, analysis of the system and identification of the challenges, the definition of possible objectives, the mobilization of social and political forces around them, and so on. As to the longer term, I have already said that in my view post-capitalist society (a deliberately imprecise term) will be desirable only if it liberates humanity from economistic alienation and global polarization. I would also call this society 'communist', in the tradition of Marx. But I accept that the social and cultural imagination mobilized around these same two objectives draws upon a variety of humanist sources, and that there is no reason to dismiss any one of them. Dogmatism on this score must be combated. It is necessary to accept, indeed to wish for, diversity in the sense I am using here: that is, diversity turned towards the building of the future, not inherited from a past to which one neurotically clings. Convergence, yes, but convergence within diversity.

Proposals in this spirit stem from the logic of what we might call creative Utopianism. History is not governed by infallible laws of 'pure economics', but results from social reactions to the tendencies that those laws express – reactions which in turn define the social relations within whose framework those laws operate. 'Anti-systemic' forces – if that is the term for the organized, coherent and effective refusal to submit entirely to those supposed laws (here the law of profit peculiar to capitalism as a system) – shape real history as much as does the 'pure' logic of capitalist accumulation. They govern the possibilities and forms of expansion, by organizing the framework within which it is deployed.

Two projects potentially stand opposed to each other: the project of dominant sections of capital to establish their dictatorship, and the project that might emerge if the struggles of the peoples of the world and the working classes successfully converge. The conflict between these two deserves to be called 'civilizational' in the strong and genuine sense of the term, since it involves nothing less than the invention of a system that deliberately situates itself 'beyond capitalism'.

For my part, I have no hesitation in seeing here that conflict between capitalism and socialism which, in view of the risks of barbarism inherent in the survival of obsolescent capitalism, is today more necessary than ever, certainly more than a century or even fifty years ago. For this to be true, however, socialism must be understood not as a ready-made formula but as the outcome of a plural inventive imagination, and the transition from world capitalism to world socialism must be conceived as a lengthy process, not the kind of leap envisaged by the successive historical Marxisms of the last century. I can only refer the reader to the ideas I have developed elsewhere on the subject.

At this early stage in the recomposition of a front of anti-systemic forces, it is not so important whether its various components agree to engage in theoretical debate about the nature of the society they envisage (capitalism with a human face, post-capitalism or socialism). The practice of democracy is alone capable of gradually answering the challenge in question. Without it, nothing good or stable can be achieved in this necessarily long march to a better future.

By democratization I mean not only the adoption of formal rules for the running of political life according to the rule of law and the multi-party principle, but the construction of democratic relations in every sphere of social life (equality between the sexes, respect for national rights, and so on). It goes without saying that, unless there are effective social policies to integrate everyone into economic life and to ensure real and growing equality of access to the material means available in the modern world, democracy will remain vulnerable or even be devalued – a possibility I invoked earlier in speaking of the 'low-intensity democracy' advocated in practice by liberals. On the other hand, democratization in the sense I have outlined offers the only hope of reducing the number of conflicts – their total abolition belongs to the realm of bad Utopian-ism – and therefore of establishing systems of security that effectively guarantee peace.

In this civilizational conflict, each of the two camps is pitched at the level of universality, albeit within radically different perspectives of global-ization. To the globalization of capitalism, anti-systemic forces oppose another project with a global ambition. The capitalist camp invokes free enterprise and 'the market', the opposite camp democracy and equality – in both cases, as universal values. This is why the term 'anti-globalist', used by the media to describe opponents of the wild globalization of liberal obsolescent capitalism, is so misleading, even if here and there some of the protesters may hanker after an impossible 'withdrawal'.

At the present stage, I see no disadvantage in saying that the alternative front that needs to be established is a 'front for social and international justice', leaving open the social horizon within which it might advance.

In any event, it should be stressed once again that concept of a civilizational conflict has nothing in common with a Huntington-style 'clash of civilizations'; indeed, it is poles apart from it.

As I see it, the kind of polycentric, democratic world system I have advocated signifies not the 'end of history', but only a stage in the long transition to world socialism. Achievement of the goals pertaining to this stage would prepare the advance of the values of a better, post-capitalist society, one based on human solidarity rather than individual or national egoism.

In this transition, the emphasis is on three principles largely neglected in the twentieth century that take account of deep tendencies of global transformation. The first is the principle of democratization as an open-ended, multidimensional process through which people begin to become more aware of the economistic alienation that has to be combated. There is thus a gradual progression from projects and visions of ongoing liberation within capitalism to ones of liberation from capitalism. The second principle is what we might call a humanist globalism, which involves placing in command the many-sided right of individuals and collectives (instead of 'business law' in the service of capital) and helping to create an internationalism of the peoples as a counterweight to the transnationalism of capital. The third principle is that of regionalization, seen as an effective means to reduce the polarizing effects of the deployment of capital.

However fragmented they may still be at the present time, the political and social struggles waged in both South and North against various aspects of the dominant system are sufficiently evident and numerous for us not to have to list them here. Evidently, too, they are growing in number and strength with every day that passes.

But the crisis is also sharpening contradictions within the ruling-class blocs, all around the world, and in the societies of Europe these might even blow apart the left–right unanimity that presently characterizes political life there. Nothing guarantees in advance, however, that the contradictions will be overcome by democratic means. In general, dominant classes at bay try to prevent any popular intervention in debates, either by manipulating public opinion (to keep up the appearances of democracy) or by directly resorting to violence and various forms of autocracy. The conflicts are set to take on more and more pronounced international dimensions, as they oppose different states and groups of states to one another. The main question here is to know how the conflicts and social struggles will combine – that is, conflicts among dominant classes and states (whose possible geometry has been outlined above), and the kind of social struggles we have been considering. Which will prevail over which? Will the social struggles be subordinate to the conflicts, so that the ruling powers are able to control them and even to manipulate them to their own advantage? Or will the social struggles become autonomous and compel the rulers to adapt to their demands?

A positive advance in response to this challenge would mean putting politics back in command, repoliticizing movements and struggles.

The dominant forces of transnational capital, which underlie the Triad's collective imperialism and wild, obsolescent capitalism, know that they cannot ignore the existence of their new adversaries. The wrongly termed 'anti-globalization' movements of the First World, from Seattle to Genoa, have shown that they are daily gathering strength, while the growing revolt of the peoples of Asia and Africa points to a rebirth of the Bandung spirit of solidarity.

These two sets of anti-systemic forces should be able to converge, thereby permitting a crystallization of alternatives at every level, from the national to the global. The ruling apparatuses react to this danger by seeking to demonize them.

To politicize struggles is to build the necessary bridges that will help them converge within each nation, as well as at a regional and global level. These credible intermediate objectives, both local and international, will then help in the crystallization of genuinely alternative projects for society.

Building convergence within diversity

To build the convergence of all social and political movements that give expression to the victims of global neoliberal capitalism certainly demands respect for their diversity. Here I propose to categorize all social and political forces active in the contemporary world (on both the left and the right) by plotting their positions on five axes corresponding to five major criteria of possibility.

1. The OX axis measures the degree to which a position involves a radical critique of capitalism. Unconditional supporters of the new liberal order thus find themselves at point O, close to those who, while accepting its key demands, advocate cosmetic reforms to save capitalism from the excesses of neoliberalism (George Soros's formula). The discourse of the World Bank, and of programmes to alleviate poverty that do not question the neoliberal system that generates it,

are part of a right-wing strategy whose real aim is to weaken, not strengthen, popular movements. Further along the axis are those moderate reformists who currently seek to defend established rights from attack (workers' rights, social security, education and health), and still further towards point X are radical reformists whose positions on society point beyond capitalism and bring them close to those whose perspective is to bring about a socialist society.

2. The OY axis measures the degree to which a position involves a radical critique of capitalist globalization. Unconditional supporters of globalization as it is thus lie close to point O, as do all those who see 'no alternative' and generally regard it as positive (or as offering 'opportunities' that should be taken). Further towards point Y are those who are aware of the imperialist dimension of actually existing capitalist globalization, particularly in its neoliberal form, and of the reality of US hegemonism.

3. Axis OZ1 measures the radicalism of conceptions of democracy. Openly anti-democratic positions are to be found right across the contemporary world: not only in the South and the former Eastern bloc (particularly among new comprador classes and regimes aligned with the neoimperialist and neoliberal projects, or among those who are nostalgic for national populism or Sovietism), but also in the United States (where the so-called Christian, para-fundamentalist right, with a strong whiff of McCarthyism about it, musters nearly half the Republican electorate) and in parts of Europe with a certain tradition of democracy (witness the neopopulism of Haider in Austria or Berlusconi in Italy). Towards the centre of this axis lie the mainstream currents that are content with the practices of minimalist democracy, ranging from electoral farce (in the USA and throughout the Third World) to 'low-intensity democracy' based on a supposedly depoliticized consensus. (Here, it has no meaning whether votes are cast for the left or the right, since the resulting government accepts its powerlessness in the face of 'market laws'.) The left on this axis defines itself by fighting to give democracy its rightful emancipatory sense, encompassing all dimensions of the challenge to affirm human and civil rights, the rights of individuals and groups, and the right to control the economic system. As its demands become more radical, this left draws closer to projects for a society 'beyond capitalism'.

4. Axis OZ2 measures the radicalism of positions on gender issues. Close to point O are openly anti-feminist ideologies (usually associated with religious fundamentalism in the United States or in the

Islamic, Hindu, Confucian or other worlds), as well as macho types of behaviour. Further along are political currents willing to accept feminist demands, so long as these do not question the capitalist (or neoliberal) order. Radical feminism, like radical democracy, situates itself within an emancipatory logic that necessarily opens out towards perspectives 'beyond capitalism'. The strong parallelism between positions on the OZ1 and OZ2 axes derives precisely from the close link between democratic or feminist demands and the emancipatory perspective. Emancipation requires radicalization of both democratic and feminist demands.

5. It would finally be useful to consider a fifth dimension of these challenges by measuring the degree to which various positions involve a radical ecological critique of the dominant world order. Close to point O are those who ignore the challenges – the establishment position in the United States, where the future of the planet is sacrificed to the short-term profits of transnational corporations and preservation of the wasteful 'American way of life'. Further along are those naive ecologists who refuse to weigh up this destructive side of capitalism, itself inseparable from the short-term financial calculations that define the (highly limited) 'rationality' of this mode of production. Radical ecologists, who do not ignore this link, come close to the radical critics of capitalism. Since these two criteria – critique of capitalism and ecological critique – have closely related logics, axis OX2 (which measures the radicalism of positions on the environment) might tend to merge with axis OX.

All the ideological positions, political forces and social movements have a location on one of the two planes defined by the OX–OY and OX–OZ axes, or within the three-dimensional OX–OY–OZ space. Each of the two planes may be divided into four quadrants, while the three-dimensional space is made up of eight three-dimensional components (see Figure 1).

In this space, some regions are virtually empty, as the relevant combination is too contradictory to exist in reality. Other combinations mark where the dominant forces of the right cluster, while many still-fragmented social and political movements – which at least partly constitute the potential base of a left alternative – are spread around the space in question.

In the world today, to rally to the theses of neoliberalism and the associated view of globalization means to be on the right, even if one's

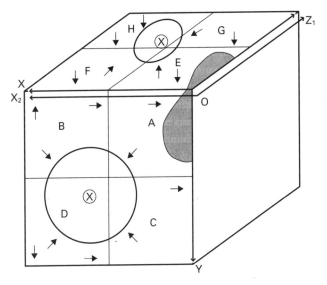

OX	degree of radicalism in relation to the critique of capitalism
OX2	degree of radicalism in relation to ecological critique
OY	degree of anti-imperialist consciousness
OY1	degree of radicalism in the conception of democracy
OY2	degree of radicalism in relation to feminism
X	left-of-centre point of junction
shading	concentration of hegemonic bloc of right-wing forces

The arrows indicate the direction necessary for convergence, or contrariwise the direction of backsliding and deadlock.

Figure I The schema of convergence in diversity

election ticket is that of a party of the left (a common case in Europe) and even if one makes speeches (only speeches) that claim to be nationalist/anti-imperialist (a possibility in the South). The mainstream right, located in quadrants A and E (the AE cube), is at best moderately reformist and bases itself on the democratic consensus, in the ordinary sense of the term. This right, forming a majority in Europe across the political parties, is outflanked further to the right (especially in the United States) by undemocratic, violently anti-feminist and racist ideological and social movements. The neo-McCarthyism of the Republican establishment has incorporated this supposedly 'moral' front into the ruling alliance. In the peripheries of the South and the former Eastern bloc, a comprador right holding most of the power has its social base among the 'wheeler-dealers' promoted by neoliberal globalization. The concept of 'wheeler-dealers' – or another of the terms commonly used to denote the same phenomenon – well illustrates the character of this fragile, artificial, barely democratic or even entrepreneurial 'bourgeoisie'. The hatched areas in quadrants A and E mark the regions where these hegemonic rights are located.

The left that needs to be built – radically anti-neoliberal, at least anti-hegemonist (if not anti-imperialist) and democratically advanced – should be found at the opposite end, in quadrants D and H (cube DH). But not all the forces and movements involved in today's struggles against right-wing dominance are necessarily located in this region. In the capitalist centres there is a left, even a radical left, which shows little sensitivity to the imperialist dimension of the system. Anti-imperialist consciousness has been greatly weakened throughout the North, as national liberation movements in support of which young 'Third Worldist' Westerners used to mobilize have disappointed their hopes. In the peripheries, some still feel nostalgic for Sovietism and various kinds of undemocratic populism, yet are critical of neoliberalism or imperialism or both. Other political and ideological forces there, with greater future potential, seek to defend legitimate national interests, while a number of governments really do seem to have embraced globalization or accepted US hegemony only 'under duress', on the grounds that the relationship of forces did not allow them any other choice. At the present time, such forces are steering a middle course between, on the one hand, the illusion of (to put it mildly) undemocratic right-wing nationalism that alignment with the neoliberal global order can still leave room for 'negotiation', and, on the other hand, the option of siding with a democratic, anti-imperialist people's front. Only if they choose the latter will they acquire any real power and link up with the global left that awaits construction; otherwise they will be left with their vague and ineffectual impulses. Or they may even drift along with such anti-democratic aberrations as ethnic chauvinism or pseudo-religious fundamentalism (political Islam or Hinduism, for example), which, for all their verbose 'anti-Western' culturalism, have agreed to subject their peoples to the demands of capitalist globalization and are in effect part of the global right-wing alliance.

The building of a left alternative requires strategies and tactics to rally all political forces, ideological currents and social movements struggling against neoliberalism and imperialism, or for democratic advances, women's liberation or sound ecological management of the planet's resources. Such left-of-centre unity – marked by a cross in quadrant D is the main starting point for the strategy and tactics that have been suggested here.

Many of the movements spread around the figure's three-dimensional space can be attracted to this perspective. There is no reason to believe that reform-minded currents upholding democracy, women's and national rights, or the cause of ecology and peace are – or will remain – incapable of learning from the failure of the 'moderate' options that still characterize many of their own positions. Not all will be capable of it: that has to be accepted. There will remain reformists who, content with merely cosmetic reforms, are unable to see that they are being used by the dominant right, just as there will remain revolutionaries who shut themselves up in dogmatic ghettoes to avoid the question of how to move humanity forward towards their alternative vision for society.

It is also possible for anti-imperialist currents of opinion, even organizations, in the South to be helped towards more consistent positions that win them widespread popular support. But there will always remain fragments of such forces that are attracted to the camp of the compradors, just as there will remain popular movements that stray down the paths of culturalism.

The hegemonic right-wing front is much less stable than it appears; its internal contradictions are bound to grow deeper and to result in actual fissures as it scores more apparent successes for its project. The South – to which it has nothing to offer – still contains a series of 'weak links' (China, India, Brazil, South Africa, and others), while in the North a historically rooted democratic, humanist and socialist tradition presents a growing obstacle to the awesome prospect of US hegemony. Capitalism is certainly not the absolute horizon that many ideologues and leaders of progressive popular movements still think it to be. In the short term, struggles may only be directed against neoliberalism (an ultra-reactionary form of capitalism) and the arrogant hegemonism of the United States (the spearhead of the new imperialism). But their own advances in that direction will lead them to become more radical.

The world will continue to abound with 'surfer politicians': that is, active, knowing men and women who have an essentially opportunist conception of politics, as the art of getting the best out of the existing relationship of forces (contrary to the radical or revolutionary view of politics as the art of transforming the relationship of forces). Surfer politicians are not, however, insensitive to the opinion of those sections of society upon whom they depend for success, whether in an electoral-democratic or another context. They surf 'on spec', in a sea filled with reefs, without always knowing where this will lead them. Many will eventually join the camp of the left, if it manages to reconstitute itself and to turn around the relationship of forces. They will not always do this out of crass opportunism or careerism, but perhaps because they find in that left the values to which they are attached. Reformists here, anti-imperialists there are, in part at least, moved by the same values as ours.

Building convergence means rebuilding this much-needed left. The gradual strengthening of convergence in diversity will therefore manifest itself through a widening of the circle around the left-of-centre point in quadrant D. There is also a corresponding left-of-centre point in quadrant H. These two points come together to form the centre of the sphere of convergence within the three-dimensional space of the figure. When the relevant circle in each of the surfaces ABCD and EFGH, or in the sphere corresponding to them, finally occupies a respectable part of the surfaces (or the volume) in question, the battle will have been won and the relationship of forces will have been reversed in favour of the working classes and the peoples of the world.

The building of convergence may be formulated in a number of different but complementary political terms.

For a united front in support of social and international justice. This emphasizes that the two epithets are inseparable, that social justice in the centres must go together with a resolutely anti-imperialist consciousness, that anti-imperialism in the peripheries has no future if it is not backed up by popular classes aspiring to social justice and democracy.

The democratic state, in the long transition beyond unbridled capitalism, is a state that imposes regulation by citizens and society. Or: *Socialization through the democracy of citizens and society is integrative, whereas socialization through the market tends to exclude people.* Or again: *There can be no answer to social needs without democracy, and no democracy without an answer to social needs.*

These 'slogans' draw the lessons from recent history. In the South, governments that have agreed to keep democratization within the limits imposed by neoliberalism serve to undermine the credibility of democracy itself (see the tragic Argentinean example), either by encouraging a return to authoritarian populism or by paving the way for a violent dictatorship in the service of imperialism. In the North, the left–right consensus of electoral majorities around economic liberalism substitutes the American form of 'low-intensity democracy' for the democracy grounded on citizens and society which has been the programme of the historical lefts. It thus perpetuates the conditions for a fragmentation of resistance and destroys hopes that an anti-imperialist consciousness will mature.

Convergence – that is, a widening of the central circle – does not exclude diversity but strengthens it and unleashes its potential; the circles in question then cover major areas of the quadrants in our figure. The challenge is to build a convergence of forces that speak for the victims of unbridled capitalism, modern imperialism, US hegemonism and the war it wages against the peoples of the South. None of those forces can fail to realize that it will advance its limited short-term or longer-term objectives only by affirming the solidarity of all sections of the global united front for social and international justice.

Notes

1. *The Lugano Report: On Preserving Capitalism in the Twenty-First Century*, with an annex and afterword by Susan George, London: Pluto Press, 1999.

2. See Samuel P. Huntington, *The Clash of Civilizations and the Remaking of the World Order*, New York: Simon & Schuster, 1996.

3. See Samir Amin, *Les régionalisations*, forthcoming (FTM).

Appendices

I. The challenges of modernity

Modernity is the outcome of a break in human history that began in Europe in the sixteenth, seventeenth and eighteenth centuries but is by no means complete, either in its birthplaces or anywhere else. The multiple facets of modernity form a whole that, though consistent with the reproductive requirements of the capitalist mode of production, would also allow progression beyond it.

Modernity was based upon the demand for the emancipation of human beings, starting with their liberation from the straitjacket of previous forms of social determination. This meant giving up the prevailing forms of power legitimization – in families, in the communities where the modes of life and production were organized, and in the state – which had until then rested upon a generally religious metaphysic. It therefore involved radical secularization, the separation of state and religion, as the prerequisite for modern forms of politics. This did not require the abolition of religious faith, but it did exclude the subordination of reason to any dogmatic interpretation of religion. Any reconciliation of reason and faith was left to unhindered individual reflection; religion was to be a strictly private matter, and no credibility was given to any form of it imposed by the state or by social convention.

The fact that modernity and capitalism grew up together was no accident. The social relations peculiar to the new capitalist system of production involved free enterprise, free access to markets and an inalienable ('sacred') right to private property. Once economic life had shaken off the kind of political controls typical of pre-modern regimes, it established itself as an autonomous area of social life with its own distinctive laws. For the traditional determination of wealth by power, capitalism substituted a reverse causality that made wealth the source of power. But modernity as it has existed up to today – that is, modernity confined to the framework of capitalism – remains ambivalent on this question of the relationship between power and wealth. For it is grounded upon the separateness of two areas of social life: the economy has a logic of its own governing capital accumulation (private property, free enterprise, competition), while state power is exercised through the institutionalization of political democracy (civil rights, a multi-party system, and so on). This arbitrary separation vitiates the emancipatory potential of modernity.

The modernity deployed within the constraints of capitalism is therefore contradictory: it creates unfulfilled hopes by promising much more than it can deliver.

Modernity inaugurated a progress of society (summed up in the term emancipation) that is of potentially huge proportions; even the limited advances of political democracy are testimony to that. Modernity legitimized action by the dominated, exploited and oppressed classes, gradually enabling them to wrest from the rule of capital a series of democratic rights that have never spontaneously flowed from capitalist expansion and accumulation. The resulting capacity for political transformation permitted the development of class struggle, so that an equivalence was established between the two terms – politics and class struggle – which gave them both their full force. At the same time, however, modernity invented and developed the means of cutting back the potential of emancipatory democracy.

The capitalism that grew up together with modernity brought development of the productive forces at a rhythm never before seen in history. The potential contained in this development would allow the major material problems of humanity to be solved, but the logic governing capitalist accumulation forbids any such resolution – indeed, it constantly polarizes wealth on a scale previously unknown in the history of the world.

Humanity today thus faces the contradictions of that modernity, the only one we know so far, which began with the capitalist stage of history. These contradictions express the three destructive dimensions of capitalism and therefore of its accompanying form of modernity.

Capitalism and its modernity are destructive of human beings, reducing them to the status of the commodity labour-power. The economistic alienation through which this reduction is expressed empties democracy of its emancipatory potential. When democracy exists at all under these conditions – which means, in practice, in the centres of the system, the only areas to benefit from the development of the productive forces – it suffers degradation and loss of meaning. Genuine politics, expressing the capacity of the inventive imagination, is replaced by the hollow consensus of low-intensity democracy, a media spectacle constructed and manipulated by the capital dominant within the economic system.

With its short-term rationality of economic calculation, capitalist modernity is destructive of the natural foundations both of social reproduction and of life itself, as we see from the grave problems affecting the environment and the stream of minor disasters (mad cows being a perfect case in point).

The global polarization induced by capital accumulation means that the majority of human beings on earth – those living in the peripheries of the system – have no prospect of satisfying the needs that modernity has promoted, and hence of enjoying even the degraded democracy practised in the heartlands of the system. For most of humanity, capitalism is a hateful system, and the modernity accompanying it a tragic farce.

The contradictions inherent in the capitalist phase of modernity cancelled the rational Utopian project formulated at the time of its birth – a project, in fact, through which only the rationality of the reproduction of capital was able to find expression. The framework in which the dominant capital had to develop was constantly reshaped by conflict between its own requirements and the demands which victims of the system managed to impose at various times and places. Instead of the 'pure capitalism' of the economics textbooks, a more pragmatic capitalism adapted to market regulation imposed by the prevailing social relations and to international conflicts that challenged the existing hierarchies within the world system. In this sense, too, whereas the ideology of modernity that grew up with capitalism claimed to make a 'clean break with the past' by replacing it exclusively with the Utopia of capitalist rationality, capitalism actually had to make do with what it found in the real world. Modernity thus became a patchwork quilt that contrasted sharply with the cohesion of its theoretical foundations.

The peoples of today's world therefore have to face the twin challenge of actually existing capitalism and actually existing modernity. The attitudes and postures through which the various political and ideological currents find expression should be evaluated according to how they respond explicitly or implicitly to this challenge.

The dominant ideology simply tries to ignore it. Anglo-American liberal ideologues, however sophisticated their language, express this ignorance in a naive manner. Their well-fed chatter reduces modernity to the only human value they know: freedom of the individual. What they overlook is that, in the context of capitalism, this freedom allows the strongest to impose their law on everyone else; that it is an illusory freedom for the great mass of people (the liberal idea that everyone can become a Rockefeller is like the old refrain that each soldier carries a marshal's baton in his backpack); and that it clashes with the yearning for equality which is the foundation of democracy.

All those who uphold the system share this same basic ideology that capitalism is an unsurpassable horizon, the 'end of history'. Extremists among them do not hesitate to picture society as a jungle filled with 'individuals', or to sacrifice the possibility of the state's pacifying intervention to management principles in which the public authorities are no more than an instrument serving the 'winners' – a Mafia-like conception of the dictatorship of capital. Others would like to give this dictatorship a human face by mixing the principle of individual freedom with pragmatic considerations of social justice, community identity and the 'recognition of difference'. Postmodernism is another way of denying the challenge: it suggests that we all 'accept' or 'adjust to' contemporary reality, that we 'run' things simply in the light of what is possible in the very short term.

For the great majority of people in the world, this modernity is simply detestable, hypocritical, based on cynical double standards. Therefore, they violently reject it, and the violence of their rejection is perfectly legitimate. Actually existing capitalism and the modernity that goes with it have nothing to offer them.

Yet rejection is a negative act. A positive alternative is also required. If reflection is inadequate and gives rise to misguided projects, the result can be to nullify the effectiveness of revolt, yielding a new submission to the demands of capitalism and modernity that the revolt claimed to reject. The principal illusion here feeds on nostalgia for a pre-modern past, which has its defenders in both the centres and the peripheries of the system. In the centres, it may pass for inconsequential reverie, an expression of conservatism enabling people with full stomachs to take the sting out of emancipatory demands, so that modernity becomes a patchwork quilt combining manipulated vestiges of the past with demands thrown up in the present. In the peripheries, the backward-looking posture derives from a violent, justified revolt; it remains at the level of neurotic impotence, however, because it is based on simple ignorance of the nature of the challenge of modernity.

Of the languages in which nostalgia may be expressed, the most common are those of religious fundamentalism (which actually masks a conventional conservative option) and ethnic affirmation of virtues transcending class and other dimensions of social reality; the common denominator is thus a transhistorical culturalist vision in which religion or ethnicity defines some intangible identity. Although these postures lack a scientific basis, they are quite capable of mobilizing large numbers of people who have been marginalized and dispossessed by capitalist modernity. This very fact makes them effective instruments of manipulation, when they are inserted into strategies of *de facto* submission to the joint dictatorship of globalizing capitalist forces and their local transmission belts. Political Islam is a good example of this in peripheral capitalism (see Appendix VI). In Latin America and Africa, the proliferation of obscurantist sects – supported by apparatuses in the United States as a barrier to liberation theology – exploits the confusion of excluded layers and manipulates their revolt against the conservative official Church.

On the other hand, to take up the challenge of modernity means to address the contradictions of capitalist-inaugurated modernity and to develop a future-oriented project for society that is capable of overcoming them. Such a position, then, would have to focus not on differences inherited from the past but on those that the invention of the future generates through its own movement (see Appendix VII).

The conservative and reactionary forces which dominate the contemporary scene, both globally and at the level of particular societies, are making great efforts to roll back the unfinished project of modernity. To this end, they seek to foster responses which, though essentially incoherent, can be effective in the short term by combining the reproduction of past appearances with the present requirements of the destructive accumulation of capital.

II. Imaginary capitalism and actually existing capitalism

The dominant forces are dominant because they succeed in imposing their language on their victims. Thus, the 'experts' of mainstream economics have sown the belief that their analyses and conclusions are valid because they are scientific: that is, objective, neutral and inexorable. But that is not true. The so-called 'pure' economics on which they base their analyses does not deal with the real world, but operates with an imaginary system that does not even come close to it. Actually existing capitalism is something quite different.

This imaginary economics runs different concepts together, conflating progress with capitalist expansion and the market with capitalism. If the social movements are to develop effective strategies, they must free themselves from such confusions.

The confusion of two concepts – the reality (capitalist expansion) and an end that is desirable (clearly defined progress) – lies behind many of the setbacks encountered by critics of present-day policies. Dominant discourses systematically make the amalgam, by describing as 'development' either the actual outcome or one they consider plausible. Logically, however, the expansion of capital does not presuppose any outcome that could be described as 'development' – for example, full employment, or a predefined level of inequality (or equality) of income distribution. The driving force, rather, is the firm's quest for profit, which, according to circumstances, may result in either growth or stagnation, expanding or shrinking employment, lesser or greater equality of incomes.

Here, a confusion between 'market economy' and 'capitalist economy' is at the root of a dangerous weakening of criticisms of present policies. The 'market' – which, by its nature, refers to competition – is not the same as 'capitalism', whose content is defined precisely by the limits to competition that monopolistic (or oligopolistic) private property entails. 'Market' and 'capitalism' are two distinct concepts. In fact, as Braudel convincingly showed, real-world capitalism is the opposite of the imaginary market.

Furthermore, capitalism does not actually function through systematic competition on the part of those who hold the monopoly of property – that is, competition among them and against others – but requires the intervention of a collective authority representing capital as a whole. The state, then, cannot be separated from capitalism. The policies of capital, and hence of the state in so far as it represents capital, are driven by distinctive logics in different periods. This explains why the expansion of capital results at certain moments in the growth of employment, and at others in its decline. The driving forces in each case are not some abstract 'laws of the market' as such, but the profitability requirements of capital in a particular set of historical conditions.

There are no 'laws of capitalist expansion' that assert themselves with a quasi-supernatural force. There is no historical determinism prior to history. Tendencies inherent in the logic of capital always clash with the resistance of forces in society that do not accept their effects; real history is the result of this clash between the logic of capitalist expansion and the logic of resistance to it. In this sense, the state is rarely just the state of capital; it is also the product of the conflict between capital and society.

Thus, if we take the case of post-war industrialization in the periphery (1945–80), we can see that it was not the 'natural' result of capitalist expansion but the product of conditions created by the national liberation victories to which global capital had to adjust. Similarly, the declining effectiveness of the national state under the impact of capitalist globalization is not an irreversible force shaping the future; on the contrary, national reactions to globalization can impose unexpected trajectories, for better or worse according to the circumstances. Or take the ecological concerns that, though clashing with the intrinsically short-term logic of capital, may yet leave a major imprint on adjustment tendencies within capitalism. These are but a few of the many examples we might mention.

An effective response to the challenges can be found only if it is realized that there are no infallible laws of 'pure' economics guiding the course of history. Rather, it is social reactions to the tendencies expressed in those laws that give history its shape, and define in turn the social relations within whose framework those laws operate. 'Anti-systemic forces', which reject in a coherent, organized and effective manner any total submission to the requirements of those laws (in fact, the simple law of profit inherent in capitalism as a system), shape the real course of history just as much as does the 'pure' logic of capitalist accumulation. They govern the possibilities and forms of expansion, by organizing the framework within which it is deployed.

The method advocated here excludes any ready-made prescriptions for the shaping of the future, for the future is produced by changes in the social and political relationship of forces, and such changes are brought about by struggles whose outcome is not known in advance. Nevertheless, thinking about the future can help to crystallize coherent and feasible projects through which society may be able to overcome the false solutions that threaten to block its advance.

A humanist response to the challenge posed by capitalist globalization is not 'Utopian'. On the contrary, it is the only realistic project, in the sense that the first steps towards it would soon rally powerful social forces in all parts of the world that could actually bring it about. If there is a Utopia, in the banal and negative sense of the term, it is the idea of running the system simply through market regulation.

III. The destructive dimensions of capitalist accumulation

Capitalism is neither the end of history nor even the unsurpassable horizon of the future. It is more a historical parenthesis – one that opened around the year 1500 and urgently needs to be closed. As it subordinated all aspects of social life to the logic of accumulation – or 'the markets', as vulgar theory has it – capitalism permitted a qualitative leap forward not only materially but also politically and culturally, achieving rates of growth quite unlike any seen before in human history. It also created the means whereby the major problems facing all nations in the world could be solved, but at the same time its governing logic made it impossible for the potential to be used for that purpose.

This fundamental contradiction gave to capitalism destructive dimensions that have now grown so extensive that they constitute a real threat to the future of humanity; the resulting crisis is thus a veritable crisis of civilization. All these destructive dimensions, which have been abundantly described at various times, centre on the key element of 'market expansion' or 'marketization' (in the language of vulgar economics), commodification or commodity alienation in more scientific terms. It is expansion that knows no limits, and that benefits only the dominant (oligopolistic) capital.

The programme of capitalism involves a growing commodification of all aspects of existence: of human inventive and artistic capacities, of health and education, of the riches offered by nature, culture and politics. This produces a threefold destruction of the individual, nature and whole peoples. The areas in which the present threat of destruction is most manifest cannot be separated from one another; they are all interconnected by the same logic of accumulation.

Bovine spongiform encephalitis (BSE) or 'mad cow disease' is one tragi-comic example of the devastation that can arise when food production is guided entirely by 'profitability' and 'market deregulation'.

Commodification and privatization of health is a sure invitation to organize a 'human organs market', which, as we know from the case of Brazil, leads to the killing of children to satisfy demand. Even in their own terms, such health systems are inefficient: the United States, for example, spends 14 per cent of GDP on (private) health care, with results inferior to those achieved on half that expenditure in Europe's largely public services. Yet the profits of the drugs and insurance oligopolies in the United States are far higher than those in Europe.

Commodification and privatization of education is a royal road towards greater social inequality and a society of general apartheid. Although there certainly needs to be a fresh look at education, the path of privatization will not bring any answers to the problems.

Commodification and privatization of pension funds is a means of absurdly fanning generational conflict between people at work (tomorrow's pensioners) and people in retirement (yesterday's workers).

Commodification and privatization of scientific research – false privatization, if one considers that government military expenditure creates profits only for the ologopolies – is a certain guarantee that research will be guided not by social needs (the elimination of Aids in Africa, for example) but by short-term profit, and that biotechnical research will serve to strengthen oligopolistic control over the farmers' agribusiness (the source of BSE). It also ensures the abandonment of basic precautions and ethical concerns.

The commodification and privatization of intellectual, industrial, cultural and artistic property guarantees the maximization of oligopolistic profits by robbing popular layers (especially the peasantry) of the know-how for which they have never before had to pay, and selling it 'back' to them as a possession of the oligopolies. This boost to the false subculture of homogenization represents a further obstacle to the diversity and wealth of cultural and artistic creation.

Commodification and privatization of natural resources guarantees waste to the disadvantage of future generations.

Commodification and privatization of the environment through trade in 'licences to pollute' guarantee the total sterility of ecological critique and serve to deepen inequalities on a world scale.

Commodification and privatization of water guarantees a worsening of inequality in access to this vital resource, and will programme the destruction of whole swathes of irrigated agriculture in the Third World.

Commodification and privatization in general make of competition an absolute principle; a false competition limited to the oligopolies. This is an absolute guarantee of immeasurable waste: exorbitant marketing costs; 'economic' sterilization of seeds to keep the peasantry dependent on the oligopolies, as pawns of agribusiness; organization of artificial scarcity through secret deals among the oligopolies to regulate competition, destruction of biodiversity, and so on.

Polarization on a world scale, which is inherent in the global expansion of capitalism, is the most dramatic dimension of destruction associated with the history of the last five centuries: just think of the hundred million Native Americans and the same number of Africans exterminated to put the system 'in place'. But unbridled accumulation was not only 'primitive'; its constantly renewed forms have included colonization and wars (from conquest down to independence), coercive selling of opium to the Chinese, forced labour, apartheid and the new pillage centred on debt. The book of actually existing capitalism is truly black. Today we have reached a stage of polarization at which most of the world's population is 'superfluous' to the needs of capital. A demographic revolution means that Asia and Africa have been catching up on their lag at the time of European expansion, rural worlds have disintegrated under the impact of 'the market', and new forms of industrialization have been incapable of absorbing the exodus of the village poor. With the help of all these factors, capitalism is taking us towards a 'shantytown planet' within the next 20 years, when 25 megalopolises will each pack in 7 to 25 million people reduced to abject poverty without any prospects for the future. Is this anything other than the destruction of whole peoples? How, then, can we not believe Susan George when she says in her Lugano Report that the horsemen of the Apocalypse are cynically planning the destruction of capital's 'useless mouths', through famine, endemic diseases and Aids, and 'tribal wars'. But in that case who is really superfluous? The billions of human beings for whom capitalism has nothing to offer? Or capitalism itself?

The market economy, to use the vulgar textbook term, is also necessarily market society. To accept the former and reject the latter may fit in with some 'third way' Sunday speeches by the likes of Clinton, Blair, Schröder or Jospin. But it lacks all credibility, when we know that the market economy they celebrate has allowed the oligopolies to double their profits over the past decade. Basic arithmetic tells us that, if profits rise faster than national product, the result can only be rising inequality – which is indeed the aim of liberal policies. The pious speeches about 'poverty' are just dust in the eyes of the gullible.

Market society, then, an inexorable result of market economy (that is capitalism), cannot be other than it is. Market society nullifies citizenship and replaces it with a manipulable mass of consumers – passive spectators. The 'alternation' of government teams to continue the same policy (wholly subordinate to the requirements of capitalist profit) does away with any real alternative (any conscious choice between different policies). Self-styled political theorists take it upon themselves to analyse electoral 'choices' with the same instruments that mainstream economists use to analyse consumer choices or that others use to pick out the winner in a competition.

We must be logical about this: if the law of the market is made the only criterion of rationality, it fully legitimizes the part of the economy that is hypocritically called criminal. The demand for hard drugs creates its own supply, which the Mafia controls by regulating the market in accordance with the rules taught in business schools. Such regulation is opaque, as is the regulation practised by the oligopolies. (The term 'deregulation' is used only because they cannot call it by its real name.) And why should we not describe as criminals those financial speculators who are fully aware of the damage that their operations inflict on society? Tax havens serve both alike, and with the same efficiency.

Their citizenship negated, the mass of ordinary people are invited to fill the void by withdrawing into their 'community'. This is an invitation to obscurantism, ethnic or religious fanaticism, racist hatred and, in the end, 'ethnic cleansing'. In the most dramatic situations, in the Third World, it is an invitation to permanent 'tribal warfare'. Self-styled theoreticians try to legitimize such practices by pointing to the conflict inherent in cultural diversity, while nice people think they can answer them with nice appeals for a 'dialogue of cultures'. What neither understand – or pretend not to understand – is that the logic of capitalism and its markets lies behind what they denounce or think they are merely pointing out.

It is high time that these destructive dimensions of obsolescent capitalism were properly assessed. The time has come to say loud and clear that a different system must be invented, one in which human beings individually (their health, education and inventiveness), peoples collectively, and nature and its resources are not treated as commodities. The terms of the choice are no different today from those Rosa Luxemburg formulated in 1918: socialism or barbarism!

IV. The development paradigm

Development is an ideological concept that requires some definition of the societal project for which it is deployed. Fearing that the project is the merest Utopianism, 'realists' see 'feasible development' in terms of intelligent adjustment to the spontaneous tendencies of the capitalist system and reduce the very concept to one of market expansion on the basis of the social relations peculiar to capitalism. Obviously this rules out any goal of qualitative transformation going beyond the basic logic of the system.

Since, however, globalized capitalism produces polarization by its very nature, making futile any hope that its peripheries might one day catch up with the centres, development faces a challenge both at the level of the productive forces ('catching up' at least some of the ground) and in terms of 'doing something else' (moving outside the strict logic of capitalism).

The problem of the development paradigm involves a number of elements: the concept of self-reliant development, identification of a social content (bourgeois, statist, national-popular) consistent with its objectives as well as historically possible, a set of means towards that end, including 'delinking' from the dominant logic of global capitalism, and the long-term project of a world society incorporating earlier advances and transformations (socialism, or however one prefers to call such an overall project). The paradigm is therefore critical of the world as it is today, in all its dimensions, and mobilizes the inventive imagination characteristic of creative Utopianism.

Actually existing global capitalism produces polarization by its very nature. Capitalism, considered abstractly as a mode of production, is based on an integrated market with three dimensions (social products market, capital market, labour market). Considered as an actually existing global system, however, capitalism is based on global expansion of the market in only its first two dimensions; the formation of a genuinely global labour market is excluded by the frontiers between states that persist in spite of economic globalization and restrict its scope. For this reason, actually existing capitalism necessarily produces polarization on a world scale, so that uneven development becomes the most violent contradiction of modern times and cannot be overcome within the logic of capitalism. This means that we have to think in terms of a protracted transition to world socialism. For, although capitalism has created the bases for an economy and society spanning the whole planet, it is incapable of carrying globalization through to its logical conclusion. Socialism, as a qualitatively higher stage of humanity, can only be universal. But its construction will involve a lengthy historical transition, requiring a strategy of contradictory negation of capitalist globalization.

An analysis of globalized capitalism must distinguish between the law of value and its specific form as a global law of value. World capitalism is not governed by the law of value *tout court* (which grounds the capitalist mode of production conceived at the highest level of abstraction); it is governed by the globalized law of value (the form of the law of value stemming from the two-dimensional world market). The law of value *tout court* would imply that the remuneration of labour was everywhere the same for the same level of productivity. The globalized law of value yields uneven remuneration of labour for the same level of productivity, whereas the prices of goods and the remuneration of capital tend to level out on a world scale. Polarization is the outcome of this. The strategy of a long transition to world socialism therefore implies delinking the system of criteria of economic rationality from the system of criteria derived from submission to the globalized law of value.

Translated into the terms of political and social strategy, this general principle means that the long transition is an obligatory, inescapable period involving the construction of a national-popular society and the associated construction of a self-reliant national economy. Every aspect of this is contradictory: it combines criteria, institutions and procedures of a capitalist nature with social aspirations and reforms that conflict with the logic of world capitalism; it combines a certain openness to the outside (as controlled as possible) with demands for progressive social changes that conflict with the dominant capitalist interests. The ruling classes, by their historical nature, fit their visions and aspirations into the perspective of actually existing capitalism, and willy-nilly keep their strategies within the constraints of the global expansion of capitalism. This is why they cannot really imagine delinking. For the popular classes, however, delinking becomes a necessity as soon as they try to use political power to transform their conditions and to free themselves from the inhuman consequences of the polarizing global expansion of capitalism.

The option of self-reliant development cannot be ignored. Self-reliant ('auto-centred' or 'endogenous') development, driven mainly by the dynamic of internal social relations and reinforced by ancillary external relations, historically characterized the capital accumulation process in the capitalist centres and has shaped the resulting forms of economic development there. In the peripheries, by contrast, the capital accumulation process mainly derives from the evolution of the centres; it is grafted on to that evolution and is in some sense dependent upon it.

Self-reliant development therefore presupposes what we may call the five essential conditions of accumulation:

- *Local control over the reproduction of labour power.* In an initial phase, this requires the state to ensure that agriculture develops sufficiently to generate a surplus at prices that meet the profitability conditions of capital, and, in a second phase, that the mass production of wage goods keeps up with the expansion of capital and the total wage bill.
- *Local control over the centralization of surplus.* This requires not only the formal existence of national financial institutions but their relative autonomy from flows of transnational capital, so that the country in question is assured of the capacity to steer investment of the surplus.
- *Local control over the market largely reserved for national production,* even in the absence of high tariffs or other forms of protection, and *a capacity to compete on the world market, at least selectively.*
- *Local control over natural resources.* This requires that, whatever the formal ownership, the national state has the capacity either to exploit resources or to keep them in reserve. Oil-producing countries do not have such control unless they are actually free to 'switch off the tap'

(which would mean that they preferred to keep their oil under the ground rather than hold financial assets that could at any moment be taken from them).

- *Local control over technologies.* This requires that the technology in question, whether locally invented or imported, can be quickly reproduced without the indefinite import of essential inputs (equipment, know-how, and so on).

The concept of self-reliant development, as opposed to dependent development resulting from unilateral adjustment to tendencies that govern the deployment of capitalism on a world scale, cannot be reduced to the antinomy between import-substitutionism and export-led growth. The latter two concepts come from the textbooks, which ignore the fact that economic strategies are always implemented by the hegemonic social blocs in which the interests dominant in society at a given time find expression. Furthermore, even for vulgar economics, all strategies implemented in the real world combine import substitution with an export orientation, in proportions that vary with the conjuncture.

The model of self-reliant development is based upon a close and important interdependence between output growth of production goods and output growth of articles of mass consumption. Self-reliant economies are not self-enclosed; on the contrary, they are aggressively open, in the sense that their export potential helps to shape the world system as a whole. The correlation we have just defined corresponds to a social relationship whose main terms are constituted by the two fundamental blocs in the system: the national bourgeoisie and the world of labour. By contrast, the dynamic of peripheral capitalism – the antithesis of self-reliant central capitalism by definition – is based on a different fundamental correlation: between export capacity and minority consumption of imports or goods produced locally by import substitution. This defines the comprador (as opposed to national) character of the bourgeoisies of the periphery.

A critical reading of historical attempts to achieve popular or socialist self-reliant development. Over the last three-quarters of a century, the question of self-reliant development and delinking was posed in practice by all the great popular revolutions against actually existing capitalism: the Russian and Chinese revolutions, as well as national liberation movements in the Third World. The answers that each gave on this question were closely related to all other aspects of the development of the productive forces, national liberation, social progress and democratization; critical assessment of these experiences is constantly necessary to draw the appropriate lessons from their successes and failures. At the same time, and because capitalism continually changes, evolves and adapts to the challenges posed by popular revolts, the terms of the questions are themselves subject to constant evolution. Self-reliant development and delinking can thus never become ready-made formulas valid for all situations and moments; they have to be considered afresh in the light of the lessons of history and the evolution of capitalist globalization.

The long wave of national liberation that swept the Third World after the Second World War ended in the establishment of new regimes, mainly based on national bourgeoisies, which in varying degrees exercised control over the movement. A veritable ideology of development came into being, as these bourgeoisies generated modernization strategies with the aim of securing 'independence within global interdependence' – not, that is, delinking in the real sense of the principle, but only active adaptation to the global system in ways that well expressed the national-bourgeois character of the development projects in question. History would show the Utopianism of this course, which ran out of steam after a number of apparent successes between 1955 and 1975. Opening-up policies, together with privatization and structural adjustment to the constraints of capitalist globalization, then imposed a kind of re-compradorization of the economies and societies of the periphery.

By contrast, the so-called experiences of actually existing socialism in the USSR and China achieved delinking, in the sense we have given to the term, and established a set of criteria for economic choices independent of those imposed by the logic of global capitalist expansion. These options, and others accompanying them, reflected the genuinely socialist intentions of the political and social forces at the origin of the revolutions in question. However, when the societies of the USSR and China faced a choice between 'catching up at any price' through development of the productive forces (which dictated organizational systems along the lines of those in the capitalist centres) and the objective of 'building a different (socialist) society', they gradually placed the accent on the former and drained the latter of any real content. This evolution, itself the product of a social dynamic, went together with the gradual formation of a new bourgeoisie. History has shown the Utopian character of that ostensibly socialist project, which in reality involved the construction of a state capitalism without capitalists in which the new bourgeoisie aspired to a 'normal' status comparable to that of the bourgeoisie in the capitalist world. At the same time, and quite logically, the new bourgeoisie put an end to delinking. This did not solve the problem of the historical backwardness of those countries; on the contrary, their reversion to a normal capitalism integrated into the world system directly led to their 're-peripherization'.

The erosion and eventual failure of 'developmentalist' projects in the Third World and 'actually existing socialism', combined with the deepening of capitalist globalization in the West's dominant centres, left the field wide open for mainstream discourse to claim that there was no alternative to capitalist globalization.

This constitutes a reactionary kind of Utopia. For, by submitting to the requirements of two-dimensional world market expansion, it becomes impossible to go beyond polarizing globalization. Self-reliant development and delinking therefore remain the essential response to the challenge of the new stage of polarizing capitalist globalization.

The new stage of capitalist expansion does not make the options of self-reliance and delinking less essential. Does the globalization that seems to be establishing itself through the redeployment of capitalism replace the opposition between self-reliant and peripheral development with a new form of globalized development? Does the rallying of a great majority of ruling classes to the project of neoliberal globalization indicate that there is no longer 'national capital' (and hence national bourgeoisies), and that the principal, most dynamic dimension of capital is already transnational or 'globalized'?

A lot of controversy surrounds these two questions, in an already abundant literature. But first it must be said that, even if the answer is 'yes' in both cases, the transnational capital at issue remains a monopoly of the Triad from which the countries of the East and South are excluded, and that in the latter there are only comprador bourgeoisies acting as transmission belts for transnational capital. That is indeed the picture today, in many if not all the countries of the East and South. But again it has to be asked whether it reflects a lasting change. If it does, then the 'new world' is only a new stage of an older imperialist expansion, still more violently polarizing than what has gone before. Will that be acceptable to, and accepted by, the dominated classes which endure massive impoverishment as well as sections of the ruling classes (or social and political forces with ambitions to become part of the ruling classes)?

In the new phase of capitalist globalization that we have entered, polarization manifests itself in new forms and through new mechanisms. From the Industrial Revolution until the middle of the last century, it manifested itself in the contrast between industrial and non-industrial countries. But industrialization of the peripheries, though highly uneven, has shifted the focus of the contrast or opposition to the issue of control over technology, finances, natural resources, communications and weapons. Does this mean – as the new expression of modernization theory would argue – that it is necessary to give up any idea of building a self-reliant economy, and to concentrate instead on the creation of highly efficient sectors capable of directly competing on the world market? To make such a choice would be to perpetuate the contrast between modernized segments (which soak up local resources) and unusable reserves that are left to rot. Any development worthy of the name would call for deep and extensive transformation, so that agriculture was able to clear a path for itself and a dense network of minor industries and towns could give indispensable support to the general progress of society. Of course, the step-by-step choices made within this general perspective would depend upon the outcome of social struggles: they would require the success of popular-democratic national alliances capable of breaking the mould of compradorization.

In the actual implementation of phased policies, it would also be necessary to develop concepts of social effectiveness in substitution for the capitalist concept of narrow market 'competitiveness'.

At the same time, we must not lose sight of the long-term universalist perspective. Preparatory steps would have to include a certain opening to the outside (selective imports), although this would have to be as tightly controlled as possible to ensure that it served, rather than hindered, the general progress of society. The need here would be for large regional groupings, especially in the peripheries but also elsewhere (as in Europe), and in this connection for priority targets to pave the way for modernization on a world scale that was gradually freed from the narrow criteria of capitalism. This would require, in turn, that the process went beyond narrowly economic arrangements and began to construct large political communities, as the building blocks of a polycentric world. Of course, delinking and self-reliant development on this scale would involve the negotiation of a web of relations among the major regions, in connection with commercial exchanges (including the terms of trade), the control and use of natural resources, financial issues and political-military security. It would thus entail reconstruction of the international political system, so that it liberated itself from hegemonism and embarked on the path of polycentrism.

The terms 'self-reliant development' and 'delinking' should be looked at again in the light of the perspectives outlined above.

V. Culturalism, ethnicism and the question of cultural resistance

Culturalism is a way of thinking based upon the notion that each 'culture' has a number of invariable, transhistorical specificities. Although these invariables find expression in various fields of social existence, such as religious beliefs or national traits, they operate in the same way that genes do in racist ideology and have the same power to transmit themselves across time.

Culturalism refuses to take seriously the evolution and change which clearly mark all aspects of social and cultural life, including aspects with a sacred quality. In its religious expressions, culturalism presents itself as 'fundamentalism' – actually more akin to stubborn (reactionary) prejudice than to good theological tradition. Certain 'postmodern' tendencies – those that, in the name of relativism, treat all 'beliefs' as irreducible truths on an equal level with one another – fuel the penchant for culturalism; while political or social currents such as American communitarianism, which give 'community identities' precedence over other dimensions of identity (class membership, ideological conviction, and so on), have their basis in culturalist thinking and reinforce its impact on the groups concerned.

The specificities in question are rarely spelled out, and when they are they usually prove to be paltry in the extreme. Ethnic culturalism may thus break up larger identities constructed in the course of history, aggressively splitting the 'nation' into ethnic groups, tribes into clans, and so on.

The recent emergence of powerful social movements based on religious or ethnic culturalism has its roots in the erosion of nationalist, class or 'developmental' legitimization of political rule. The irruption of ethnicism cannot be traced back to spontaneous demands on the part of communities on the ground, to their assertion of some 'irrepressible and primordial' identity against other communities. In reality, ethnicism has largely been constructed from the top down, by segments of ruling classes at bay who were seeking a new legitimacy for their rule. As the African proverb says, a fish starts to rot at the head. The social disasters resulting from neoliberal policies created the conditions in which ethnicism could play its decisive role in breaking up the USSR and Yugoslavia, unleashing war in the Horn of Africa (Ethiopia, Eritrea, Somalia), triggering massacres in Rwanda, and producing so-called tribal wars in Liberia and Sierra Leone. The mediocrity of many of the established regimes, the democratic deficit that made them incapable of handling diversity (whose reality as such is not in question), also played their part in such aberrations, which hit not only the most fragile regions of the world system but the very heart of Europe (Northern Ireland, the Basque country, Corsica, Northern Italy, and so on).

All these negative and often criminal expressions of culturalism were perfect material for manipulation. And manipulated they were, by the dominant forces in the system.

The phenomenon of cultural resistance is quite different. Capitalist globalization does not homogenize the world but, on the contrary, organizes it on the basis of ever stronger and more pronounced hierarchies. The peoples which are its victims are thereby deprived of active and equal participation in the shaping of the world.

By encouraging culturalist responses, globalization strategies make as much use as they can of diversity inherited from the past. At the same time, however, capitalist globalization imposes on the dominated some of the 'specificities' that characterize its dominant centres. It is a question not only of the English language or fast food, but also, for example, of the presidentialist political system that the United States exported to Latin America and is now exporting to Europe itself.

Any resistance on the part of the victims can therefore only be multi-dimensional, involving cultural resistance (if only implicitly) and an idea of diversity in the invention of the future (see Appendix VII).

French-speaking areas provide a good example of this positive cultural resistance, which it would be wrong to scorn. It already has to its credit various kinds of support for the cinema in French-speaking and other parts of the world, while the US movie oligopolies have vociferously denounced it as an illegitimate curb on their superprofits. Such resistance will remain limited in scope and liable to attack, however, so long as political leaders in the French-speaking countries treat culture as a special case and accept that the laws of the market should hold sway in every other area. The resistance should take place in many dimensions – in culture, to be sure, but also in politics and the running of the economy.

VI. Political Islam

The fatal mistake is to think that the emergence of Islamic political movements with a mass following is an inevitable result of the irruption of culturally and politically backward peoples on to the arena, who are incapable of understanding any language other than that of their almost atavistic obscurantism. Unfortunately, this mistake is widely disseminated in the simplifications of the mass media, and taken up in the pseudo-scientific discourse of Eurocentrism and 'orientalism'. It involves a prejudice that only the West could invent modernity, whereas the Muslim peoples have remained shut up within an immutable tradition that makes them incapable of grasping the scale of what needs to be changed.

Just like others around the world, the Muslim peoples and Islam have a particular history that includes various interpretations of the relationship between reason and faith, as well as a shifting pattern of mutual adaptation between society and religion. But the reality of that history is denied, not only by Eurocentric discourse, but also by contemporary movements that claim to speak in the name of Islam. They share the culturalist prejudice that the specific trajectory of their peoples and religion belongs to them as an intangible and transhistorical fact of nature incommensurable with any other. To the Eurocentrism of Westerners, contemporary political Islam opposes only an inverted Eurocentrism.

The emergence of movements laying claim to Islam is the expression of a violent revolt against the destructive effects of actually existing capitalism, and against the deceptions of the truncated modernity that goes together with it (see Appendix I). It is the expression of a perfectly legitimate revolt against a system that has nothing to offer the peoples in question.

The Islamic discourse presented as an alternative to capitalist modernity (and, without any distinction, to the experiments with modernity of historical socialism) is a political and in no way theological discourse. Often enough, the 'fundamentalist' label corresponds to no content of the discourse; only a number of Muslim intellectuals actually speak in such terms, and then more with Western public opinion in mind than because it comes to them spontaneously.

In this case, the Islam on offer is the enemy of any theology of liberation: political Islam calls for submission, not emancipation. The only reading that went in the direction of emancipation was that of the Sudanese Mahmoud Taha, and he was condemned to death and executed by the regime in Khartoum. No party belonging to the broad Islamic movement, whether 'radical' or 'moderate', has identified itself with Taha; nor has he been defended by any of the intellectuals who speak of an 'Islamic renaissance' or who merely wish for 'dialogue' with Islamic movements.

The heralds of an Islamic renaissance are not interested in theology, and they never refer to the major texts concerning it. What they understand by 'Islam' seems to be no more than a conventional social version reduced to formal respect for all ritual practices; it is a community to which one belongs by heritage, like an ethnic group, not by deep personal conviction. All that matters is the assertion of a 'collective identity'. Hence the term 'political Islam', which is used in the Arab countries to describe such movements, is certainly more accurate than 'Islamic fundamentalism'.

Modern political Islam was invented by orientalists in the service of British rule in India, and was then taken up as such by the Pakistani Abul Ala Al-Mawdudi. The aim was to 'prove' that Muslim believers are not allowed to live in a non-Muslim country, because Islam does not recognize any possible separation between the state and religion. What the orientalists failed to mention was that the thirteenth-century English would also have been unable to conceive of their living outside Christendom!

Mawdudi argued that, since power emanates from God and God alone (*wilaya al faqih*), citizens have no right to legislate and the state's only task is to apply the law handed down for all time (the *sharia*). Joseph de Maistre wrote similar things when he accused the French Revolution of the crime of dreaming up modern democracy and individual emancipation.

In its dismissal of the concept of emancipatory modernity, political Islam rejects the very principle of democracy – the right of a society to build its own future through the freedom to legislate for itself. The principle of *shura*, which political Islam claims to be the Islamic form of democracy, is no such thing, as it forbids innovation (*ibda*) and at most accepts some degree of interpretation of tradition (*ijtihad*). In fact, *shura* is only one of the many kinds of consultation that one encounters in all pre-modern, pre-democratic societies. It is true that interpretation has sometimes been the vehicle for real change, imposed by new historical exigencies. But its very principle – rejection of any right to break with the past – is a barrier to the modern struggle for social transformation and democracy. Hence the alleged parallel between Islamic parties (whether radical or moderate, since both adhere to the same 'anti-modernist' principles in the name of Islamic specificity) and the Christian Democratic parties of modern Europe has no validity, although the US media and diplomatic institutions constantly play it up in order to legitimize the support they might feel called upon to give to 'Islamicist' regimes. Christian Democracy is part of modernity: it accepts the fundamental concept of creative democracy as well as the essence of secularization. Political Islam rejects modernity. Or, this is what it proclaims, without having the capacity to understand what it means.

The Islam on offer certainly does not deserve to be called 'modern'. Arguments to the contrary, such as those put forward by the friends of dialogue, are platitudinous in the extreme: for example, that the propagandists of political Islam use cassette recorders, or that they come from 'educated' groups such as engineers. Besides, the discourse of such movements often betrays no contact with anything other than Wahhabi Islam, which rejects the whole legacy of interaction between historical Islam and Greek philosophy and is content to regurgitate the dull writings of the most reactionary of medieval theologians – Ibn Taymiya. Although some trumpet this as a 'return to the sources' (or even to the Islam of the age of the Prophet), it is actually a return to ideas that had their day two hundred years ago, those of a society already arrested in its development for several centuries.

Contrary to a sadly widespread misconception, today's political Islam is not a reaction to the alleged abuses of secularism. For no Muslim society of modern times – except in the former Soviet Union – has ever been genuinely secular, still less stricken by the bold innovations of an aggressively 'atheistic' regime. The semi-modern state of Kemalist Turkey, Nasserite Egypt or Ba'athist Syria and Iraq was content to tame people of religion (as others had before it) by foisting upon them a discourse that legitimized its own political options. The elements of a secular idea existed only in a number of critical intellectual circles. It had little purchase on the state power, whose nationalist projects sometimes involved a retreat on this score – a disturbing trend, already begun in the time of Nasser, which marked a break with the policies of the Wafd since 1919. Perhaps the explanation is simply that, in rejecting democracy, the regimes in question were led to seek a replacement for it in a 'homogenized community', the dangers of which have now spread to the declining democracy of the West itself (see Appendix VII).

Political Islam proposes to round things off by combining a nakedly conservative theocratic order with a Mamluk-style political regime. The reference is to a military ruling caste that, until two centuries ago, placed itself above the law (by claiming to know nothing other than the *sharia*), monopolized the benefits of economic activity, and agreed in the name of 'realism' to occupy a subaltern position within the capitalist globalization of the time. It is a historical analogy that immediately springs to the mind of any observer of the region's debased post-nationalist regimes and their twin brothers, the new 'Islamic' forces already in power or bidding to replace them.

In this fundamental respect, there is scarcely any difference between the supposedly 'radical' currents of political Islam and those that would prefer to present a 'moderate' face. The projects of the two are essentially the same.

The case of Iran is no exception to the rule, despite the initial confusion when the rise of an Islamicist movement coincided with the struggle against the Shah's socially reactionary and politically pro-American dictatorship. Early on, the excesses of the theocratic regime were offset by its anti-imperialist positions, which gave it internal legitimacy as well as a powerful resonance beyond the frontiers of Iran. But gradually it revealed that it was incapable of meeting the challenge of innovative economic and social development. The 'turban dictatorship' of the clergy that replaced the 'helmeted dictatorship' of the generals and technocrats – to use terms often employed in Iran itself – ended in a stunning dilapidation of the country's economic apparatuses. Iran – which used to pride itself on being a 'second Korea' – is today among the countries of the 'Fourth World'. The insensitivity of regime hardliners to the problems facing the popular classes is at the root of the emergence of self-styled reformers. But, although their project might soften the rigours of theocratic dictatorship, it will not depart from the constitutional principle of *wilaya al faqih* underlying the monopoly of power by a regime that has come to renounce its anti-imperialist postures and to rejoin the banal comprador world of peripheral capitalism. The system of political Islam has reached a dead-end in Iran. The political and social struggles on which the Iranian people has now openly embarked will sooner or later lead them to reject the whole idea of *wilaya al faqih*, which places the clergy's collegial rule above all the institutions of political and civil society. That is the condition for its success.

In the end, political Islam is nothing more than an adaptation to the subaltern status of comprador capitalism. Its supposedly 'moderate' variants are thus probably the main danger facing the peoples in question, since the violence of the 'radicals' serves only to destabilize the state and to pave the way for a new comprador regime. The farsighted support that US and other Triad diplomats give to this solution is perfectly consistent with their aim of imposing the globalized liberal order in the service of dominant capital.

The two discourses of globalized liberal capitalism and political Islam do not conflict with each other but are perfectly complementary. The American-style 'communitarian' ideologies which are so much part of the Zeitgeist seek to obliterate social consciousness and social struggles, entirely replacing them with 'collective identities'. This plays straight into the hands of capital's strategy for domination, because it transfers struggles from the realm of real social contradictions to the absolute, transhistorical realm of the supposedly cultural imagination. Political Islam is, precisely, a form of 'communitarianism'.

The foreign-policy establishments of the G-7 powers, particularly the United States, know what they are doing when they choose to back political Islam. They did it in Afghanistan, hailing its Islamicists as freedom fighters against what they called communist dictatorship (in reality, a modernizing national-populist project of enlightened despotism, which had the audacity to open schools to girls). And they continue to do it today, from Egypt to Algeria. They know that the rule of political Islam has the great virtue of rendering popular classes powerless, and hence of ensuring that their compradorization can proceed without difficulty.

With its characteristic cynicism, Washington knows how to profit twice over. For it can happily exploit the aberrations of its sponsored regimes – aberrations built into their programme from the start – whenever it is useful for imperialism to intervene with as much brutality as it takes. The 'savagery' attributed to popular forces, who are actually the first victims of political Islam, serves as a pretext to spread 'Islamophobia' and thus to gain wider acceptance for the 'global apartheid' that is the logical and necessary result of an ever more polarizing process of capitalist expansion.

The only political Islamic movements that the G-7 powers condemn without reservation are those which, because of the objective local situation, form part of an anti-imperialist struggle: Hezbollah in Lebanon, Hamas in Palestine. That is no accident.

VII. Inherited diversity and future-oriented diversity

All human societies have a history in the course of which they have undergone either gradual minor changes within the logic of an existing system, or major qualitative changes of the system itself. Protagonists in the second type of change – which we may call revolution – have always declared their resolve to take over nothing from the past: the Enlightenment proposed to destroy the *ancien régime* root and branch; the Paris Commune and the socialist revolutions wanted to make 'a clean break with the past'; Maoism set out to write a new history for China 'on a blank sheet of paper'.

In reality, however, it has never been possible to wipe out the past completely. Some of its components have always been incorporated or transformed in the service of a different logic; others have survived as means of resisting and slowing down change. The specific combination of new and old in each historical trajectory under consideration is the first source of (partly inherited) diversity. Here, a good aspect on which to focus is the way in which secularism is conceived and practised in societies that have entered capitalist modernity. Taking France as a reference, we can say that the more radical the bourgeois revolution, the more radical the degree of secularism; when capitalist transformation proceeded by way of compromises between the new bourgeoisie and the old ruling classes (as it did almost everywhere else in Europe), secularization did not exclude the survival of some religious dimension in public behaviour. Some national Churches (in the Protestant countries) were actually moulded in the new capitalist system, and have survived as such even if they have lost the coercive power they used to enjoy before modernity. Thus the separation between state and religion, which defines the concept of secularization, is asserted with varying degrees of formality. Let us note in passing that modernity involves the separation of state and religion, not negation of the latter. 'State atheism' (only ever really attempted in the Soviet Union) functions somewhat like a state religion: it violates the basic principle of modernity, that philosophical, religious, political, ideological and scientific opinions are a matter for the free judgement of individuals.

On the other hand, insistence on the need to recognize and respect inherited diversity – which is a feature of the dominant discourse today – most often serves to legitimize policies for the strengthening of conservative regimes (as we have seen in the European debate on secularism). What is the purpose of a reference to Christian values in a declaration of rights? Why not also refer to the role of Europe's non-religious tradition in the rise of modern humanism?

Many other areas of social reality are marked by diversity, and the variety of languages and religions indicates that its roots often lie in the remote past. Diversity has survived even when its constituent elements have changed in the course of history.

Does the existence of several nations or cultures within a modern state – that is, a state made up of citizens with an equal right to build their future – pose a problem for the practice of democracy? Does it represent a challenge? Quite different approaches are taken to this question.

Those who fiercely support national and cultural homogeneity, seeing it as the only way to define the common identity necessary for the exercise of civil rights, do not hesitate to propose either the 'forced assimilation' of recalcitrant groups (often minorities) or, if they are democrats, the physical separation of ethnic groups and the partition of the state. Meanwhile, as second best, they will accept only the 'toleration' of diversity – the inverted commas being there to remind us that we tolerate only what we do not love ('you've got to tolerate your mother-in-law'). This leads to the American idea of a multicultural society, although in fact it is always a *hierarchical* multiplicity within the national system. The essential point is an inherited communal identity that cannot be the object of personal choice. The assertion of a 'right to difference' comes at the price of denying equal status to its complementary opposite: the right to similarity and equal treatment, and, more generally, the inalienable right of individuals to choose not to be defined by their membership of an inherited community.

Emancipatory modernity is based on a quite different concept of democracy, one that involves both strict equality of rights and duties (including the creation of conditions for this to be a reality) and respect for differences. Respect is a stronger term than tolerance. It implies that state policies create the conditions for equality in spite of diversity – for example, by opening schools that teach in various languages. Here 'in spite of diversity' means only that there is no attempt to freeze it; history is left to do its work, possibly through assimilation that is no longer forced. The policy goal is that diversity does not end in the juxtaposition of closed, and therefore mutually hostile, communities.

It scarcely needs to be recalled that various socialist currents, whether influenced by Austro-Marxism or Bolshevism, have advocated this kind of tactful approach; nor that modern classes (working classes and significant bourgeois fractions) have tended to favour large states in which the existence of several nations is a source of wealth, not of impoverishing oppression. Supporters of 'homogeneous communities', on the other hand, have tended to come from older classes and traditional peasantries.

This helps us appreciate the regression, the veritable betrayal of emancipatory modernity, which is involved in the currently fashionable insistence on 'communities'. Such discourse goes together with a degradation of democracy and a denial of the multiple dimensions of identity (not only nationality, but also social class, gender, ideological and perhaps religious affiliation, and so on). The Zeitgeist no longer recognizes citizens who are at once individual and multidimensional; it substitutes 'people' ('consumers' for economists, TV viewers for politicians), who can thus be manipulated both as amorphous individuals and as subjects of inherited and imposed communities.

Inherited diversity poses a problem, because it is there. But if one becomes obsessed with it, one loses sight of other, more interesting forms of diversity that the invention of the future necessarily throws up. These are incomparably more interesting because they derive from the very concept of emancipatory democracy and the unfinished modernity that goes together with it.

There is a need for policies to ensure that the freedom of individuals does not detract from their equality and that the two values can advance hand in hand: to say this is to say that history is not over, that systemic change is necessary, and that we have to struggle for it to lead towards real emancipation. How could anyone argue, then, that theirs is the only path or formula corresponding to this need?

The creative Utopias that may afford a real perspective for the crystallization of struggles have always found their legitimacy in a number of different value systems – from various kinds of secular humanism to others with a religious inspiration (theologies of liberation). The systems of social analysis that are their necessary complement also draw their inspiration from a variety of scientific social theories. Strategies to achieve real progress in the agreed direction cannot be the monopoly of any one organization.

Given the incomplete nature of our knowledge, these types of diversity in the invention of the future are not only inevitable but positively welcome for anyone who does not rest on a dogmatic and empty certainty.

VIII. Capitalism and the agrarian question

All societies prior to capitalism were peasant societies, and the various logics governing their agriculture were all alien to the one that defines capitalism (maximization of capitalist profit). Historical capitalism took shape in large-scale commerce and then in the new forms of industry, before eventually launching into the transformation of agriculture. In the present day, half of humanity still lives in the agrarian world of the peasantry, but its production is divided between two sectors quite different in their economic and social natures.

Capitalist agriculture, governed by the principle of the profitability of capital, is located almost exclusively in North America, Europe, the Southern Cone of Latin America, and Australia. It employs no more than a few dozen million farmers (no longer 'peasants'), whose large landholdings and almost exclusive access to mechanization mean that they can achieve output between 10,000 and 20,000 quintals of cereal-equivalent per worker/year.

Peasant agriculture encompasses nearly a half of humanity – three billion human beings. It is in turn divided between those who have benefited from the Green Revolution (fertilizer, pesticide and seed selection, though still little mechanization) and achieve 100 to 500 quintals per worker, and those who continue to operate with older methods and remain stuck around 10 quintals per head of the active population.

The productivity gap between the best-equipped agriculture and the poorest peasant agriculture has shot up from 10:1 before 1940 to 2,000: 1 today. In other words, the rate of productivity growth in agriculture has largely exceeded that in other areas of the economy, bringing with it a fall in real prices from 5 to 1.

In these conditions, to accept the principle of competition for agricultural and food products (as the WTO demands) is to accept that billions of 'uncompetitive' producers will be eliminated in the brief historical space of a few dozen years. What will become of these billions who, though already mostly the poorest of the poor, have in the past been able to feed themselves well or badly? (Badly in a third of cases – three-quarters of the world's undernourished living in a rural context.) No reasonably competitive development of industry that is likely to take place in the next fifty years, even in the fabulous scenario of 7 per cent annual growth for three-quarters of humanity, could absorb as much as a third of these human reserves. This means that capitalism is by its nature incapable of solving the peasant question, and that all it offers is the prospect of a shantytown planet with five billion 'excess' inhabitants. The optimistic doctrine of 'creative destruction', which is supposed to be an intrinsic feature of capitalism, clearly falls down here. It was accepted by historical socialism, as can see from Karl Kautsky's *The Agrarian Question* (first published in German in 1898), the bible of the Second International and even of Leninism, though not of Maoism. But, although modern urban development and mass emigration to the Americas soaked up Europe's peasant reserve, capitalism today does not permit a similar evolution in the peripheries of its world system. This is one of the main factors in the polarization that characterizes the system (see Appendix IV).

So, what is to be done? It is necessary to accept that peasant agriculture will continue to exist in the twenty-first century that is our foreseeable future – not for romantic reasons, but simply because a solution to the problem will require going beyond the logic of capitalism, in a long transition to world socialism stretching over a century or more. Policies must therefore be devised to regulate relations between 'the market' and peasant agriculture. Specifically adapted to national and regional levels, these relations must protect each country's output by delinking internal prices from world market prices, so that it has the food security it needs to neutralize the imperialist use of food as a weapon; and they must enable the slow but sure growth of productivity in peasant agriculture that will make it possible to control the transfer of population from countryside to towns. At the level of what is known as the world market, regulation should probably take place through interregional agreements – for instance, between Europe on the one hand, and Africa, the Arab countries, China and India on the other. This would correspond to what is required for development that integrates rather than excludes. Marcel Mazoyer has developed at greater length this analysis, which I have been able only to touch upon here (see Mazoyer and Roudart 1997). Of course, the combined development of peasant agriculture and modern industry should be part of a perspective in which free rein is given to the social imagination, for it is hard indeed to conceive how the model of waste peculiar to capitalism could be extended to a world population around ten billion.

Select bibliography

Other writings by the author

To keep the main text as tight as possible, I have placed some supporting arguments in appendices (referred to in this section) and refer the reader to some of my recent writings on the main themes in this book.

Theme 1: Capitalism, basic critical concepts

Samir Amin, *Critique de l'air du temps*, Paris: L'Harmattan, 1997: i) The concept of underdetermination in history (pp. 47–61); ii) Critique of 'pure economics' (pp. 125–36); iii) Critique of the dominant ideology of the political economy of capitalism (pp. 27–46) and of postmodernism (pp. 87–113).

Specters of Capitalism: a Critique of Current International Fashions, New York: Monthly Review Press, 1998.

Appendix II: Imaginary capitalism and actually existing capitalism.

Theme 2: The world capitalist system and polarization

Delinking: Towards a Polycentric World, London: Zed Books, 1990.

Maldevelopment: Anatomy of a Global Failure, London: Zed Books, 1990.

Les défis de la mondialisation, Paris: L'Harmattan, 1996: i) Re-compradorization of the Arab world (pp. 249–60); ii) Origins of the African catastrophe (pp. 261–78); iii) China (pp. 225–36) and Russia (pp. 237–48) facing the challenges of globalization.

Le monde arabe, état des lieux, état des luttes (L'Harmattan, forthcoming).

Capitalism in the Age of Globalization, London: Zed Books, 1997, esp. Chapter 1.

Appendix IV: The development paradigm (the self-reliant option and delinking have still to be addressed in a perspective of popular development).

Theme 3: Economic aspects of the present crisis and its management

La gestion capitaliste de la crise, Paris: L'Harmattan, 1995. (This work analyses the nature of the crisis and the functions of the main institutions that manage the world capitalist economy: the World Bank, the International Monetary Fund, the GATT and now the World Trade Organization, the United Nations Organization, at different stages of the contemporary period.)

Les défis de la mondilisation, Paris: L'Harmattan, 1996, esp. pp. 127–87.

Capitalism in the Age of Globalization, Chapter 2.

Theme 4: Political dimensions of the contemporary world crisis

For issues relating to the drift of liberal globalization into militarization and chaos, see my earlier works (written before the Gulf War): 'La géo-politique de la région Méditerranée-Golfe', in Samir Amin et al., *Les enjeux stratégiques en Méditerraneé*, Paris: L'Harmattan, 1992, pp. 11–112.

The Empire of Chaos, New York: Monthly Review Press, 1992.

On the thesis that Europe's liberal option necessarily entailed subordination to US hegemonic strategies within a perspective of militarized globalization: *L'Hégémonisme des États-Unis et l'effacement du projet européen*, Paris: L'Harmattan, 2000 (written before the war in Kosovo).

On the concept and the reality of hegemonism: *Les défis de la mondialisation*, pp. 85–95.

On the critique of the Soviet model: *Re-reading the Postwar Period: An Intellectual Itinerary*, New York: Monthly Review Press, 1994, Chapter 7.

Theme 5: Culturalism and ethnicism

Eurocentrism, London: Zed Books, 1989.

L'ethnie à l'assaut des nations, Paris: L'Harmattan, 1994. (This work deals with the conjunction of local ruling-class strategic options with the strategies of imperialism to break up certain countries. Yugoslavia and Ethiopia are taken as cases for study. The contemporary debate on the concept of the nation is reviewed in a conclusion: 'Nation des Lumières ou Nations des brumes?', pp. 131–54.)

Capitalism in the Age of Globalization, Chapter 4.

'Le délire ethniciste', *Histoire et Anthropologie* No. 12, 1996 (University of Strasbourg).

On the religious and ethical dimensions of contemporary issues, see: *Matérialisme historique et éthique*, Brussels: Centre Oecuménique, 1992; 'Judaisme, Christianisme, Islam', *Social Compass* 46/4, 1999.

Appendix V: Culturalism and ethnicism.

Appendix VI: Political Islam.

Theme 6: Obsolescent capitalism

For an early interpretation of the present crisis in terms of the deep structural crisis associated with the obsolescence of capitalism: 'Révolution ou décadence?', *Classe et Nation* (1979), pp. 238–45.

Critique de l'air du temps; the withering away of the law of value and problems of the transition of communism (pp. 63–85).

'Quelles alternatives à la dimension destructive de l'accumulation du capital?', *Alternatives Sud* 8/2, 2001.

Appendix III: The destructive dimensions of capital accumulation.

Theme 7: Questions concerning the transition beyond capitalism

Les défis de la mondialisation, pp. 309–43.

Appendix I: The challenges of modernity.

Appendix VII: Inherited diversity and future-oriented diversity.

Appendix VIII: Capitalism and the agrarian question.

On the contribution of social theory in the Third World to the renewal of world thought, see *Re-reading the Postwar Period: An Intellectual Itinerary*.

Other authors

Aglietta, Michel, *Le capitalisme de demain*, Notes de la fondation Saint-Simon no. 101, 1998.

Aiguo, Lu, *China and the Global Economy since 1840*, New York: St. Martin's Press, 2000.

Albert, Michel, *Capitalisme contre capitalisme*, Paris: Seuil, 1991.

Amin, Samir and Ali El Kenz, *Le partenariat euro-méditerranéen* (forthcoming).

Amin, Samir and Giovanni Arrighi, André Gunder Frank and Immanuel Wallerstein, *La crise ... quelle crise?*, Paris: La Découverte, 1982.

Anwar Raja, *The Tragedy of Afghanistan*, London: Verso, 1988.

Arrighi, Giovanni, *The Long Twentieth Century*, London: Verso, 1994.

Artus, Patrick, *La nouvelle économie*, Paris: La Découverte, 2001.

Badie, Bertrand, *La fin des territoires*, Paris: Fayard, 1995.

Baran, Paul and Paul Sweezy, *Monopoly Capital*, New York: Monthly Review Press, 1966.

Beaud, Michel, *Le système national mondial liberalisé*, Paris: La Découverte, 1987.

Beinstein, Jorge, *La larga crisis de la economia global*, Buenos Aires: Corregidor, 1999.

Bello, Walden, Nicola Bullard, Kamal Malhotra et al., *Global Finance: New Thinking on Regulating Speculative Capital Markets*, London: Zed Books, 2000.

Biel, Robert, *The New Imperialism*, London: Zed Books, 2000.

Boltanski, Luc and Eve Chiapello, *Le nouvel esprit du capitalisme*, Paris: Gallimard, 1999.

Bowles, S., D. Gordon and T. Weisskopf, *Beyond the Waste Land: A Democratic Alternative to Economic Decline*, Garden City: Anchor/Doubleday, 1983.

Boyer, Robert, Yves Saillard et al., *Théories de la régulation*, Paris: La Découverte, 1995.

Braverman, Harry, *Labor and Monopoly Capital*, New York: Monthly Review Press, 1974.

Brenner, Robert, 'The economics of global turbulence', *New Left Review*, May–June 1998.

Breton, Philippe, *L'Utopie de la communication*, Paris: La Découverte, 1995.

Bukharin, Nikolai, *Economic Theory of the Leisure Class*, New York: Monthly Review Press, 1972.

Burkett, Paul and Martin Hart-Landsberg, *Development, Crisis and Class Struggle: Learning from Japan and East Asia*, New York: St. Martin's Press, 2000.

Byres, Terence et al., *The Indian Economy: Major Debates since Independence*, Oxford: Oxford University Press, 1998.

Castells, Manuel, *The Rise of the Network Society*, Oxford: Blackwell, 1996.

Castoriadis, Cornelius, *The Imaginary Institution of Society*, Cambridge: Polity, 1987.

— *La montée de l'insignifiance*, Paris: Seuil, 1994.

Chesnais, François, *Tobin or not Tobin*, Paris: L'Esprit frappeur, 1999.

— *La mondialisation du capital*, Paris: Syros, 1997.

— *La mondialisation financière*, Paris: Syros, 1996.

Chesnais, François, G. Duménil, D. Lévy and I. Wallerstein, *Une nouvelle phase du capitalisme*, Paris: Syllepse, 2001.

Chesnais, François, T. Noctiummes and J. P. Page, *Réflexions sur la guerre en Yugoslavie*, Paris: L'Esprit frappeur, 1999.

Chun, Lin, *Situating China*, Mexico City: UNAM-Mexico, 1994.

— *China* (forthcoming).

Coker, Christopher, *The Twilight of the West*, Boulder, CO: Westview Press, 1998.

Cordelier, Serge et al., *La mondialisation au-delà des mythes*, Paris: La Découverte, 2000.

Dasgupta, Biplab, *'Structural Adjustment', Global Trade and the New Political Economy of Development*, London: Zed Books, 1998.

Debord, Guy, *La société du spectacle*, Paris: Champ Libre, 1971; trans. as *The Society of the Spectacle*, New York: Zone Books, 1994.

Delaunay, Jean-Claude et al., *Le capitalisme contemporain: des théorisations nouvelles*, Paris: L'Harmattan, 2001.

— *Le capitalisme contemporain: questions de fond*, Paris: L'Harmattan, 2001.

Diouf, Makhtar, A. Nidaye, B. Founou and S. Amin, *Afrique et Nord–Sud, co-développement ou gestion du conflit?* (forthcoming).

Dorronsoro, Gilles, *La révolution afghane*, Paris: Karthala, 2000.

Duménil, G. and D. Lévy, *La dynamique du capital, un siècle d'économie américaine*, Paris: Presses Universitaires de France, 1996.

— *Crise et sortie de crise, ordre et désordres néo-libéraux*, Paris: Presses Universitaires de France, 2000.

Duménil, G., D. Lévy et al., *Le triangle actuel: Crise, mondialisation, financiarisation*, Paris: Presses Universitaires de France (Actuel Marx), 1999.

Ebel, Robert and Rajan Menon (eds), *Energy and Conflict in Central Asia and the Caucasus*, New York: Rowan and Littlefield, 2000.

George, Susan: *The Lugano Report: On Preserving Capitalism in the Twenty-First Century*, London: Pluto Press, 1999.

Gill, Louis, *Économie mondiale et impérialisme*, Montreal: Boréal, 1983.

Gillman, J. M., *The Falling Rate of Profit*, London: Dennis Dobson, 1958.

Gombeaud, Jean-Louis and Maurice Décaillot, *Le retour de la très grande depression*, Paris: Économica, 1997.

Guerrien, Bernard, *L'Économie néoclassique*, Paris: La Découverte, 1996.

Guillebeaud, Jean-Claude, *La trahison des Lumières*, Paris: Seuil, 1995.

Guyatt, Nicholas, *Another American Century*, London: Zed Books, 2000.

Harnecker, Martha, *La izquierda en el umbral del siglo XXI*, Havana, 1999.

Hobsbawm, Eric, *On the Edge of the New Century*, New York: New Press, 2000.

Hochraich, Diana, *L'Asie du miracle à la crise*, Paris: Complexe, 1999.

Hoogvelt, Ankie, *Globalization and the Postcolonial World: The New Political Economy of Development*, Baltimore, MD: Johns Hopkins University Press, 2001.

Huntington, Samuel P., *The Clash of Civilizations and the Remaking of the World Order*, New York: Simon & Schuster, 1996.

Israel, Giorgio, *La mathématisation du réel*, Paris: Seuil, 1995.

Ivekovic, Ivan, *Ethnic and Regional Conflicts in Yugoslavia and Transcaucasia*, Ravenna: Longo, 2000.

Kunio, Yoshikara, *The Rise of Ersatz Capitalism in South-East Asia*, Manila: University Press, 1993.

Lang, Tim and Colin Hines, *The New Protectionism*, London: Earthscan, 1993.

Lipietz, Alain, *La société en sablier*, Paris: La Découverte, 1996.

Mandel, Ernest, *Late Capitalism*, London: Verso, 1978.

Marais, Hein, *Southern African Cooperation, Reinforcing the Mould* (forthcoming).

Massiah, Gustave, *Le G7 en 1993, le crépuscule d'un mythe?*, Paris: CEDETIM, 1993.

Mazoyer, Marcel and Laurence Roudart, *Histoire des agricultures du monde*, Paris: Seuil, 1997.

Michalet, Charles Albert, *Le capitalisme mondial*, Paris: Presses Universitaires de France, 1985.

Monthly Review, *In Defense of History*, 47(3), 1995.

Negri, Antonio and Michael Hardt: *Empire*, Cambridge, MA: Harvard University Press, 2000.

Parboni, Riccardo, *The Dollar and Its Rivals*, London: Verso, 1981.

Passet, René, *L'Illusion néo-libérale*, Paris: Fayard, 2000.

Plihon, Dominique, *Le nouveau capitalisme*, Paris: Flammarion, 2001.

Reich, Robert, *The Work of Nations: Preparing Ourselves for 21st-Century Capitalism*, New York: Vintage Books, 1992.

Rifkin, Jeremy, *The Age of Access: The New Culture of Hypercapitalism*, New York: Putnam's, 2000.

— *The End of Work: The Decline of the Global Labour Force and the Dawn of the Post-Market Era*, New York: Putnam's, 1995.

Robinson, William and Jerry Harris, 'Towards a Global Ruling Class?', *Science and Society*, 61(1), 2000.

Sachs, Ignacy, *L'Éco-développement, stratégies pour le XXIe siècle*, Paris: Syros, 1997.

Samary, Catherine, *La déchirure yougoslave*, Paris: L'Harmattan, 1994.

Shiva, Vandana, *Stolen Harvest: The Hijacking of the Global Food Supply*, Cambridge, MA: South End Press, 2000.

Sundaram, Jomo et al., *Tigers in Trouble*, London: Zed Books, 1998.

Taguieff, Pierre André, *L'Effacement de l'avenir*, Paris: Galilée, 2000.

Todd, Emmanuel, *L'Illusion économique*, Paris: Gallimard, 1998.

Tronti, Mario, *La politique au crépuscule*, Paris: L'Éclat, 2000.

Vakaloukis, Michel, *Le capitalisme postmoderne*, Paris: Presses Universitaires de France (Actuel Marx), 2001.

Valladao, Alfredo, *The Twenty-First Century Will Be American*, London: Verso, 1996.

Vercellone, Carlo, *La Mafia comme expression endogène de l'accumulation du capital*, Matisse University of Paris 1, 2001–58.

Vichnevski, Anatoli, *La faucille et le rouble*, Paris: Galilée, 2000.

Volle, Michel, *E-économie*, Paris: Économica, 2000.

Wallerstein, Immanuel, *After Liberalism*, New York: New Press, 1995.

Warren, Bill, *Imperialism, Pioneer of Capitalism*, London: New Left Books, 1980.

Wilke, Joachim, *Les tourments de la raison*, Paris: L'Harmattan, 1995.

Various authors, *The World We are Entering 2000–2050*, Luxembourg: Institute for International and European Studies (forthcoming).

Index

Central Asia, war in, 87–91
Central Intelligence Agency (CIA), 84, 88
centre–periphery relationship, 2, 13, 18, 19, 21, 25, 44, 52, 62, 69, 76, 77, 92, 93, 94, 96, 107, 122, 131
chaos, periods of, 12
Chaplin, Charlie, 10
Chechens, 83, 88
China, 7, 9, 10, 17, 18, 20, 62, 67, 68, 75, 81, 83, 87, 89–90, 105, 107, 108, 109, 110, 130, 132, 134, 145, 162, 171, 176; development of, 110–11; market socialism in, 92
Chinese revolution, 4, 59
Chrysler-Daimler, 71
churches, moulded in capitalist system, 172
citizenship, 158; democratic invention of, 118
clash of civilizations, 104, 123, 124, 125, 129, 139
class society, 20, 54, 55
Clinton, Bill, 80, 99, 101, 118, 125
Cold War, 66, 74, 105
collective identities, 170
collective triad imperialism, 68–72, 74–91, 93, 94, 100, 101, 110, 117, 124, 127, 140
colonialism, 66
commodification of life, 155–7
communism, 22, 24, 30, 47, 103, 137; building of, 25 see also anti-communism
communitarian identity, 74, 113, 114, 117, 123, 158, 173; American, 165, 170
community development, 114
competition: changes in nature of, 71; glorification of, 39
compradorization, 164
contradictions, 2, 48, 76, 139, 155; fundamental, 25
convergence, within diversity, 140–7
creative destruction, 94, 175
crisis, economic, unfolding of, 42–7
Croatia, 86
Cuban Revolution, 58
cultural identities, 35

cultural resistance, 165–6; in French-speaking areas, 166
culturalism, 114–15, 124, 165–6; anti-Western, 144; as antithesis of democracy, 115

debt, 17, 156; cancellation of, 133; repayment of, 94; rescheduling of, 108
decentralization, regional, 38
deflationary spiral, 46
deindustrialization, 107
delinking, 63, 68, 130, 131, 158, 159, 160, 162, 163, 164, 176
demilitarization, of the UN, 133
democracy, 14, 25, 61, 74, 99, 100, 105, 115, 133, 134, 138, 139, 141, 146, 148, 150, 161, 165, 168, 172; American, 58, 123; and market, 35; as luxury, 32; as means to socialism, 32–41; as precondition of development, 36; as rational principle, 33; Christian, 168; decline of, 93, 95, 173; emancipatory, 149, 174; erosion of, 126; low-intensity, 37, 118, 138, 141, 146, 149; rejection of, 169; subordinate to market, 34; threat to, 112–19
demographic growth: in Europe, 7; in peripheries, 14
dependency, 67; theory of, 31
deregulation, 2, 16, 123, 155
desarollismo, 32
development, 51, 129, 136, 152–3; concept of, 4, 18, 65; correlation with democracy, 35; dependent, 161; ideology of, 162; paradigm of, 158–64
difference, right to, 173
diversity, 137, 146, 166, 172; convergence within, 140–7; destruction of biodiversity, 156; future-oriented, 171–4; inherited, 171–4; management of, 114; respect for, 113, 173
division of labour, international, 96
dollar, 104, 107, 127; role of, 79
drugs, market for, 157

Durban anti-racism congress, 134–5

East–West divide, 66
Eastern Europe: integration of, 131;
 Latin Americanization of, 111
ecology *see* environmental issues
economic determinism, 42
economics: as science, 22; pure, 16,
 43, 137, 150, 152, 154;
 reductionism in, 2
Egypt, 83, 88, 109
l'Enarchie, 38
Enlightenment, 32–3, 39; grand
 narratives, retreat of, 74
environmental issues, 16, 53, 133,
 142, 144, 150, 154
equality, value of, 36–7
equilibrium, 23, 26, 28, 47, 74, 92,
 112
d'Estaing, Giscard, 96
ethnicity, 115, 122, 165–6, 173
euro, 79
eurocentrism, 24, 31, 59, 167
Europe, 95, 100, 111, 112, 127;
 military force of, 104, 105; on the
 left, 131; relation to US, 106 *see
 also* Eastern Europe
European project, 92, 128, 130;
 obliteration of, 76–7, 100, 101–6
European space, creation of, 60–1
European Union (EU), 19, 64, 65, 70,
 78, 80, 100, 109, 131; Cotonou
 Convention, 108
Eurotunnel, shareholders'
 association, 48
exports, as percentage of GDP, 42

feminism, 88, 142
Fifth Republic, 37
fin de siècle crisis, 15–17
finance capital, domination of, 68
financial hypertrophy, 43, 50, 51
financialization, 47–52, 123; process
 of, 67
France, 10, 37, 38, 39, 43, 52, 60, 88,
 102, 108, 111
Frank, A.G., 66
French revolution, 59, 112, 168, 172
Friedman, Thomas, 98

fundamentalism, religious, 144, 151,
 167, 168

G-7, 42, 43, 84, 85, 97, 108, 115, 121,
 128, 134, 171
Galbraith, J.K., 48
De Gaulle, Charles, 60, 103
GDP, growth of, 42
gender issues, 141–2
genocide, logic of obsolescent
 capitalism, 128
geometry of class conflict, 139–40
geometry of international conflicts,
 106–12
George, Susan, 121, 157
Germany, 9, 10, 11, 52, 60, 62, 80, 87,
 102, 105, 107, 109, 111, 125
globalization, 15, 17–21, 43, 44, 47,
 61, 76, 77, 79, 86, 99–100, 101,
 105, 121, 123, 134, 142, 144, 153,
 163, 166, 170; critique of, 141;
 financial, 8, 63; multipolarity of,
 130; of struggles, 133
gold standard, 10
governance: global, 113; good, 35,
 115
Green movement, 113
Green Revolution, 175
Group of 77, 75, 134
growth, 46, 66, 80, 93
Gulf War, 1, 70, 85–6, 108, 123

Hamas, 171
hegemony: compromises within, 78;
 of the left, 121 *see also* US,
 hegemony of
Hezbollah, 171
Hinduism, 144
historical materialism, 24
history, end of, 7, 12, 23, 24, 68, 139,
 151
Hong Kong, 17, 43, 132
Hoogvelt, Ankie, 94
human rights, 99, 116
humanist globalism, 139
humanitarian intervention, 61
Huntington, Samuel, 123
Hussein, Saddam, 84, 85

Ibn Taymiya, 169

imperialism, 61, 65, 76, 95, 144; collective *see* collective triad imperialism; in plural form, 68; new form of, 57–73, 76, 107; of Japan, 66; redeployment of, 52, 61–5; transformation of, 72 *see also* super-imperialism

import substitution, 161

India, 18, 83, 87, 89–90, 107, 108, 109, 110, 111, 134, 145, 176

indigenous peoples, rights of, 58

Industrial Revolution, 7, 13, 58, 62; new, 8, 11

industrialization, 13, 14, 153

inequality, social, 45, 51, 58

informal economic activity, 66

intellectual property rights, 96, 97

international business law, 97, 117

International Monetary Fund (IMF), 94, 97

intervention, duty of, 99

intifada, 86

inventive imagination, 112–13, 159

Iran, 85, 87, 109, 170

Iraq, 83, 85

Ireland, Northern, 114

Islam, 86, 87, 88; political, 115, 124, 144, 152, 166–71 (as form of communitarianism, 171; US support for, 171); rejection of democracy, 168; Wahhabi, 169

Islamic world, 18, 107

Israel, 83, 85, 90, 103, 104, 110, 124, 135

Italy, 10; modernization of, 35

Japan, 7, 10, 11, 52, 60, 62, 63, 70, 78, 80, 95, 100, 102, 105, 107, 109, 111, 112, 124, 125, 127; crisis in, 67; imperialism of, 66; 'miracle' in, 65

judges, election of, 39

Kautsky, Karl, 69, 71; *The Agrarian Question*, 175

Keynes, J.M., 14, 16, 27–30, 48

Keynesianism, 22–32, 136; historical, 29; military, 30, 127

Kissinger, Henry, 100

Kondratiev cycles, 92, 107

Korea, South, 17, 18, 20, 67, 105, 108, 109, 132

Kosovo war, 81, 99

Kurds, 85; massacre of, 110

Kuwait, 85

labour: active army of, 20; reserve army of, 19, 20–1; rigidities of, 16

labour market, global, 159

bin Laden, Osama, 84, 88, 89, 103

law, international, 116

law of value, withering of, 53

League of Nations, 99, 116

left, 131; building of, 144, 145–6; hegemony of, 121

Lenin, V.I., 9, 11, 68–9

liberalism, 8, 9, 10, 43, 44, 46, 48, 70, 82, 129, 133; economic, as enemy of democracy, 36, 59; of capitalism, 28; Utopian, 39

liberalization, of agriculture, 97, 122

liberation theology, 152

local control, 160–1

Lugano Report, 121, 157

Luxemburg, Rosa, 158

MacDonnell Douglas, 98

Magdoff, Harry, 126

de Maistre, Joseph, 168

Malaysia, 17, 43, 109

Maoism, 31, 171; demise of, 1

Marais, Hein, 110

market, 12, 29, 104, 138, 154, 156, 157; and socialism, 32–41; distinct from capitalism, 153; expansion of, 155; invisible hand of, 98; laws of, 2, 3, 43, 118, 141; local control of, 160; powers beyond, 96–7; self-regulating, 28, 47

market regulation, 44

market share, renegotiation of, 132

market socialism, in China, 68, 92

Marshall, Alfred, 8

Marshall Plan, 95

Marx, Karl, 8, 14, 16, 50; on commodity alienation, 22–3; on instability of capitalism, 23

work, organization of, 54, 55, 112
workers' movement, 8, 9
working class, 13; struggles of, 34
World Bank, 97, 108, 140
World Trade Organization (WTO), 94, 96, 97, 100, 117, 132; agriculture and, 134, 175; Doha ministerial, 134

Yugoslavia, 113–14; former, 108, 115 (war in, 70, 83, 86–7)

Zhdanov, Andrei, 69